OUT OF TOUCH

OUT OF TOUCH

*When Parents and Children Lose Contact
after Divorce*

Geoffrey L. Greif

NEW YORK   OXFORD

Oxford University Press

1997

OXFORD UNIVERSITY PRESS

Oxford New York Athens Auckland Bangkok Bogotá Bombay
Buenos Aires Calcutta Cape Town Dar es Salaam Delhi Florence
Hong Kong Istanbul Karachi Kuala Lumpur Madras Madrid Melbourne
Mexico City Nairobi Paris Singapore Taipei Tokyo Toronto
and associated companies in
Berlin Ibadan

Copyright © 1997 by Oxford University Press, Inc.

Published by Oxford University Press, Inc.,
198 Madison Avenue, New York, New York 10016

Oxford is a registered trademark of Oxford University Press

Library of Congress Cataloging-in Publication Data
Greif, Geoffrey L.
    Out of touch : when parents and children lose contact after divorce /
Geoffrey L. Greif.
        p.   cm.
    Includes bibliographical references and index.
    ISBN 0-19-509535-9
    1. Children of divorced parents.   2. Children of divorced parents—
Psychology.   3. Divorce—Psychological aspects.   1. Title.
HQ777.5.G74   1997   96-7929
306.874—dc20

1 3 5 7 9 8 6 4 2

Printed in the United States of America
on acid-free paper

Preface

Cultures are rich with tales of parents who have abandoned children. Whenever such stories have been told, whether they be mythology, folktales, or fairy tales read to children, the theme emerges of the parent who withdraws, due to some mysterious event, adventure seeking, divine intervention, death, or leaving the child to be raised by others. This absence then sets the stage for the child to overcome hardship and find success. Romulus and Remus, the mythical founders of Rome who are nurtured by wolves, survive without their parents. Zeus is raised away from both parents on the isle of Crete (hidden from his child-eating father, Cronus) before becoming king of the gods. Cinderella, living with her stepmother while her father either has died or is away at sea (depending upon the version of the story), triumphs by marrying a prince (not a politically correct victory). Stagolee sets off on his own at the age of five to make his mark in the world, parental supervision being unneeded. The message is that children can overcome a life without a parent, sometimes being cared for by others, sometimes fending for themselves. A child hearing such a story could be reassured that if he or she were left alone, all was not lost.

Almost always left unexplained is the state of the absent parents. Their reactions to and feelings about being away from their children are not described.

Fast forward to the end of the twentieth century, and we see a slightly different cultural message. Now children raised away from a father or mother not only are failing to adapt, but are suffering. Much is blamed on a parent's absence. Schneiderman believes this theme is reflected in twentieth-century novels whose protagonists are craving attention and praise because of a lack of strong parenting. By comparison, nineteenth-century Dickensian parental figures are cruel and unjust, he writes, but an overall parental structure still exists in the broader society which provides children something to push off against in their attempts to define themselves.[1] That is not the case at the end of this century. We are inundated with the message that the failures of families, whether they be rural, suburban, or urban, are due to the decline of the two parent family as well as the rise of unwed pregnancy. Crime, low academic achievement, substance abuse, and emotional problems are being linked in the community psyche to father absence and, occasionally, to mother absence. In past generations, the child pulled himself up by the bootstraps and survived despite the absence of the parent. Now it is not so simple.

What remains unchanged is that we still have little information about the motivations and feelings of the absent parent. The fathers and mothers are believed to vanish for reasons that connote weakness, lack of interest, and self-absorption. They are often seen as ne'er-do-wells who are avoiding paying child support and need to be corralled by the court system. Such absences are resulting, by most accounts, in one of the most significant crises of our times and collectively appear to be a time bomb waiting to explode in even broader dimensions on future generations.

To understand this many-sided puzzle, researchers and writers have looked extensively at single mothers and fathers struggling to raise children alone. They have inquired about the absent parent's visiting patterns and child support payment habits. They have questioned and observed the children, trying to understand how they are faring. They have made predictions about the children's future well-being. Less well known, though, are the positions of the fathers or mothers not in contact with the children. Why are they not seeing their children? What is their side of the story? How do they feel about their children, their ex-spouses, and themselves?

Having written other books on single parent families, I became interested in this topic both for its familiarity and its timeliness. In all of the other books, some discussion centered on either a nonvisiting parent or the possibility of a parent dropping out. These absent parents interested me in a profound sense because they seemed the epitome of the misunderstood and the insufficiently understood.

Once I began researching the topic, its complexity became quite apparent. There are parents from all walks of life and of all ages who are not seeing their children, ranging from the wealthy child support evader to the poor undereducated teen parent. Given the robust nature of the topic, and the lack of information on these parents, I chose to focus primarily, though not exclusively, on parents who were married at one time. I wanted to learn about the feelings of parents who were not visiting and how they came to lose contact with their children. Others will have to focus on unmarried teen parents who are not seeing their children and those who are dodging child support payments, both social problems that have grown out of proportion. A few such parents, both white and African-American, appear among the parents I interviewed, but here the focus is on the process that unfolds when relationships go bad.

I began the study with a national questionnaire sample of over 180 parents who belonged to Parents without Partners.² Two follow-up telephone surveys were conducted in subsequent years to gather more information and to watch changes over time. I found immediately that collecting quantitative data was insufficient to understand the complexity of the situations involved. Their lives could not be explained by checking off a series of boxes. I chose to interview a subset of these parents myself and to look for other parents not connected to a self-help group who might provide additional information. I first thought I might find a great number of parents who were clearly wronged by what had happened to them and were suffering because of it. I hypothesized that some parents were being deprived of the contact they wanted and that, through discussions with them, I could clearly point out the multiple injustices that had befallen them. What I ended up with was less clear cut. While many of the parents I interviewed were suffering and do not fit the common profile of the uncaring self-absorbed parent, others presented less sympathetic tales, even though they claimed to have been treated unjustly. I have not excluded people that I interviewed for the book to prove a point. Rather, what I was left with was a great appreciation for the complexity of these people's lives. Little in life is clear-cut; and when you shake in a tincture of divorce, acrimony, legal and financial disputes, suffering, and varying impressions from the family members intimately involved, the picture can be fuzzy. I have classified the most common themes that I have heard from the mothers and fathers but—and again because of the complexity of the issues—this becomes an approximation.

Editing their comments was necessary to make their words more readable. In addition, great care was taken to disguise identities of the families involved without changing the nature of their stories. But I scrupulously have tried to capture their own words, sometimes unsettling or sad, sometimes inflammatory, and sometimes contradictory.

Where is the road map for these parents? There are no frequently retold folktales to refer to that provide cultural messages about divorced parents struggling to see their children. Where is the fairy tale of the parent who is good and pure but does not have access to a child because of earlier marital problems or a seemingly unfair court system? Does that parent receive a visit from a fairy judge? When does he or she get a turn at happiness?

No culture is telling those tales. I believe we suffer as a result, because our options for self-definition are reduced. If we understand the complexity of divorced families better, maybe we will believe that some single parents who are out of contact with their children are decent people. But simple solutions, unfortunately, do not exist.

Over the past four years, many graduate social work students at the University of Maryland have assisted me in tracking down and interviewing parents and understanding the lives of the parents they have contacted. Most recently, Linda Beam and Danielle Donner helped with the three-year follow-up interviews and a further literature review. These students' interest and questioning have made this book immeasurably better. My daughters, Alissa and Jennifer, also helped along the way with editing suggestions and mythological references. The support of Parents without Partners and Mothers without Custody in publishing the questionnaire as well as articles about the findings is greatly appreciated. The research could not have been undertaken without them! Rachmael Tobesman, Jennifer Isham, and Joan Kristall need to be thanked, as do the folks at the Annapolis Child Support Project, who were extremely cooperative in helping me understand the dimensions of child support payment enforcement. To David Roll and Gioia Stevens at Oxford University Press, who supported the idea of the book, I also give a nod of thanks.

Finally, and most important, I wish to recognize the parents who participated in the original survey as well as the parents and children I later contacted and who contacted me. Many allowed me enormous access to their lives, including permission to review court documents. Sharing their experiences with me was often painful. Some interviews went on for hours at a time. Many parents stayed in touch with me for a number of years to provide me with updates. I have been following one family, discussed in chapter 6, for ten years, allowing for a view of divorce and parent-child separation that reaches from childhood to young adulthood. I thank you all and hope that I have done you, and other parents in your situations, justice.

G. L. G.

Baltimore
September 1996

Contents

OUT OF TOUCH

Divorce and How Parents Lose Contact

When Rachel left her husband, her daughter Mindy never forgave her. Mindy began splitting time between her parents' homes but became increasingly recalcitrant when she was with Rachel. Rachel tried to forge a closer relationship with her but felt her ex-husband was turning Mindy against her. The defining moment in the relationship came one evening when Rachel was reprimanding Mindy about her rejecting behavior. Fourteen years old at the time, Mindy became incensed, pushed Rachel off her bed, and told her to get out of her room. Rachel admonished Mindy by saying that if she couldn't treat her with respect, she would have to leave. Mindy packed up her things immediately, called her father who lived nearby, and left. They have not spoken for the past six years.

"I feel I did the right thing," Rachel told me. "I was not going to let her treat me that way. But it has been very painful. I would go to her basketball games just to have a chance to see her. She would ignore me. It has been especially hard for my parents, who know what has happened and have supported me. But they are very old, and I'm afraid they will die before there is a reconciliation. They're very unhappy about not seeing their granddaughter."

Rachel is a bright woman in her mid-forties. She is insightful and hardworking, and loves tennis. She lives in the same neighborhood in which she grew up and has sought support in that community for the painful feelings related to her lack of contact with her child. She ponders how to answer questions about her daughter when she meets new people, questions that many noncustodial parents have difficulty answering. "It is hard to say I have a daughter and then admit that I haven't seen her for many years. Sometimes it is easier to say I don't have any or to lie about my relationship with her. But if I don't tell the truth at first, it is hard to go back and tell it later."

When I first met Mindy, there was no outward indication that she was not seeing her mother. An outside observer would claim she was carrying on with life, engaging in such activities as working for her high school newspaper. I attended an event at her school; we played guitar together. But children, like adults, can be very skilled at hiding feelings.

One of the more pressing social problems facing America today is the absence of the father from the family and the attending economic and emotional hardships that may befall the family as a result. In a similar vein, though much less of a widespread demographic phenomenon and concern, is the absence of the mother from the single-father-headed family. A loss of contact usually grows out of an unsatisfactory family breakup and after a custody decision has been or is being finalized. It also can follow an unplanned pregnancy. It is the premise of this book that, in most cases, society is ill served when parents and children stop speaking or visiting after a breakup; and families in particular are the big losers. The focus of this book will be on learning from parents who are no longer in touch with their children why they believe the contact stopped. Their impressions were gained during in-depth interviews and from the results of a survey questionnaire. The voices of children involved in these relationships will also be heard.

How prevalent is the single-parent family? By the mid-1990s, according to a Census Bureau report, 7.6 million women were raising children without the father in the household, and 1.3 million fathers were raising children without a mother.[1] There has been a steady increase in the ranks of single parents over the past twenty-five years and thus in the number of parents living away from their children (many of whom have lost contact). In 1970, 2.8 million single mothers had custody of their children. By 1994 the figure had almost tripled. The number of fathers with sole custody practically quadrupled during that same time period. The rise in African-American families headed by one parent was more dramatic during this time span than the increase among white families. (Only incomplete data is available on Hispanic families).[2] For the same years, the number of children under eighteen living with a single parent more than doubled, going from 8 million to almost 18 million, while the majority of children, 47 million, live with two parents.[3]

As a nation we have become most concerned with the financial ramifications of this phenomenon and the impact on the national budget. Single mothers, especially those who are owed but do not receive child support, frequently live in poverty[4] and need government support. Divorced mothers had a median income of $17,014 in 1993, whereas never-married mothers had a median income of $9,277.[5] Welfare often makes up the deficit. Slightly under half of the single mothers in the United States were awarded child support, with never-married mothers less apt to be awarded support than once-married mothers. While three-quarters of those who were awarded it received some payments, full payment was received by only half of those due money. When there is no contact between the absent father and the family, the likelihood of payment is apt to be even lower. It is not just fathers who avoid this responsibility. One-quarter of noncustodial mothers were court-ordered to pay support to custodial fathers. They were less apt to pay some portion of it, with 63 percent of noncustodial mothers making some payment versus 76 percent of noncustodial fathers.[6]

While the headlines focus on child support, the damage to the family far exceeds the monetary hurt. Living with one parent in and of itself places a child at risk for a host of negative experiences.[7] When the child whose parents split up is not even seeing the other parent, the consequences can be more severe (as will be discussed). In neighborhoods with a high rate of father absence, there are higher rates of poverty, public assistance families, and high school dropouts.[8] Fatherlessness (and to a lesser extent, motherlessness) cuts across all races and economic classes.[9] While the rate of fatherlessness is great among African-Americans, according to one source, it is spreading more rapidly now among whites.[10]

Numbers do not fully reflect the sense of loss that pervades the lives of parents and children affected by family breakup.[11] I recently called the home of a roofer who had been working on my house for the last few years. His six-year-old daughter answered the phone. When I asked for him she said in a sad voice, "He's not here, and I haven't seen him in a very long time." Her mother confirmed he had dropped out. But, when I asked him about his divorce, he told me his ex-wife had made it difficult to visit. Regardless of the truth, that kind of feeling expressed by a young child is hard to quantify and painful for me personally to hear. What will she grow up thinking about her father or herself? If she hears his version of the story and decides that is the truth, what will she think of her mother? What will concepts such as "making a commitment" and "keeping a promise" mean to her?

Regardless of the circumstances that have led to the loss of contact between parent and child (discussed in depth in the following chapters), family members go through life wondering what has happened to the other person: A parent wonders what his child now looks like and if the child will recognize him; a child wonders if her mother is ever thinking about her; a son worries about whether his father will return; a mother sends a card on a holiday hoping it will be read. Absence, rather than connection, becomes the dominant theme. Keeping people out rather than letting them in becomes the operating principle. The emotional toll, unlike the financial, is hard to document, but it is ever present.

Estimates of the number of fathers who have stopped visiting their children at least annually after a breakup run from as high as two-thirds[12] to slightly under 10 percent, with the Census Bureau placing the figure at 47 percent.[13] Never-married fathers are reportedly more apt to drop out than once-married fathers.[14] Many of these men would appear to have shunned their responsibilities to their children. Often called "deadbeat dads," they are depicted in the press as shirkers, bums, and con artists, abusing society's financial resources as welfare ends up supporting their children when they do not pay the child support they owe. Much less data exist on mothers' rates of nonvisitation, though it is estimated by the Census Bureau to be 30 percent.[15]

A second premise of this book related to the first (that society is ill served by the absence of a parent from a child's life) is that not all parents should be in touch with their children after the breakup. There are "bad" parents who, through contact with their children, will foster more harm than positive growth. I am speaking specifically about parents who are uninterested in change and are incapable of healthy parenting. Until they decide they want to get their lives back on track, they are unlikely candidates for divorce mediation or therapy. They may have a history of incarceration, domestic violence, severe emotional problems, substance abuse, or child abuse. Despite the pain of no contact, visitation between these parents and their children should be denied or significantly restricted.

But what about the rest of the parents, those who for other reasons are out of touch with their children? Is it fair to say that not all parents who are not seeing their children are deadbeats, substance abusers, child maltreaters, or criminals? Or that a parent and child's relationship cannot be rehabilitated in most cases? Is it fair to assume that some parents have ceased visiting for reasons other than their own behavior? These parents are the focus of the book. It is these parents, where a relationship perhaps could be reestablished between a parent and child, that are of vital interest.

Our society has never seriously explored these questions. The parent who is out of touch with his or her child (I will use the male and female pronouns interchangeably to make the point that I am speaking about both fathers and mothers) is often tarred with the "deadbeat" parent brush. In fact, this is a catch all categorization that is used commonly for parents (usually fathers) who do not visit but pay support, parents who visit but do not pay, and parents who *neither* visit *nor* pay child support. By lumping all parents into the same category, ABSENCE = DEADBEAT, we are ignoring the diversity of their experiences. Even using subcategorizations calling a parent emotionally absent or financially absent, does not do justice. There are subtle as well as significant differences between parents who casually walk away from their families for self-serving reasons and those who turn away or are turned away for other causes. These differences are hard to understand because it is the custodial parent and the child who control the dialogue about these complex relationships. We do not know from the absent parent's point of view what has happened because that parent is missing from the scene. We are left with only part of the story. For an issue so significant to our society's well-being, this is insufficient.

Two purposes of this book are to examine why some parents are not seeing their children and to increase the dialogue on this topic. The attempt is to hear from the unheard population, the parent who has ceased having contact. These stories do not always fit with what we have come to believe about this group of parents. In some cases, their stories do not even fit with the information I have gained from their children. This book is not meant to praise or defend these out-of-contact parents. Not all of those I interviewed are heroes and heroines who have been misunderstood or are victims of an unjust system. Sometimes the situations are much murkier, and the reader may be left feeling that the custodial parent's or child's cessation of contact is understandable. Yet, in other cases, the impression will be left that the relationships did not have to evolve in the direction of decline, and that, to use therapeutic jargon, the situation was "workable."

The Research

Locating a sample of parents who were out of contact with their children proved a daunting task. They are a stigmatized population, particularly the mothers, and are often loathe to discuss their parenting situation. While these parents have some representation among advocacy groups, such as Mothers without Custody and Fathers United for Equal Rights,[16] an attempt was made to garner a more representative sample. A forty-item questionnaire was placed in the *Single Parent,* a magazine published by Parents without Partners (PWP), a national organization begun in the 1970s to assist single parents in raising their children and improving their social lives. PWP is the largest self-help organization of its kind in the United States, with membership approximating 150,000. Members join PWP for a variety of reasons, ranging from a desire to socialize to a need for parenting information. The questionnaire specifically asked for parents who had been out of contact with one or more of their children for at least six months following separation or divorce to complete the instrument and mail it to me. This approach yielded a sample of 185 (109 fathers and 76 mothers) who hailed from forty states and Canada.

Two years later, one-third of the fathers (36) and the mothers (25) were contacted by telephone and interviewed extensively by graduate assistants. Half of the members of this sample were contacted again a year later, in 1995, for a brief follow-up concerning their level of involvement with their children. (See Chapter 8).

Given the nature of the survey approach and the lack of any official count of members of PWP who have little contact with their children, a response rate of the potential pool is impossible to estimate. It is important to note that this is not a random sample or one that is necessarily representative. Rather it is one that offers a chance to build hypotheses for further study of this population. The findings form the basis for some of the findings reported in the next four chapters. But the situations of these parents are more complicated than what could be encapsulated solely in written questionnaire responses. I spent the next three years tracking down parents to interview in depth. These mothers and fathers came from the sample, and also from other sources ranging from advocacy and self-help groups for fathers and mothers to parents who are part of a state run program designed to increase child-support compliance, to people I met at social gatherings or other professional contacts who were interested in being interviewed. While I ended up interviewing more than 40 people in depth who represent a broad diversity of race, culture, regional and economic diversity, I chose 26 to present here (11 mothers and 11 fathers without contact, and four parents who have reconciled with their children).

Many of the interviews unfolded over time. In some instances I interviewed families over the course of one to two years; I have followed one particular family for ten years. This afforded me an opportunity to learn how these relationships evolve. I have interpreted the findings from the questionnaires, the research assistants' interview data, and the interviews I conducted after lengthy discussions with the research assistants, feedback from audiences to whom I have presented the information, and from my own previous work on divorce.

It is hoped that investigation and discussion of these situations will help prevent future families from losing contact after a breakup and suggest ways to reconcile when they do. While child support is discussed by a few of the parents, this book is not geared toward social policy experts interested in reversing the high numbers of parents who do not pay child support or who consciously avoid support by running away. (Child support is discussed later in this chapter and again in chapter 7). It is also not geared specifically toward the never-married population or the teenage unwed parent. Rather, the hope is to provide information and insight for professionals interested in these issues and to give help and hope to the families themselves (the last chapter offers self-help suggestions) who are experiencing the potential for a loss of contact or are already living with such a situation.

Men and Women, Fathers and Mothers, Are Different

To set the context for what is to follow in this book, we need to acknowledge that the circumstances of men and women, fathers and mothers, are different. Gender is one of the great dividers in our society. Because of this, the experience of being a parent and of *being a parent out of contact* hold variegated meanings for mothers and fathers.

Because males and females are not raised the same and are not expected to fulfill the same roles in every facet of their adult lives, fathers' and mothers' experiences vary when they become parents. Of course "times have changed" and greater flexibility in gender roles has arrived. More mothers have joined the workforce, and the income gap between men and women has narrowed for those working full-time outside of the home.[17] More fathers than at any time in recent history are involved in single-parent childrearing.[18] Yet gender distinctions still exist, some biological and some social. Neonatal differences have been found between males and females in stress reactivity (obviously even before the possible effects of social conditioning can take hold);[19] life expectancies are shorter for men than women regardless of race;[20] women are more apt to be *seriously* hurt in domestic violence than men;[21] men outearn women;[22] single mothers are poorer than single fathers and thus are more reliant on child support;[23] mothers are more apt to take time off from work for maternity leave than fathers are for paternity leave to be with new-borns;[24] when both parents work outside of the home full-time, women still perform more of the child care and house chores;[25] mothers and fathers play with children in different ways; and, as anyone who has observed children knows, the way little boys play and participate in sports is unlike how little girls play and participate. While more females have entered into traditionally male jobs than vice versa and males have increasingly entered into female domestic areas, gendered expectations about behavior remain. The message about what it means to be masculine is not the same as what it means to be feminine. The list goes on and on.

As a result of these dissimilarities, the father who is not seeing his child would have traveled to that point down a number of twisted paths that may not look a lot like the twisted paths that a mother would have traversed to the same point. And, once at that point, their experiences and their attempts at resolving the lack of contact would also vary.

Single Parenting across the Spectrum

Descriptions of children living away from one parent or another have abounded in mythology, literature, and history since early accounts of civilization. In millennia past, fathers trudged off for months at a time to participate in the tribal hunt. War has compelled men to leave home, often for years, to protect their families or to conquer new territory. Quests, holy and otherwise, have also separated fathers from their children and wives. Hunting and war could be considered a separation of the father and children sanctioned by the existing culture, though, as recently as World War II, single men were selected for service before married men.[26] Whether serving voluntarily or involuntarily, such service was viewed as a duty, a necessity, or a rite of passage. The point I wish to convey is that a father's separation from his family was often approved by society. He was acting within the roles defined by his culture when he left their wife and children. (Exceptions do exist. Fathers wandered off their farms or away from their small villages, often leaving their families destitute. How many of the men who went off to seek their fortune, supposedly for the good of their family, never returned? Desertion was the poor man's divorce before changes in family law and greater availability of legal help made formal separations possible.)

Mothers have historically been separated from children less often because it was the mothers who would stay behind to care for the family and whose role it has been to nurture. Separations did occur, of course, yet, with the exception of children farmed out to be nursed, poor women turning over their children to orphanages and foster care, or women wandering off the farm seeking a different and less harsh life in the city, they were rarely voluntary. Poverty and religious persecution forced some teen-agers and young adults in Europe to enter indentured servitude in Colonial America. Their options were few and governed by class. Families were also ripped apart by slave owners.

Separations of mothers and children continued after the abolition of slavery. By the end of the nineteenth century, among the waves of immigrants from foreign shores were teens coming to America to earn enough money to send for their families back in their homelands. Native American children were sometimes removed from their reservation-bound parents and sent to boarding schools to receive the "right" upbringing.[27] Poor children were sent away from noxious urban environments to be raised in the country, where it was hoped they would learn good habits.

Prior to this century, the father would gain custody after divorce because women had few rights and few options for supporting a child, and children were often considered the property of their fathers. Mothers were turned out of their homes for such "sins" as infidelity, sexual incompatibility, and mental illness.

By the beginning of the twentieth century, women and children had achieved new rights and greater equality with men. Custody no longer automatically was given to a father if there was a divorce. Theories pertaining to the psychological importance of the mother in the development of the child gained ascendancy. The term "the tender years' doctrine," came to mean that, for young children, a mother should be the primary parent.

At the twentieth century's midpoint, divorce, replacing death, became the primary reason for the separation of parent and child, splitting apart a father and child more frequently than a mother and child. The father's role, which had evolved over the previous 150 years from moral guide and teacher to breadwinner, now took on the definition of gender-role model, particularly for sons.[28] Divorce rates during this century skyrocketed in the United States. The number of divorced adults more than doubled between 1970 and 1980 while the number of married people grew by 10 percent.[29] The precipitous rise in divorce did not start to level off until the mid 1980s.[30] By the mid 1990s, over 40 percent of all first marriages were ending in divorce, and approximately 1.5 million children were affected by divorce annually.[31]

The reasons for the rise in divorce are many. As previously mentioned, when legal aid permitted affordable divorces and divorce laws were simplified, desertion was no longer as necessary. Following World War II, Americans had a greater sense of impermanence. The security that marriage offered was no longer as attractive. Religion, a cohesive force in many families, began playing a less important part in American life as attendance at services declined between 1958 and 1980 by almost 20 percent. The number of people who affiliated with any religion also declined during that time period.[32] Women's economic situations improved so much that many no longer felt they had to remain in an unhappy marriage for their own survival. The ease with which one could travel and experience new cities and countries, the advent of the birth control pill, which greatly increased sexual experimentation outside of marriage, rising expectations for personal happiness, and a reviving women's movement all contributed.

Perhaps fueling the divorce fever further were some of the high-profile divorces and custody trials that attracted media attention, as unpleasant as these cases often were. Famous divorce cases sparked interest in divorce as well as custody and made something that was unthinkable to previous generations possible and likely. In the 1930s it was the separate custody trials of Gloria Vanderbilt and Mary Astor's children. In the 1970s, Cary Grant and Dyan Cannon fought over their daughter. Ten years later it was Roxanne Pulitzer fighting for her children and then the battle for Hilary Morgan between Drs. Eric Foretich and Elizabeth Morgan.

Over the last 150 years, the obscure as well as the famous have dropped out of contact with their children after a breakup. It is not just the fellow on the corner and the woman who works down the block who are not visiting their children. For example, the wife of Charles Dickens apparently lived apart from her children for many years while he raised them.[33] Alfred Steiglitz, one of the greatest American photographers of the early twentieth century, did not see his daughter, Kitty, for years following his divorce from her mother and his marriage to Georgia O'Keeffe.[34] John Lennon suffered severely from the breakup of his parents' relationship and his lack of contact with his father. Yoko Ono's daughter, Kyoko, was kidnapped by her father; and mother and child went for years without seeing each other. Actress Jodie Foster has seen her father only a few times since her parents divorced over thirty years ago.[35]

As divorce has been on the rise, the probability that mothers will have sole custody has been dwindling. One outgrowth of the women's movement has been a diminution of the presumption of sole mother custody. Gender-neutral laws are less likely to favor mothers. Mothers are less likely to feel the necessity to seek sole custody as workplace opportunities provide other options for how they wish to define themselves. The growth of joint custody, which provides fathers with increased access to their children after a breakup, has further chipped away at the chance of a mother raising a child alone. This approach has not been found to be a panacea. While contact with both parents is generally agreed to be beneficial in most, but not all situations, joint living situations are not always the answer. If there is extreme hostility, anger, an inability to separate one's own feelings from those of the child, a belief the other parent is essentially a bad person, or physical or substance abuse, joint custody is given a bad prognosis.[36]

Finally, sole mother custody has been decreasing as fathers appear to be seeking custody more often. Fathers are being encouraged to stay involved on many fronts. Television shows portray dads in nurturing roles, social scientists talk about the importance of the father in all aspects of child development, and recent presidents have vowed to go after "deadbeat dads."

The passive father who willingly gives up custody at the time of the breakup is vanishing slowly from the courthouse, though mothers still overwhelmingly get custody.[37]

Fathers in general are showing increased interest in parenting their children. According to one professor, "'Young men are much more cognizant of parental responsibility than the generation of men from the 60's and 70's.'"[38] Mental health workers familiar with the situation of young fathers in Baltimore report that fathers want to be involved but that the cycle of poverty and poor education, which lead to underemployment and an embarrassing inability to pay support, makes connection to their children uncomfortable.[39] These last points are especially important when we consider the situation of the noncustodial father and what he feels living away from his children at a time of increased interest in fathering.

As the calls for fathers to increase their involvement have grown, there has not been a comparable lessening of stigma surrounding mothers who do not have custody. The options for women's self-definition have increased to include the work world, but these options usually do not replace the pressures on mothers to be involved with their children. Maccoby and Mnookin even argue that gender equity has declined after divorce as mothers still handle the bulk of the child care and are assuming increasing financial responsibility. Fundamentally, people still believe that children are women's work and that fathers should help out but not replace them in this endeavor. This works against the best interests of mothers, fathers, and children. All this sets the context for understanding how some children are separated from their parents in the 1990s.

The Dark Side

There is a dark side to these issues that increases our need for solutions. Violent episodes between warring parents unfortunately remain common events. Too often, a parent, almost always male, who is denied custody or visitation or is pursued to pay child support, uses that as justification and erupts with murderous rage. One study found that most of the murders that occurred within the courthouse in one recent year are family-related.[40] This should not be surprising if we consider what we are learning every day about the violent nature of family relations, even among the rich and famous.

A few years ago in New York state, a father killed four workers in a child support office, workers whose job it was to find parents who were in arrears. When trapped, and before killing himself, he said that he could not get a wife or a job because he owed so much child support. The father had been pursued for over twenty years to support a child he did not believe was his and whom he rarely saw.[41] A few months later, a veterinarian poisoned his five children after having told his ex-wife that he would kill them and himself if denied custody. All five survived.[42] More recently in New Jersey, a divorced father, unhappy with his ex-wife's plans to move to Florida with their two children, killed the children. Acquaintances of the father recounted how he often complained bitterly about the unfair treatment he had received at the hands of the courts during the divorce and custody proceedings.[43]

Child support enforcement has even resulted in at least one father in arrears robbing and murdering a total stranger. The father, described by his ex-partner as distraught because he had lost his job and could not pay the child support he owed her, killed a woman unrelated to him in a fit of rage.[44]

Cases such as these point up the need for gaining a clearer understanding of what the divorce process can do to people who feel emotionally stretched to the limit. Obviously, some of them react irrationally and commit acts that range, on the minor end, from needling the other parent, to the more extreme of not seeing the children and committing acts of violence. The experiences of the fathers and mothers interviewed for this book bear out distinctions between the sexes. For this reason, the fathers and mothers are discussed separately. It is important to emphasize that when a father is not seeing his children, the meaning for society is not the same as when a mother is not. Before further explaining this, I will talk about the meaning of parenting after divorce in general.

Entering Divorce: The Stepping-Stone to Losing Contact

Because it is the norm for mothers to have custody after divorce (I recognize that joint custody allows for both parents to have equal contact, but usually the mother ends up with more time with the children), it is often the father and child who struggle to maintain meaningful relationships. I will talk here, though, about the struggles of visiting fathers and mothers, as what can happen to pull apart a father-child relationship is often similar to what can happen between a noncustodial mother and child.

Divorce is a difficult transition for most family members, and so at least a modicum of trouble with adjustment can be anticipated. These struggles can be emotionally draining even in the best of circumstances. When there is trouble in these areas, as will be seen later, contact between parent and child can trail off and the stage may be set for an eventual loss of contact. Think of visitation as on a continuum. In effect, the divorce begins a process that starts with some contact, often goes to less visitation, and may end up with little or no contact.

The struggles between parent and child tend to occur around six broad areas. These are

1. parent-child relationships
2. physical visitation
3. telephone contact
4. visitation at another site (for example, attending school meetings or sport events)
5. interparental conflict
6. differences about parenting.

Parent-Child Relationships

Perhaps the best, but by no means the only determinant of how the parent-child relationship will develop once the mother or father has moved out of the home is how emotionally close they were prior to the breakup. If there is good communication from the outset between, for example, the father and child, and if the parents handle the actual separation without a great deal of acrimony, it will be easier for the father and child to remain close.

Handling the actual separation smoothly is not easy, though. The beginning of the transition from a two-parent to a one-parent family, the period during which the parents are making the actual decision to split up, is often touted as the most traumatic part of the divorce process and can set the stage for what follows. If the parents were fighting openly before the breakup, things are likely to escalate. Sides are chosen, ultimatums thrown down, and joint property is evaluated for later division. Children are not always consciously aware of problems between their parents during a marriage. But with a breakup, angry feelings that may have gone unnoticed by the child now enter the child's consciousness and may be unsettling during this transition period.

In the best of circumstances, the issues that caused the parents to divorce do not include the child. Subsequently, the child will not be inappropriately caught between the parents during the separation transition or after the breakup. Ideally, parents are able to negotiate their settlement and continue to parent the child without drawing the child into any lingering controversies.

At the same time, many things can go awry in this new relationship. If the father defined his role as breadwinner and disciplinarian, a traditional and prevalent notion about fatherhood, he may have trouble with the transition, which will require him to spend time alone with the child. His contact with the child may always have been mediated by the wife. He may have no idea how to nurture or talk about his child's or his own feelings. His role model of fatherhood may not include a picture of a single father spending time with a toddler in the sandbox or "giving space" to a moody teenager pining over unrequited love.

If the mother's role was defined as primary nurturer, and her day revolved around the child, she will have trouble adjusting to having less contact. She may be slow in learning how to fill up her time in productive ways; she may continue to focus on time with her child beyond the point at which such a focus is adaptive. As the mother or father in these situations struggles to find sea legs, boundary issues are apt to emerge. Boundary problems, which vary by culture, occur when family members become overly invested in each other's lives and attempts at healthy separation are impeded.

What might that look like? It might mean that the father's or mother's own sense of well-being is too tied up in the well-being of the child. In healthy parent-child relationships, the parent draws a sense of self and feelings of competence from a variety of sources—for example, past successes, work, parenting, and adult relationships. If the parenting side of the equation becomes too important, and the child is not progressing well during visitation, the visiting parent may become upset to the point of being unable to parent effectively. This can spoil other aspects of life, too. That parent may blame the custodial parent, and by attacking the custodial parent verbally, may hurt the ability of both parents to work together. When parents have fought for custody or visitation, they often feel they must prove to themselves and to others that they are effective parents. If the child experiences ups and downs, the parent with less contact may interpret those variations as failure on his own part, particularly if he or she does not understand a child's developmental changes.

At other times, boundary issues are illustrated by the noncustodial parent being overly interested in the child's life during visitation. For example, the father may try to cram in information about the child's life he does not normally receive. The child, seeking privacy, resents this. Curiosity about the child's friendships and behavior in the mother's home becomes obsessive, rather than healthy interest. Conversely, the child may be overly solicitous of the father's attention. Feeling abandoned or unsure of where he or she stands with the father, the child may be demanding more during visitation than the father can realistically provide in terms of attention and affection. This need on the child's part may stem from the inherent nature of the child, past gaps in the child's upbringing, or a combination of this nature-nurture axis.

With an understanding of this process, we can see how visitation between the parent and child can become problematic. Once the relationship takes on an unhealthy quality, a series of dominoes can fall slowly on top of each other. Each behavior becomes a stepping stone for more miscommunication and failures in relationship building. For example, simple difficulties scheduling visitation (discussed next), are incorrectly interpreted as much more: They are viewed as wounds to the parent's or child's psyche. Low school grades may be viewed as punishment of the parent rather than a child's legitimate problems in grasping a subject. False readings of actions escalate out of proportion. If there is little contact occurring, there is scant opportunity to resolve the misreading of the situation.

Struggles around Physical Visitation

Visitation often becomes the first and primary arena in which parent-child conflict is played out. We all know how difficult it can be for parents to find a regular time to spend with their children even when they are all living in the same household. Schedules conflict, work interferes, and social dates crop up, as do interesting TV shows, family crises, and homework assignments. Now imagine how much more difficult it is when the parent and child are living apart. In many cases, the divorced parents or the court have fixed on days of the week when visitation must take place. These days are often regulated down to the hour. "Pick-up the child at school at 4:00 P.M. on Friday, return the child Saturday evening at 6:00; spend Tuesday evening with the child from 3 until 9:00 before return to mother's home!" If one of the parents does not adhere closely to the schedule, a return visit to the court may loom, with its accompanying lawyers' bills. If the child is invited to a sleepover Friday night, whose time does that come from—the father's or the mother's? What if the child is a teenager and wants space from both parents, but is living with Mom? Finally, suppose there is a great distance between homes? A late meeting at work or a slight shift in a factory worker's schedule can wreak havoc in getting from a job to the child's home on time.

Consider visitation a two-way street. Either the visiting parent or the child can have a tight or changing schedule that can affect it. Now, add to the equation a mother and child who are not getting along well. They may be having the normal peaks and valley that all parents and children go through. Or, they may be having more problems communicating because of the divorce and their own reactions to it. In any case, visitation may not be something the child is interested in on a particular day. The mother may be reluctant to see a child who is not interested in seeing her or who was testy the last time they were together. Imagine again, a mother or child who, because of visitation, has missed out on an important business meeting or party. If they were still living in the same home, they each may more easily have given the other permission to attend. But now, with visitation mandated by the court and seen to be meaningful in light of the breakup, they are forced to spend time together.

Finally, visitation often includes "doing something" together. Depending on the age of the child, this can vary greatly. Finding interesting things to do together week after week can be quite a task. The sooner a visiting parent and child get into the routine of not having to entertain each other, the better off each will be. But if they feel their time together has to be spent doing special things, they probably will not have much fun. For these reasons, physical visitation can be a normal area of trouble.

Struggles around Telephone Contact

There are good times and bad times to get a telephone call. In some cases, the time of telephone contact is regulated by the court. In many cases though, noncustodial parents and children call each other spontaneously and attempt to speak on perhaps a weekly basis. It is the wise parent who does not call during his child's favorite TV show or when there is a major test in math the next day. Weekend evenings can be problematic if friends are over or the child is getting ready to go out. In some cases, telephone contact is timed to coincide with the absence of the custodial parent. This is especially likely to happen if that parent is monitoring calls or if the calling parent feels the child will not speak freely in the other parent's presence.

Some children are naturally uncommunicative with their parents. If the divorce has been acrimonious and has placed the child in the middle of a parental war zone, the child may be particularly reticent about talking. In turn, some parents (fathers in particular) may be uncommunicative. The child may want to talk late at night when the father is sleepy, occupied with work, or entertaining a friend. The child may know this about the father and use it as a test of the father's commitment.

When the visiting parent and child are feeling uneasy with each other, carrying on a meaningful telephone conversation may be impossible. Instead, telephone machine messages are left as they play telephone tag. Once they do speak with each other, the result can be unsatisfying. Because the parent is out of the home and out of daily contact with the child, she or he may not understand the context for the lack of communication as well as in the past. The custodial parent may be unwilling to interpret or may offer an interpretation that the calling parent does not trust or knows to be unrealistic. Within these parameters, it is easy for the calling parent or the child to feel rejected. As a result, one or both may make the decision to speak on the phone less frequently.

Visitation at Another Site

Sometimes an area of conflict is the visiting parent's ability to attend a child-related activity such as a teacher's meeting, sporting event, or school play. When all systems are running smoothly, the visiting parent and child enjoy spending time together at these events and they become a way for the relationship to deepen. But this does not always work and can misfire in two different ways. Most frequently, a child wants a parent to attend an event, but the parent is unavailable either because of a work conflict or miscommunication about the time and place of the event. Here the opportunity is missed for the growth of the relationship. If the child has felt abandoned before by a father, that father's absence heightens this feeling. If the father has felt excluded from other important events in the child's life, not being invited to a graduation, for example, heightens his own feelings of displacement.

As in the example given at the beginning of the chapter by Rachel, who had to attend basketball games to see her child, such events may take on another meaning. A mother and child may be out of contact altogether. A public forum such as a basketball game may be the only chance for her to see her child, even if it is across a gym floor. The child may not want the mother there but is unable to prevent it. Whereas the mother sees this as an opportunity, the child may see it as an intrusion.

Interparental Conflict

The struggles between a visiting parent and child are also affected by the third side of these relationships, the custodial parent. He or she interacts both with the child and the visitor and can be a facilitator or impediment. The custodial parent has the capacity to simplify visitation by helping the child be available on time, offering reminders of the visitation schedule to the child, and reinforcing the importance of seeing the other parent.

But it is often not that straightforward. For example, a custodial father can block visitation overtly or covertly. How does the father respond when the child says he would rather see a friend than spend the night with his mother? Does he subtly reinforce being with the friend rather than the mother? Or does he encourage the child to visit? Another common exchange to consider is what the mother says to the child if the father misses the scheduled visitation? Think of the implications for the father-child relationship if she takes a negative approach, such as "Your father used to stand me up, too," "I told you he was irresponsible," or "What did you expect?" A mother working to encourage visits could say, "This is not like your father; I wonder what happened," "It must not feel very good to have a visitation scheduled and then missed," or "I know he has missed in the past, but I also believe he really wants to see you."

Child support, too, can play a large part in these relationships. Mothers and fathers have been known to hinder visitation when child support is not paid. While this is illegal in many states (see chapter 7), it is not unusual and leaves the child feeling like a chip in a poker game. When children are drawn into battles over child support, as will be illustrated in the case studies, money becomes a substitute for love. "Why doesn't Daddy pay child support if he cares about me?" "Why does Daddy have things that we don't have?" and "Why is Mommy late with the payment?" are common refrains that the child may feel on his own or repeat from his custodial parent's mouth. For the visiting parent (typically the father), the battle around child support is usually not with the child but with the mother. The father may be unhappy with the way support is being spent. He may feel he is being viewed as a meal ticket and is not appreciated in his own right for being a caring, nurturing father.

Within an acrimonious atmosphere strained by child support issues, every cent is a down payment on an argument. A father-child dinner becomes a debate about why money is being spent on an expensive restaurant (or fast food) and not on clothing. Gifts are scrutinized for their price and not for the thought behind the selection of the gift. It is *possible* for parents to disagree about financial issues, yet agree about how to parent—but it is rare.

Differences about Parenting

Even when parents have a strong marriage, disagreements about parenting are natural. These stem in part from each parent's own background. For example, a father who had a happy childhood with a strict upbringing may want to raise his child as he was raised. The mother who also had a happy childhood may want to follow her roots, which happened to have been more permissive than the father's. If they each follow personal family history, there will be conflict. Additional disagreements can stem from conflicting impressions of the needs of the children, disparate impressions as to the level of closeness each parent wants with the children, and different perspectives on the role that parents should play in assisting their children with life's vagaries.

If parents who love each other disagree about parenting, it can be expected that divorced parents would have enormous problems agreeing how to parent. Disputes about religious upbringing, education, summer camp attendance, homework and part-time work expectations, and behavior in Mom's home versus Dad's home are just some of the common areas of disagreement.

As parents lock horns over these issues, their battles spill over into the relationship between parent and child. Perhaps one day the child sees things Dad's way and the next he sees things Mom's way. Maybe Mom's permissiveness works for an older child but not for a younger sibling, thereby adding another variable into the parenting equation. Perhaps the father resents the child choosing the mother's religion. However it happens, a strain is placed on each parent when the mother and father cannot agree.

As a result of these factors, the relationship between the visiting parent and child may be destined for trouble. It may be easier for visitation to cease than for a child to have to choose sides between his mother or father. It may be easier for the child or parent to withdraw.

In considering the struggles between the visiting parent and child (and why contact can eventually break off), we finally must consider the pain from the marital split, if the custodial parent is still loved, and the pain of the noncustodial parent's separation from the children. Anger or hurt feelings from the breakup almost always affect parenting decisions.

A Word about Fathers

In thinking about fathers, we do not tend to think of men feeling and expressing much emotional pain. It is not that men do not feel pain, it is that they express it differently than women do. Study after study has documented the loss of role, anger, frustration, depression, and anxiety that result when men are separated from their children. Of course there are unfeeling fathers, those who walk or run away and do not care. But the pain most fathers experience should not be minimized or denied. It becomes a driving force in the relationships they build with their ex-spouses.

A Few Words about Mothers

The pain mothers feel when separated from their children is often more enormous. Mothers who are conditioned as the nurturing and feeling member of the family are denied that expression to some extent when they become noncustodial. Society frowns upon these women and, in so doing, robs them of their ability to connect with others around this most excruciating hurt. In fact, when we look at the situations of mothers, a different lens can be used. Because of the socialization of women and mothers in the United States, it is much rarer for a mother to be noncustodial than a father, though their numbers are increasing. A brief discussion as to the reasons for this increase would be helpful in understanding their current situations. According to some research, mothers become visiting rather than custodial parents for four primary reasons:

1. They are not as financially solvent as the father. As a result, they choose to turn the children over to the father so that the children can live a better life, the children choose to live with the father who is better able to provide for them, or the mothers cannot afford to hire a legal team as competent as the father can, and so lose custody in a battle or do not contest it.

2. They are not as emotionally competent as the father. Noncustodial mothers and custodial fathers agree that in about a quarter to a third of these situations, the mother is having emotional problems that incapacitate her as a parent, or she is functioning adequately but not as capably as the father.

3. The children choose the father. Given a choice, the children either elect to stay with their dad or, after living a few years with Mom after the divorce, want to build a relationship with their father and go with him.

4. The mother loses custody in court. She may fight tooth and nail and come up on the short end of a custody decision for a variety of reasons.

Once she starts living away from her children, a noncustodial mother would be more open to criticism than a father. For example, noncustodial mothers were almost ten times as likely to receive negative feedback from others because of living away from their children than noncustodial fathers.[45] Rachel's situation, discussed earlier, provides one way of understanding what can happen. She is suffering in part because of not knowing what to tell new acquaintances about her situation. She fears the inevitable first or second question: After you meet someone and are asked what you do, you're then asked if you have children. Fathers who are noncustodial and out of touch with their children do not suffer in the *same* way, though the pain of the loss of contact can be great; it is not a pain that is reinforced constantly by society as it is for mothers, however.

Of the noncustodial mothers that I have known and written about, those in the most pain have been rejected by their children. When a child is given the choice of where he wants to live, and then chooses the father, the mother is often devastated. Typical is the mother who is shocked to find that after she has dedicated so much of her life to raising the children, they want to live with the father. Of course, in some cases, that is exactly the reason why the father is chosen: He is an unknown quantity, or the child wants to shore up a shaky relationship with him and already feels secure with the mother. The mother's attempts to establish a visiting-parent relationship are affected by this feeling of rejection and the feelings associated with rejection.

There are exceptions to the difficulty just described in building a mother–child bond. When the mother willingly turns the child over to the father because she believes it is in the best interests of the child, the foundation is often set for a positive relationship. In this situation, the mother has often accepted her circumstances and has moved into them voluntarily. There is usually little recrimination on anyone's part, thus freeing all parties (mother, child, and father) to work together as a team.

Why Stay Involved after Divorce?

With so many impediments blocking the road for the noncustodial parent, why stay involved? What is in it for a parent? Certainly love of a child is the most compelling reason. Add to that the desire to protect, nurture, and help someone you love as well as the fulfillment of the sense of personal and moral responsibility most parents feel. A need to have someone carry on the family name and the wish to leave a legacy are often mentioned, too. Noncustodial parents also stay involved in an effort to diminish their own loneliness and sense of guilt.[46]

Despite these reasons for staying involved, some parents do not. Before I give the stories of such parents I wish to briefly present one way of thinking about this process, through the use of a social exchange approach.[47] In such an approach, people behave in ways that are pleasurable to them and avoid interactions that are not. For example, when the problems in a marriage begin to outweigh the benefits the couple begins to consider divorce. It gets more complicated when applied to the noncustodial parents. As long as staying in touch with the child feels good to them, characteristic of any healthy relationship, parents will do it. But when visitation becomes a horror show, a parent may reconsider. Awkwardness and discomfort may occur if time together is not pleasurable. Such uneasiness may engender anger and conflict with the other parent, cause problems in establishing new adult-adult relationships if the child is seen as an interference, and underscore the inconvenience and costs of arranging visitations.[48]

Visiting also brings up a mirroring for the parent who suffers from low self-esteem. A parent who believes he is worthless or believes he has behaved in a shameful way is reminded of that every time he sees his child. The child is a painful reflection of the parent, and if the parent does not like what he or she sees, the cost of visiting can be too great.

While this may help explain theoretically the situation of parents in this book who have voluntarily removed themselves from contact with their children, what about those who perceive that they have been denied contact? This is a tricky group to theorize about because it includes not only parents who have been denied visitation despite continuing to fight for it, but also those who have fought and then have given up. It could be argued that this second group voluntarily walked away from the battle after a few losses, having assessed the emotional and financial pros and cons of continuing it (an example of social exchange theory).

The Context of Child Support

One topic that needs discussion is that of child support and its relation to visitation. Because married men usually earn more than women, the payment of child support when the mother becomes a single parent is vitally important to her well-being and that of her children. In some cases (though a statistically smaller number), payment by a noncustodial mother is also vitally important. Why do parents choose or refuse to pay child support?

A spokeswoman for one private organization in California that attempts to collect child support from parents in arrears[49] describes two groups of non-payers: Those who were once married and those who were never married. Based on the cases that she sees, she believes mothers and fathers who were once married do not pay because of visitation disputes stemming from the breakup of the marriage. Among the never-married population, fathers are not paying because they never wanted the child and in some cases have never seen the child. Because they do not see their children, they do not want to pay for them. A few complain that they want to see them but are blocked by the mother. The spokeswoman's response to this is to tell them to "put their money where their mouth is!"

What is the feeling toward their children, I wondered, among the parents she and her organization are pursuing for child support? "The ones who have had prior relationships with their children are angry, frustrated, sad, and lonely. But they also feel it is too costly to them to try and get visitation so they don't try."[50] Lawyers may be discouraging them from pursuing contact because of the large fees they charge. If no prior relationship was established with the child, the parents do not appear to care about the child and are angry at paying support. This is the impression of one person working in the netherworld of private child support collection.

Child support has become a cause célèbre. Advocacy and support groups throughout the country, such as Fathers United for Equal Rights, often target legislators for child support and custody reform. "Deadbeat" dads have been a target of legislators for years as denial of paternity by some fathers and lack of child support payments by others have caused many mothers to spiral down into poverty. Child support is needed to help stop the financial drain.

What affects whether fathers pay? They often pay out of obligation—because they have been ordered to and fear the penalties of not paying, or because their salaries are being garnished and they have no option. When they do not pay, there are various reasons: They may feel they are being asked to pay too much; perhaps they are unhappy with the way the money is being spent by the mother; possibly, they are being ignored by the child; and they could view themselves as being "loved" or "needed" only for their financial resources.[51] One study, using reports of mothers, concludes that fathers do not provide a great deal of assistance (clothing, gifts, medical care, et cetera), other than child support.[52] But if fathers do contribute in other ways, they are likely to maintain more harmonious relations with the custodial mother.[53]

Several approaches have been tried to increase child support, from the garnishing of wages and tough compliance laws to enrollment in state-supported programs that work with the nonpaying parent. The method for calculating what child support payments should be varies greatly both within and between states.[54] A Wisconsin-based study of nonmarried mothers found that strict enforcement increased fathers' child support compliance. As also might be expected, higher income among the fathers was associated with a greater likelihood to pay. Correctly setting payment levels is key. Very poor fathers who were ordered to pay a small amount were more apt to be compliant than fathers asked to pay a higher percentage.[55]

Whereas most of the child support discussion focuses on nonpaying fathers, mothers also may be in arrears. My own research with noncustodial mothers indicates that those who are ordered to pay often do so because they feel it is their obligation to support their children or out of a fear of legal reprisals. Those who initially had custody after the breakup but became noncustodial will then pay the father if he had paid them during mother custody. Conversely, mothers sometimes do not pay if they were not supported by the father when they had custody. They also do not pay if they perceive a great income gap between themselves and a higher-earning father, or if they are specifically asked by the father to not pay. In this last situation, the father may feel it is unnecessary for the mother to pay because of her less solvent financial position or because he was the financial provider during the marriage and feels uncomfortable accepting money from her. Occasionally a father will discourage payment of support so that if there is future custody litigation custody, he can use a lack of payment against her.[56] Because mothers are a smaller population and are less likely to cause a custodial father to fall into poverty, little attention is paid to them.[57]

Up to this point I have described some of the difficulties that can arise to make visitation difficult. I will now briefly discuss situations in which parents have little or no contact. Two questions will be explored: (1) What is known about children of divorce and contact with their parents? (2) What is known about parents who stop having contact with their children?

When Children Grow Up without Regular Contact with Their Fathers

Social scientists have long been interested in the development of children who grow up seeing one of their parents either occasionally or not at all. Debate has raged about the necessity of having contact with a parent, particularly a father, in order to insure adequate growth and development. Still unresolved is the definition of contact. For example, should it be defined by the number of visits or the quality of the father-child relationship? Who defines the amount and quality of contact is also at issue: Should it be the custodial parent, the visiting parent, the child, or an outside observer such as a teacher?[58] Even the role that a substitute father, a man other than the biological father, can play in the life of a child has been raised as a critical variable in assessing the impact of fatherlessness.[59]

Contact between a child and a father following divorce frequently trails off. In one study from the early 1980s, one-third of a nationally representative sample of separated and divorced mothers reported that their children had not seen the father in the last five years. Another one-sixth reported their child's last contact was one to five years before the interview. Only one in six reported at least weekly contact, and another one in six reported at least monthly contact. Visiting mothers, a much smaller proportion of the sample, maintained more frequent contact with their children.[60] As might be expected, the longer the time period since the end of the marriage, the more likely there is to be no contact. Of the children whose parents had been divorced for ten years or more, two-thirds were out of contact with their fathers, a frightening statistic! Children whose parents were married at one time are as likely to not have contact as children whose parents never married and separated shortly after the birth.[61] Neither age nor gender of the child seemed to have a specific effect on visitation in this study, though it has been hypothesized elsewhere that fathers see sons more often than daughters post-divorce and play a more important role in their development.[62] Another study looked at the psychological issues involved in noncustodial dads staying in touch with their children three years after divorce. The more competent the father felt (which meant how needed he felt) and the easier it was to arrange visitation, the more apt he was to stay involved. Further, a father who remained involved with his children one year after the breakup was likely to stay involved at the three year post-divorce mark.[63]

A different body of research, based almost exclusively on samples in which fathers were absent, has looked at how children do when they have little contact with a noncustodial parent. A high correlation has been found between adolescents without fathers or other male substitutes and the personality traits of young offenders. However, boys living away from fathers but in contact with a significant male substitute fared as well on a battery of psychological tests as boys living with fathers.[64]

Other studies are less clear about the positive influence of a father.[65] A recent review of thirty-three studies examining the hypothesis that children's well-being is positively associated with contact with the visiting parent found that eighteen supported the hypothesis, nine found no correlation, and six concluded frequency of visitation was associated with more problems in the children.[66] One group[67] concludes there is little to support the notion that contact with a father after a marital breakup has either positive or negative effects on children's well-being. (They do suggest, and it is something for parents who worry about the long-term effects of divorce to remember, that single events such as a family breakup, while significant, may have less of an impact over time on a child's well-being than previously thought. Later events in a child's life that are positive can mitigate the impact of any one experience).[68]

The age of children and how they experience the departure of a parent can help us understand how they may cope later. Children in one study were reported to be terrified by the departure of the father, even when there had been family violence. For young children, the departure was similar to a magical event: They wondered what had happened to him. Visitation both in the home and at the father's new residence helped reassure the children. Older children, while cognitively more aware of the father's removal from the home, still experienced anxiety about his whereabouts.[69]

Despite the subtleties of the research findings, experts generally agree that children adjust better to divorce when they have contact with both parents *and* those parents are getting along well, and when each parent is content with his or her life. Yet this is unfortunately far from the usual order of the day, which leads to the second question, "What is known about fathers who stop having contact?"

While we look at this group, we should remember that it consists of divorced people. Divorce in and of itself is fraught with stresses, from increased risk of psychiatric hospitalizations (greater for divorced men than women), to car accidents, suicides, homicides, and deaths due to diseases.[70]

When the divorced man is a father and children are involved the stress is greater. A comparison of eighty noncustodial fathers from Canada and Scotland who were divided into two groups—those with continuing involvement and those without contact—revealed that those with the greatest attachment to their children prior to the divorce were the ones most apt to reduce contact afterwards. The interpretation was that, in order to deal with their unhappiness over their changing parental status, fathers withdraw. An overwhelming number of these fathers experienced a great deal of distress from their noncustodial status and went through a period of mourning after they moved out.[71] This sense of pain and loss experienced by fathers out of daily touch with their children has been reflected in other research that surveyed fathers.[72]

The hurt from separation can continue for years. It can lead to a cycle of infrequent visitation because depressed men have been noted to find it very painful to visit, as do those who feel guilty at having ended the marriage. Fathers who visited less, according to Wallerstein and Kelly, were those who felt unappreciated by their children and were blamed for the breakup. In addition, men who viewed the mother as psychologically intact visited less, as did men who themselves were psychologically unstable. Finally, when the parents were not getting along, dads visited less often.[73]

One study of eight-four fathers with infrequent or no contact with their children concluded the low level of visitation was due to the former spouse impeding visitation, the father having emotional problems, the children's desire for independence, and the great geographic distance separating father and child. Of particular interest, most of the fathers who cited emotional problems as the reason for no contact said they were satisfied with this lack of contact. The author believes that these fathers may feel inadequate as parents, may be discouraged from maintaining contact by a new wife or a close friend, or may feel it is in the children's best interests if they drop out.[74]

In some African-American communities, according to Charles Ballard, the founder of the National Institute for Responsible Fatherhood and Family Development and himself an African-American, young males are not in touch with their offspring because they often do not *perceive* themselves as fathers. There is little to tie them to the mother and the child. He recounts approaching a group of teenagers on a playground and, after talking to them for awhile, asking how many of them had children. The hand of almost every boy went up. Then I asked, 'Okay, now, how many of you are fathers?' And the hands wavered and fell."[75]

It is important to note that not all fathers who stop having contact with their children are upset by this consequence. Some are content and do not want more contact with them.[76] This harkens back to the social exchange theory stated earlier: When the costs outweigh the benefits or the father believes he is a bad influence, he may stop visiting if it is too hard or painful.

When Children Grow Up without Regular Contact with Their Mothers

We have much less information about children being raised by fathers away from mothers. What has been ascertained so far is tentative. Some early thinking maintains that children do better being raised by same-sex parents.[77] Sons, then, would seem to not be hurt by living away from mothers as much as daughters would be hurt. More recent and rigorous research indicates that no such benefits accrue to children being raised by a same-sex parent.[78] In general, the research on father-headed families attests to the success of this family form as a viable living arrangement for children of both genders.

Similarities have been established between what noncustodial mothers and what noncustodial fathers experience,[79] though, as mentioned earlier, I believe the pain for the mothers to often be even greater. The reasons are manifold. Societal pressure, what some people believe is a greater nurturing instinct in mothers than fathers, the intense bonding between mother and child, especially when younger, all contribute to make separation from the child extremely painful. Loss of custody often occurs at the time of termination of the marriage, so other losses are being experienced simultaneously. These can include dismantling the home, separation from friends, loss of financial support, destruction of the dream of a married life, and loss of a loved husband if the divorce was unwanted. Many mothers lose their sense of self when they lose contact with their children. In addition, their families may be unsupportive. They often are derided by their own mothers.[80] Some feel oppressed by the court system and their ex-husbands and marginalized by society.[81] They may have little means of support (particularly if they were full-time homemakers and have no marketable job skills). They are not apt to receive alimony if the father has custody and is financially supporting the children.[82]

As a result, this loss of contact, unlike the fathers', is more likely to be a double whammy: They suffer from the separation and feel further under attack from friends, family, and an economic situation that makes access to opportunities more problematic. Certainly, as with noncustodial fathers, we can estimate that when a noncustodial mother is adapting well to her status, there is a greater possibility of her children also adapting.

I am not concluding that children need both parents in the home to be healthy and that a motherless or fatherless family is less than whole. Many single parent families have marvelous and successful lives. Rather, I am saying that the odds of children and parents adjusting more smoothly after the breakup increase if both parents remain involved.

Mourning is one final issue that needs mentioning. As will be seen in the interviews with the mothers and fathers, many parents have a mourning or grief reaction to their loss of contact with their children. It is difficult for them to express this because society does not have a mourning ritual for parents who are not visiting their children. Death is a clear marker for beginning to mourn. Funerals as rituals help people make a public statement about a loss. But how should the divorced parents in this book behave, parents who are also in mourning over their loss? And how can neighbors and friends react to them in a way that is nurturing and will assist in adaptation? The answers do not exist at the moment.

While I have focused on each parent's part in effectuating visitation, a note on the children is needed. Custodial parents sometimes block visitation and noncustodial parents find it difficult to visit or choose not to, but children also get turned off to seeing the visiting parent. It is easy to understand from the child's perspective. If parents are fighting a great deal over visitation, some children are going to absent themselves from the dispute. But such a move hurts the noncustodial parent. More on this appears when I discuss the children in chapter 6. But consider for now, that the child's reaction to the noncustodial parent as well as visitation conflicts in general can have a significant bearing on how the parent behaves and how strenuously the parent wants to fight to see the child.

If the literature overwhelmingly concluded that contact when parents *are* in conflict is harmful to the child, the solution would not be to stop contact, it would be to attempt to improve the parents' relationship (except when there has been violence). Learning that children do not fare well when parents are fighting should not result in the child not seeing one of the parents, it should result in the parents working to resolve their differences so that access to both parents continues. As will be seen in the stories that follow, children and parents need each other.

A Brief Look at the Book

I use the results of the study and twenty-six interviews in the next four chapters and in chapter 8 as beginning points and as a way to make broad statements about what some parents experience being away from their children and why and how they have reached this point. In chapter 6, ten children from six different families are interviewed, thus adding stories to those that we hear from children in the previous chapters.

Chapter 7, written by Rebecca Hegar, a social policy expert, focuses on legal issues facing these families. She also addresses the changes in social policy that affect these families. In chapter 8, discussion focuses on families who have resumed contact with each other. The chapter concludes with general proposals for fixing the issues raised in the book. The final chapter takes a different approach by speaking directly to family members who are struggling with these issues. Self-help advice is offered to parents, children, and grandparents about how to prevent the loss of contact in the first place and how to resolve it when it does occur.

Finally, we must consider the following: *Why believe them?* In most instances I have not interviewed both the noncustodial and the custodial parent. As in most divorces, we do not know whose side of the story is the truth, and it is uncertain that any amount of interviewing of all the parties concerned would yield a single truth. Have the parents I interviewed built a Potemkin village that I have stopped to admire? Have they merely constructed a façade of a life that makes them the more admirable?

What we have known about these parents in the past comes largely from the custodial parent. Are their descriptions always accurate? It is time to hear from this population without assuming they are necessarily lying because they are out of contact. There are parents who claim to have been shut out of their children's lives. I am not always convinced I have heard the truth. What I am convinced of is that this information may help us to better decide where to go from here in breaking this debilitating cycle. We will not stop divorce and families from splitting up. The question is this: Can we improve the divorce process and, in some cases, make contact more likely to continue?

Chapter 2

When Fathers and Children No Longer Visit

Feelings of Inadequacy and Rejection

Why do fathers lose contact with their children after a divorce? What do they say is the reason for their seeming abandonment of their sons and daughters? Whereas the first chapter set the groundwork for understanding the situations of noncustodial parents, and cites studies that report that fathers are absent in between 30 percent and 66 percent of separated families, in these next two chapters I pursue 11 fathers' stories and examine them in light of the survey of 109 fathers who were out of contact. I have chosen to divide the fathers into two chapters. This chapter focuses on the less acrimonious instances of how fathers come to be noncustodial, situations in which the father seems to be the root cause of the loss of contact or in which the child is viewed as rejecting the father. In the next chapter, where the level of rancor is much higher, the mother is blamed for lack of contact or allegations of abuse have been leveled against the father.

It is almost impossible to turn on the TV or radio news, or pick up the newspaper these days, and not hear a sound bite or see some headline leaping out about fathers who are ducking child support payments and abandoning their children. One father, Jeffrey Nichols, was recently vilified for not paying the $580,000 he owed his ex-wife for the care of their two children. He also did not visit them.

Fathers have also been framed more sympathetically. In one newspaper article, a man is featured who left a middle-class existence for life in a run-down home, the only lodging he could afford, after his wife asked for a divorce. He pays almost half his monthly salary in child support. His greatest concern is losing contact with his youngest daughter, who, at the time he was interviewed, he had not seen for seven weeks. When she went to camp, she wrote him a letter begging him not to come to parents' visiting day because it would be awkward with her mother there. The father reports he has been depressed and at times suicidal since the divorce. He feels at fault and unable to bridge the widening gap that could result in an eventual loss of contact. "My impression is that they don't give a damn about me," he said. "Zero. Absolutely nothing. I have become completely irrelevant. And it hurts very much."[1]

Not all stories, as this chapter shows, are as dramatic as these. Some fathers I have met over the years removed themselves and make no serious attempt to see their children. They withdraw because they are angry at their ex-wives and blame them for rejecting them, mismanaging family finances, mistreating the children, making friends with the wrong crowd, remarrying, and so on. (Blaming the other spouse is common in divorce). It is not only anger that causes the fathers to drift off, it can also be hurt. They are upset at being unloved, being replaced by new people, and being perceived as unimportant. One father told me he stopped visiting his daughter because it was too painful: she reminded him of his ex-wife who he still loved! Sometimes they accept responsibility for their part in the dissolution of the relationship, sometimes not.

Other fathers make consistent attempts to see their children and are thwarted. They believe they have acted in a manner that should allow them access to their children, but because of a variety of circumstances, many of which they perceive as related to the behavior of their ex-wives, they are unable to maintain contact. The eleven cases presented in this chapter and the next, arranged under four separate headings, include both those who have voluntarily withdrawn and those who report they have been forced out of the picture.

As I was beginning my interviews with these dads, I spent some time with a leader of a local chapter of Fathers United for Equal Rights,[2] a support group for parents who feel mistreated by the court system. The leader offered a not surprisingly sympathetic view of what happens to fathers during the legal machinations that follow divorce. He also put his finger on many of the key issues they face. "Many of these guys have no clue about how to raise children and need to be more active in pursuing custody or visitation at the time of settlement." They are bewildered, he believes, by parenting and by the divorce process.

After the breakup, they become estranged from their children because of the mother who, for whatever reason, is perceived as not fostering contact. Additional issues interfere. Some fathers, already unsure of their parenting abilities, are easily convinced that they have significant shortcomings as parents. Others withdraw because they feel they are being harassed over child support. Allegations of child abuse occasionally are raised to prevent the father from having contact. The father is kept away from the child during an investigation and finds it difficult to resume visitation if he is exonerated. Finally, he believes the legal community discourages fathers from pursuing custody unless the case for them and against the mothers is airtight.

Is my source on target? Certainly he presents a picture of victimized fathers that is commonly seen at fathers' rights groups. But a little expansion is necessary. Many parents enter the court system for the first time in their lives when they divorce. They do not understand the adversarial nature of the proceedings. Accusations are made, epithets hurled, and property and children divided justly and unjustly. Emotionally and financially the process can be terribly debilitating. They start out hoping for something and end up with nothing and quite embittered. Some fathers are emotionally immature. Ill-prepared for marriage in the first place, they are unable to handle the painful rejection and loss of family that accompanies divorce. They do not know what to do with themselves and do not respond in ways that build a sense of continuity with their children or that recognize the importance of co-parenting.

Some fathers are accustomed to having the mother mediate their relationship with the children. They do not understand all the demands of parenting either within a marriage or as a single parent. (The youngest fathers are the most unaware). During the marriage, the mother has often served as a traffic cop. She sets up the times that the father and children spend together. She often relishes this role, and the father is happy to turn it over to her. His abdication of a more equal parenting role is based on his belief in his own financial importance to the family juxtaposed with his belief that the mother should be more central with the children.

With the mother more removed from the father-child interaction, things do not flow smoothly unless the father is emotionally prepared. Very often, without a compass, the father and child are misdirected. They may not know how to handle the nuances of their relationship without the mother's input. As my source indicated, the stage is set for problems.

A word about allegations of abuse brought against the fathers. It has been well established that some men abuse and sexually molest their children. It has also been well established that some men have been falsely accused of such actions either intentionally, to increase the mother's leverage in a court battle, or mistakenly. For example, in 1992, agencies designed to protect children received a total of nearly two million reports of abuse and neglect involving almost three million children. Following investigation, 59 percent were found to be unsubstantiated.[3] Other studies, including one cited in chapter 7, have found a much higher rate of substantiation of charges when they are made in cases where custody is being disputed. Abuse charges need thorough investigation and should be examined with the best interests of the child in mind. Such interests need to include continued contact, when warranted, with both parents.

Finally, to what extent are lawyers discouraging fathers from pursuing custody? In the sample surveyed for this book, when lawyers were consulted, three out of four discouraged the father from pursuing custody. By comparison, two out of three mothers were encouraged to pursue it. These findings may confirm the impression that fathers supposedly get about their chances in court, though without knowing a great deal more about each case it is hard to draw any definitive conclusions.

A Look at 109 Fathers

What can we learn from the fathers in these out-of-contact situations? I will first describe some of the characteristics of the 109 fathers in the research before going to the 11 in-depth cases.

The fathers in this study, 96 percent of whom are white, with an average annual income of thirty-one thousand dollars (a range of eight thousand to eighty thousand dollars) earn almost exactly the same as the average divorced man living away from his wife in the United States.[4] They tend to be in their mid-forties, with occupations most predominantly in business or sales, followed by laborer, and then professional. The fathers had been separated or divorced on average for nine years at the time of the survey. They were living away from two hundred children, 59 percent of whom were daughters. More than half had children age eighteen and under.

The actual patterns of contact between father and children sometimes varied by child (if he had fathered more than one). Almost one in three fathers had other biological or stepchildren, and, in over 80 percent of those situations, the fathers had more contact with those other children than with the child from whom the father was estranged. This becomes particularly important when one considers that a parent who is still in touch with some of his children is potentially in a situation much different from that of one who has no contact with all of his children. Fathers with differential contact clearly have demonstrated the capacity for a relationship and cannot be classified as easily as being an emotional deadbeat.

The fathers were asked to indicate their level of contact with the child and whether it was in person, by telephone, or by letter. Telephone and letter contact were included because many parents who live a great distance from their children and have a good relationship with them may not visit the child but substitute another form of communication. This allowed for a cross-check of whether a parent was truly out of contact. Over half the fathers reported they had absolutely no physical contact and rarely had telephone contact with their child in the previous year. The remainder had phone or written contact that varied up to a few times a year, though they had no contact of any kind within the previous six months, the time frame required to participate in the study. The sense is that they all felt effectively out of touch with their child.

The fathers were also asked how long ago the relationship ceased. The most frequently mentioned length of absence was eight years, with periods of two years and four years mentioned next as most frequent. Thus, these were fathers who in many cases had gone for substantial lengths of time without seeing their children.

The courts played a significant part in resolving custody disputes in almost half of the cases, a point that will reappear in the case studies. Two-thirds of the fathers were required to pay child support, and 80 percent said they always paid what they owed. Finally, six out of every seven fathers reported they wanted more contact with their child than they were having.

Why do these fathers say contact ceased? This was explored in two ways to gain the maximum information. The fathers could select from four choices for why contact had ceased. They also could write in a reason. Sixty-two percent blamed the other parent, 30 percent contributed it to distance, 16 percent blamed their own issues, and 16 percent blamed the children's issues, with no consistent write-in answer given.

The fathers were also asked to write in their own words why they were not seeing the children. The chief reason they gave was that *the other parent interfered* with their relationship with their children by poisoning the child against them or by not allowing visitation. Distance was mentioned only occasionally.

A note is needed here about the role that the court system plays in preventing a father from having contact. Courts get involved in disputes and often appear unhelpful to the fathers. I decided to not consider the court system as a separate reason for a father losing contact because frequently the court was involved *and* was perceived as unhelpful. By definition, these fathers would not have participated in the research if the court had been helpful.

Other facts about the sample were also gathered. Nineteen percent admitted to a history of substance abuse (twice as high as estimates of substance abuse in the general population).[5] Nine percent said they alone had been violent during the marriage toward their spouse, another 9 percent said violence had been perpetrated by both spouses, and 17 percent said only their ex-spouses had been violent. In total, 35 percent of the marriages included a history of domestic violence, somewhat above one estimate of 28 percent of marriages being so characterized[6] (though the estimate of violence in marriages that end in divorce may be higher). In relation to their children, 24 percent said there had been an allegation of child abuse lodged against them, which is not the same as admitting to abuse. (In chapter 7 allegations of sexual abuse are noted to arise in 2 percent of custody disputes). Almost 80 percent described themselves as "involved" or "very involved" with their children during the marriage. Finally, three-quarters felt unhappy (angry, guilty, lonely, abandoned) about not seeing their children. The remainder felt indifferent or happy about being out of contact.[7]

To briefly recap, these 109 fathers (remember, they are members of Parents without Partners and may not be representative) earn an average income and have a great deal of experience with being out of contact with their children; it is not a new phenomenon for them. The majority said they had been involved parents during the marriage and are unhappy with the lack of contact now. Their marriages were marked by substance abuse and domestic violence as well as allegations of sexual abuse that occur more often than the norm. The ex-wives are blamed for the lack of contact in the majority of cases. It will take a comparison with the responses given by the mothers, discussed in chapter 4, to help us to better understand these responses.

A quantitative study of this sort does not provide the richness that is needed to better understand the ins and outs of the fathers' situations. For this reason, I embarked on the interviews. Who were the men I interviewed? Some came from the study just cited. Others came from specific attempts to find a more racially and economically balanced sample. I went to a fathers' rights groups as well as a government program that attempts to rehabilitate fathers who were in arrears on child support. Others I met by accident, people not associated with any organization, who agreed to be interviewed. It seems whenever I began talking about my research someone popped up who either fit the description or had a family member or friend who did.

What I found from the more than twenty interviews I completed, eleven of them case studies presented here, are four patterns that lead to loss of father-child contact. These patterns encompass most, but not all, of the situations I have come across. I begin with the more usual cases in this chapter and then proceed in the next to provide those associated with greater conflict, the more extreme cases. Most readers will see either themselves, their family members, or their clients in these patterns. Some cutoffs occur precipitously, while others are slow in evolving. Overlap exists between the patterns. The patterns that emerge are driven by a wealth of factors, yet all have in common that they are tinged with the pain of separation for the fathers. Two patterns are described here and two others in chapter 3.

Pattern 1: Fathers Who Feel Inadequate

Fathers in this group look the most like the stereotypical father who drops out or loses contact because of the vagaries of divorce. These would be men whose lives were affected by moves to a new city, feelings of rejection, and the pain of watching a new family develop that the father is not a part of. What I believe these fathers have in common is that they possess a basic sense of inadequacy and to some extent feel shame at their own actions. This feeling leads to or is exacerbated by emotional problems (such as substance abuse) and affects their judgment. Many believe, incorrectly, that they are not important to their children and withdraw. Attached to this type of thinking is a low self-estimate of the value of a father to children. This sometimes gets played out when the father believes a child is better off with a high functioning mother,[8] as is the case with Bill, whose story follows, and many other fathers who leave the home.

When a father is struggling with substance abuse, the alcohol or drug takes on greater importance than maintaining the relationship with the family. There is no room for anyone else in the father's life, and the father may feel ashamed about his behavior and be unwilling to inflict himself on his family (as John's example will show). Some fathers who drop out feel unneeded and ashamed if their role as breadwinner has been overemphasized to the diminution of their role as nurturer. If they are under- or unemployed, they may feel a sense of economic inadequacy because they cannot provide what they are supposed to as men.[9]

To some extent, most of the fathers I interviewed in the book *are* inadequate, though to classify all of them as such would diminish the importance of their messages about how their situations evolve.

Pattern 2: Fathers Who Are Rejected by the Children

Children sometimes decide to stop seeing the father. They may be being pulled between both parents and decide to sit out the dance their parents are performing around the struggle for custody or visitation because it becomes too stressful to be caught up in the battle. They may be at an age when spending time with any parent is not their first choice, regardless of the relationship they have with that parent. Some children pull away from a father who they see as hurting their mother emotionally, financially, or physically. The father may have a nicer home or a new family, or be taking expensive vacations, which the children resent. Other times there is a lack of communication that, with only occasional contact, is hard to resolve. It becomes easier to not speak than to try to clarify issues during an abbreviated visitation.

Pattern 1: Fathers Who Feel Inadequate

BILL

To politicians, social policy experts, and the layperson, Bill conjures up the classic image of the deadbeat father. For years he did not pay child support, and his daughter became eligible for Aid to Families with Dependent Children due, in part, to Bill's refusal. In effect, his refusal caused the taxpayer to shell out more money. The government came after him, and now he is supporting her to a greater extent than he was. I met Bill, an African-American in his thirties, through a state-run child support program established specifically to cope with parents who were in arrears for significant amounts of money.

Whereas John, the next father, made every attempt to keep up with his child support payments while out of touch with his son, Bill did not. Remarriage played a part here, as it so often does when one parent is no longer in contact with his previous family. Often the remarried parent is the one to stop contact. The previous spouse can also be the one to stop it, as in the case here.

Bill has children from two separate families, which represent two different phases of his life. He has not seen his daughter from his first marriage for over ten years. This saddens him but, at the same time, he believes she is being raised well by her mother. He also has three children from a second marriage who are the focus of his attention now.

Raised primarily by a mother and stepfather, Bill's own father was a figure he saw only occasionally in the neighborhood. Their connection was not strong but it was acknowledged. While it could be hypothesized that someone who has only a tenuous tie with a parent may in turn have peripheral contact with their own child, Bill does not draw any such link. He views the issues as separate.

At seventeen he enlisted in the military and was stationed in Louisiana, where he met his first wife. After they were married, they lived happily together for seven years before deciding to have a child. With the birth of

Sandra, their only child, their living situation and their marital relationship shifted. Bill recounted, "We had done everything we wanted to, so we felt it was time to become parents. Problems between us started after Sandra was born and I was sent overseas. It got to be your normal disagreements. We tried to keep things inside, and then they would just blow up. We were young when we married, and after a while we began to nag each other."

When Sandra was one year old, they decided to separate. At the time they were living in Florida, where Bill had been reassigned. Custody was a forgone conclusion and was decided without rancor. "My wife wanted to move back [to Louisiana] to be with her family, and I agreed a daughter should be with her mother, so they left. She was a good mother. Our differences were between her and me, and there was no reason to put the child in the middle. There were also things I still wanted to do."

Because Sandra was quite young when she and her mother moved away from Bill, contact between daughter and father was problematic. "I would call on the phone, and her mother would put the telephone to her ear, but it was hard for her to know who I was. I would call three to four times a month, but I never went out to visit her. I knew they were alright, I didn't worry about them. I was paying child support directly out of my check. I would write, and her mother and I talked about getting back together. Then I wondered if it would be the right thing for us to do and would things escalate again.... So I haven't seen her since and we got divorced three years later."

Bill remarried shortly thereafter. He left the service, and soon became the father of three other daughters. He thinks that his remarriage was upsetting to his first wife and that she made future communication with Sandra more difficult because of it. Sandra began to recede further from his thoughts as he juggled the daily demands of three other younger children. Eventually he lost direct contact with Sandra and heard about her only occasionally from his mother, who maintained sporadic contact. He is not even sure if his mother has seen Sandra and his ex-wife, saying, "I don't want to interfere with them."

Ironically, it is Bill's other daughters who want to meet their half sister. "I know how my other daughters feel about seeing Sandra because I recently found out I have a sister that I never knew about. If it all works out, I would like them to see each other at some point. My younger ones ask about Sandra, and I now have a picture of her that my mother was sent. I can't do much because I don't know exactly where she is. I don't think it will be a lost cause, but I think I will see her again. I would love to see her again. After not seeing her for ten years, I would love to even just talk to her. Money is still being taken out of my paycheck for support. I don't resent paying it because that is my daughter; she is still a child, and children are innocent, and she deserves the money."

In trying to understand Bill's thoughts and feelings, it is important to highlight a few points. First, he believes Sandra is being well taken care of. Second, he has the demands of other children on his mind. Third, he never established an especially close bond with her because she was quite young when the separation occurred, and during the first year of her life he was stationed overseas, away from the family. Yet here, with the garnishing of his wages and his enrollment in a child support program for parents who are in arrears, he is back in contact in some form. His statement that, on the one hand he does not want to interfere with her life, but on the other he would love to talk with her and has her picture, is emblematic of the ambivalence he must feel. Because he loves his new family, he also must reexperience the possibility of loving Sandra, too. Bill did not "screw up" the way that John in the next case did. But he also undervalued his own role as a father, did not know how to express his love and affection for such a young child living a great distance away, and believed that Sandra would be well taken care of even if he were out of the picture. While this may be true, his withdrawal may also have caused more problems for Sandra than she needed to experience. Because I didn't talk with her or her mother, it is hard to know.

Does knowing his side of the story make a difference? Is this a situation in which the role of father has been diminished by distance and by his acceptance of the prevailing assumption at the time that fathers are not needed? Bill does not seem to suffer from not seeing Sandra, though it may be hard for him to allow himself to experience the suffering, given the pressing demands of a new family. But from the outside, this is a man who has dropped out of sight and has not seen his child for ten years.

This next case is another common situation: the father who, because of significant personal problems, believes his son is better off without him.

JOHN

John had everything: A job résumé that read like that of a regional star in management, a Ph.D. in education, and an exemplary work history. He was the boss. Articulate and bright, in his late forties, he presented himself as being warm and supportive to his staff and visitors. He could walk out of one job one night and into another almost literally the next week by calling on old friends. In fact, that happened once when the politics at one organization necessitated him leaving for another.

But there was one major problem with this picture. He was an alcoholic. He told me that before he sobered up, he lived in fear all of the time. That fear affected his relationship with his coworkers, his wife, and his son. He arranged his work schedule around his drinking. He tried to arrange his home schedule around his drinking, too, but that was impossible.

John's wife divorced him. Because of the fear that was now ruling his life, John withdrew. He refused to see his son, whose approval he needed, for three years. He didn't want to be seen as an alcoholic. "I was ashamed of who I was, so I stayed away." It was not until he went to AA that he began to consider visiting him again. Alcoholics, as mentioned earlier, have a diminished capacity to care for someone else as they become a slave to drinking. A drug addict suffers from the same tendencies. Putting aside the substance to work on a relationship with a child is all but impossible and leads to a cycle of further denial—denying the important role the parent can play for the child and denying the pain that is inflicted on the child by the parent's absenting behavior.

John fits the stereotype of the alcoholic who drops out and stops seeing his children. Except he did care about his son. It was, in part, his caring about him that convinced John his son would be better off with him out of his life. While this could be said to be a loving position to take, to protect one's child from the parent's dark side, it could also be seen as a misguided perception and an inability to show love and acceptance, a significant weakness. Parents with problems such as alcoholism often have feelings so negative about themselves that they feel unloveable. Rather than be rejected by their children, and thus confirming their beliefs, they pull away first.

From the outside, he is the father who has dropped out. From the inside, he is the tortured soul who does not feel good enough about himself to talk to or visit his child. With time, John did begin seeing his son again. But it was an uncomfortable reconciliation and one that is still problematic. John hoped his son would want to talk to me, but my two attempts over the course of a year proved fruitless. Yes, his son told me, he was back in touch with John, but, no, he would rather discuss his feelings with John than with me. He was not even sure he was ready to do that, the hurt ran so deep.

These fathers give up their children believing they as parents are unneeded, that the children are better off without them. In many cases, such as Bill's, they have been conditioned to believe that mothers are more important. They feel totally ineffectual as parents. They make the decision unilaterally to withdraw rather than helping their children to decide if they want to stay in contact with them. It is hard to know how many fathers have dropped out of their children's lives for these reasons and whether, if they *felt* as needed as they often are, they would reappear.

Pattern 2: Fathers Who Are Rejected by Their Children

As stated in the first chapter, circumstances often mitigate against parents and children staying in contact. Many things can interfere. Most important, a father, as the responsible adult, may not be creating an atmosphere or relationship that will encourage the child to stay in touch. For the father and child, a situation arises such that each party is waiting for the other to make a motion toward reconciliation. With such a standoff, and the father not acknowledging his own role in the proceedings, the atmosphere is ripe for misinterpretation and hurt feelings. At times fathers claim they never knew what the problem was, a derogation of the parent role. It is every parent's responsibility to know what the circumstances are regarding his relationship with his child.

MANUEL

Some fathers can be quite unexpressive at first when it comes to describing their situations. It is hard to know whether they do not understand what has happened to them or are just uncomfortable talking about it. Differences in culture between an interviewer and a father can also play a part. I interviewed Manuel three times over twelve months before I gained a sense of his story. He could be seen certainly as an inadequate father, but I think the major thrust of his story is that he has been rejected by his son.

Manuel, a Mexican-American by birth, was raised in Texas and moved to New Mexico just before completing high school. He met his wife, Maritza, his senior year, and they married two years later when he was completing a stint in the service. One daughter and twin sons were born within the next four years. "The marriage was happy at first, but Maritza was not interested in being a mother. She did not have maternal instincts. She took care of them but her heart wasn't in it. I was the oldest of twelve children and knew how to bathe them and feed them, and she did not."

The marriage became shaky as Maritza spent less and less time at home. They separated for six months, reconciled, and then separated for a final time when the children were fourteen and sixteen. "I got custody because she wanted to find herself. I don't know what book she was reading at the time," Manuel said, disparagingly alluding to Maritza's tendencies to follow whatever social trends were in fashion at the moment. When child support was being arranged, Manuel reported, Maritza did not want to pay it, so she maneuvered for one of the boys to live with her. A year and a half later, the second son followed. Their daughter was out of the home by this time, so Manuel moved back in with his parents.

I asked Manuel why the children left and why he lost contact with them. Manuel was vague at first but alluded to his not being "man enough" in his sons' eyes. His daughter, on the other hand, has no conflict with him and sees him regularly. One son eventually resumed contact, also. When parents are vague with me about why they are not seeing their children, I suspect that their part in the absences has been more significant than they are willing to admit. I also return to the belief that it is a parent's responsibility to know what is happening with a child.

Manuel feels the children were tired of being caught in the middle between him and their mother. "In their taking sides, they decided it was easier to not see me." When I asked why they were caught in the middle, he reported, "She would want to start fights with me when the children came home. She would put on a show. It was a trait in her family, where people were always fighting and taking sides. She bad-mouthed me, and the one son, who was the most sensitive, sided with her."

Manuel would like more contact with his son but knows it will be hard to resume it. He wrote me at one point, "My son told me that he wanted to see me dead." Strong emotions and, again, a sign of the differential relationships parents establish with their children. Manuel was rejected and is unwilling to admit what his own part may have been.

Sometimes it is hard to know when a child has been poisoned against a parent, is being blocked from seeing that parent, or is deciding on his own not to visit. In this next situation, the father perceives it one way, and the child another.

SMITTY

Smitty, forty-nine, is currently struggling to establish a relationship with two of his three children, after losing contact with them for two years. Furious at his ex-wife for interfering with visitation and his home state for its unfair treatment of fathers, Smitty is now petitioning for a change in the state's joint custody laws. To get support for his attempts to change the laws, he has formed a fathers' rights group.

The on-again, off-again nature of his relationship with his children is a reflection of his own on-again, off-again marital history. Smitty met his wife, Gail, in high school, where they dated only once. After high school he enlisted in the military during the Vietnam War but did not serve overseas. While in the service, Smitty and Gail began dating more seriously and eventually married in the late 1960s. Their first pregnancy ended in a miscarriage, which was very traumatic for them both. Gail was five months' pregnant at the time. It was six years before they gave birth to a son, in 1975.

The marriage proved to be unstable, and Gail left soon afterwards to be with another man. Smitty and Gail divorced but remarried six months later when Gail's new relationship fell apart. Smitty was just coming out of the military and began work as an electrician for the U.S. Postal Service. "We thought we had forgiven each other but I guess we carried some of that baggage with us for years later," Smitty stated. Two more children were born within the next three years. "I thought the marriage was much better then. We moved out into the country to get away from our earlier problems. We isolated ourselves and started going to church. After a while, with the two extra children, we moved back to town because I needed a second job to support us. That is when more problems started."

Like many fathers, Smitty may have had a misguided conception of what was needed in the marriage. "I got into working too much, and she had a lot of free time and was unhappy again. Gail was bored and I would encourage her, but she did not want to do anything and was also unhappy dealing with the children a lot. We got divorced again in 1987 when the children were eight, nine, and twelve. I came home from work one day and they were gone. I don't know why but she has used them against me since. She denies visitation and did so almost immediately after divorce."

Smitty reflects on his role in childrearing during and after the marriage and issues a lament that many other fathers have felt, "I did not have as big a part as I should have with the children, but I didn't know any better. I thought I was doing what I was supposed to do by working hard. We had two homes, a lot of cars, but the family was falling apart in other ways. She contributed to the problems by running around, though I don't know why. During the marriage she blocked my input into the children. I guess she wanted total control."

When it came time to negotiate a divorce settlement, Smitty was discouraged by his lawyer from considering custody. The strong presumption in his southern state that the mother was the parent of choice was the reason cited.

Smitty says he made every attempt to see the children during visitation, always paid child support, and had a good relationship with the children.

but Gail threw roadblocks in his way at every turn. At one point she changed her telephone number and refused to let him see or call the children for over a year. Eventually, he took her to court for contempt for denying visitation, and visitation was restored.

When his oldest child began having academic problems (something of which Smitty had been unaware), he moved out of his mother's house and into Smitty's. Smitty filed for joint custody of all of the children at that time and was denied it. The court did not have a joint custody law.

"With my youngest two children, the court was going to take the position to let the children decide where they wanted to live, a horrendous situation because she was going to brainwash them. Just within the last six months they are beginning to talk to me because they are seeing that I am not the bad boy their momma says I am. She would tell them that I am no good, running around with other women, and won't pay her any money. So even though I am talking to the children again, I still don't have visitation."

Smitty's anger remains unabated. He believes that his ex-wife drove a wedge into his relationship with his children, blocked him from visiting them for years, and has been bad-mouthing him continuously while the state gouges him unfairly for child support. (While this sounds like a situation best categorized under a different pattern, you can consider his daughter's views in the next section). He regrets not taking a more active role as a parent when he was still in the home, saying that he thought that fulfilling the traditional fathering role was enough. He also regrets being discouraged by the lawyer from pursuing custody.

If there is a break with the children, his advice is "Be patient. The children will come back to you if you are the right kind of father. I hesitate to recommend that parents fight it out in court because that can be hard on the children. Don't get on the defensive. Maybe after they're grown they will come back to you. I have suffered and still may from only seeing my younger two once or twice a year, even though they live only twenty miles away. Now that we are starting to talk again, I am hopeful."

Despite the reasons given by Smitty for his not seeing his children, his daughter, Hannah, sixteen at the time of the interview, provides a portrait that shades the relationship in a different direction. (Smitty gave me her name.) It is this portrait that caused me to place this case history under the heading of fathers who are unwanted. It appears that Smitty created a reality that was different from that of at least one of the children.

Hannah: A Daughter's Perspective. A high school sophomore, Hannah lives with her mother and seventeen-year-old brother. She describes herself as a typical teen, interested in a few sports and one or two subjects in school. During the interview she was shy about talking about her father. She wisely asked me first what I had heard from him about why there had been little visitation. When I recounted that he had filed for joint custody and felt that his efforts to see her and her brother had been blocked by Gail, she said, "I guess my opinion is a little bit different. Some of that is true. He filed for joint custody but didn't tell us he was doing it at first. When he did tell us that he had filed, we were at the age when *we* didn't want joint custody with him. We weren't going up there to see him. We saw him as the divorce decree read for a long while, and then a bunch of stuff wasn't right, so we stopped going to see him."

I asked Hannah what was not right about going to see him, and she explained, as many adolescents would, "We weren't happy when we were there, and we wanted to be with our friends. Going up there caused a lot of trouble. We kept having to go back to court because we didn't want to be made to go up there. If we didn't go, we kept being brought back to court."

There was never a singular event that cut Hannah off from Smitty; things happened gradually. In her mind, she was not seeing her father because it was not "fun"; she had few friends in his neighborhood, and the visitation situation became tension-filled because he would bring everyone into court when they did not visit. Was Gail blocking visitation, I asked, and thus stoking the flames of the relationship? "Dad seemed to think that my mother wasn't allowing us to go up there, but really it was us and he blamed it on her. She always encouraged us to go, despite what was going on between them with all the court battles. I was angry at him for a while for taking us to court so much. I never felt pulled between my parents. Whenever I saw they were starting to fight, I would just back out and shut it all out. I tried to avoid siding with either of them at those times."

Where is the relationship now, given the ups and downs it has had in the past? "We talk on the phone a lot. Contact has increased a little because we started to get along better than we used to. We just never had that father-daughter relationship that some people have. But we are starting to form one now!"

When I was given access to children and they were willing to be interviewed, they sometimes provided a different impression than the one so adamantly argued by the father or mother. Hannah rejected Smitty for many of the reasons that children commonly cite. The fact that his view of events is different can help in our understanding of how to combat misperceptions. As is discussed in chapter 9, if parents and children are given a forum in which to talk (a therapist's office, the home of a trusted friend), some misunderstandings can be clarified.

Parents and children often have vastly different impressions of their own interactions. A parent's attempt at discipline is seen as cruelty by a child. A child being left alone may feel rejected, while the parent may be hoping to foster independent behavior in the child. After a divorce, opposing views of parenting may also prevail: A custodial parent may be seen by the noncustodial parent as interfering, while the custodial parent may be acting protectively.

With this next father's situation we again have the opportunity to hear how a child's perception about events is vastly different.

MICK

Mick is the father of one adopted son and two other children, a son and a daughter. He has not seen his sons for two years and even had a physical fight with one concerning visitation. His story also paints a picture diametrically opposed to that painted by one of his sons.

The product of a two-parent family, the youngest of two children, Mick became a schoolteacher after college. He had met Georgia at college and married her during his junior year because she became pregnant. Mick believes they probably would have married anyway. The pregnancy ended tragically, in a miscarriage.

Wanting children, they made arrangements to adopt. "Our pastor was doing a lot of missionary work in Colombia and he convinced a few parishioners to adopt children he had seen in an orphanage there." Georgia became pregnant again as the adoption was being finalized and gave birth the same time that the adoptee arrived.

The marriage was happy in the early years. Georgia stopped working because of child care demands, and they nestled into a typical family existence. Their next child was born three years later. Family life was placid, and the couple stayed together for sixteen years. One day, though, Georgia announced she wanted a separation. She had decided, Mick told me, that she was unhappy with the relationship. "When things go bad, you start to look back, and perhaps things weren't happy for many years before that. There were underlying problems waiting to surface."

In the late 1980s (the children ranged in age from ten to fifteen), she moved out of their home and left Mick with all three children. She felt she was not getting enough respect from the children or from Mick. Mick denies this, saying perhaps she was not getting things her way. Despite her leaving, she had contact with the children every day. She also began dating, as did Mick. But a few months later, she moved back into the house.

"She made my life miserable when she moved back in, with constant arguments. So I moved out, and she got a lawyer who said I had abandoned the family. She had first said I could have the kids. Then she changed her mind and said I couldn't have the kids. I wanted to fight for them but my lawyer told me there was no way I would get custody in our state's courts. I didn't fight and I ended up paying over one thousand dollars a month in child support. I got visitation whenever the children wanted to see me, but they never got into that pattern and that is how we started to lose touch."

Mick could not understand why they were not visiting him; he had a wonderful relationship with them when they were still in the home. Georgia continued to accuse him of abandoning them and told the children he did not love them and was fooling around with other women. Within six months, they despised him.

"I visited them occasionally but she would make their life so miserable that it wasn't worth it for them to see me. My oldest son, within a matter of weeks of separation, aggressively hated me and told me he never wanted to see me, that I was no longer his father. He threatened that he would do everything he could to make sure my daughter never saw me. He felt so strongly that when I went to visit he physically attacked me. I have no idea as to why except he was poisoned.

"This still hurts. About once a month I sit in my room and cry for about an hour. If I am watching a movie about a relationship between a father and a child, it is too painful. I still try and contact them and will write letters but not as often as years past. The only good news is that my adopted son, after he graduated from college, started to see me again. He had never really gotten along well with his mom. He called me, and now we get together once a week or so. He sees his brother and sister only occasionally. His mother has told him that if he sees me, he is considered the enemy. The kids are unhappy about the new relationship I am in. They don't like my girlfriend."

Once again, this is a father that does not fully understand what happened. He is aware that Georgia cut herself off from other relationships she had, and those friends also took on the persona as the enemy. She tends to see things in black and white, and never in shades of gray, which has led to a strained relationship with her own parents. Georgia ultimately placed tremendous pressure on the children to choose, and they chose her. She has remarried; Mick is unsure what influence her new husband has on the children or on her. He also wonders whether her actions are geared toward maintaining her twelve-thousand-dollar a year child support payments. Mick said his children do not believe he even pays child support. He has explained to them he has the receipts and can prove it, but Alan (who I will introduce soon) believes that Mick faked the receipts.

"I feel the pain not only for myself but also for my parents [who have no contact]. Here, my marriage and relationship have failed, and it affects them, too. It just adds to the burden when I see my mother crying about not seeing her grandchild. I also feel let down by the court system. I let the case languish for too long before trying to pursue custody more strenuously. Sometimes the pain of not seeing the children is so great that I think about moving away so I won't have to be reminded of them."

After interviewing Mick I telephoned both his sons, first his oldest, biological child (Alan) with whom he fought, and then his adopted son (Norman). Mick was unsure whether Alan would talk, and so I called with a good deal of trepidation. When I reached Alan after many attempts, he was eager to talk. He even reassured me, saying that he had done telephone interviewing while in college and knew how tough it could be. Now twenty, he was about to enter his junior year and was still living at home with his mother.

Alan and Norman: Sons' Perspectives. Alan said he not seen his father in over a year and that there had been a long period of silence prior to that one sighting. When he did see his father, they barely spoke. Alan was waiting outside the courthouse where his mother and Mick were signing the final papers on a divorce decree that they had battled over for five years. "I just sat in the car and was reading a book when he came out and said hello. I didn't need any of that, so I ignored him."

Alan initially felt a great deal of guilt when people learned he was not talking to his father. "People would say to me, 'Oh, he's your dad. You have to talk to him.' Well, after a while I began thinking, should he not try to talk to me, too? When is he going to take responsibility?"

Alan recounted a history of emotional and physical abuse that, in retrospect, he believes he and the family suffered for years. Apparently, the abuse escalated when his parents first split up. "The divorce went on for five years, and he kept postponing it. First the settlement would be all set, and then he would change his mind. During this time he was living outside of the home, but he would sneak into the house and take things he thought were his. He was the classic control freak. I think the divorce happened in part because my mom began to spend time away from home with her job and she began to see what other relationships could be like. She started to see what was normal and how she didn't have to take his abuse. With my dad it was always our fault (a pattern that remains), and if we were punished, it was what we deserved. After going through this, it was safer for me to stay away. I got tired of being treated like a wild beast instead of a person. One time he even stuck a gun in my face. It is not something I had to tolerate."

The relationship between father and son had its ups and downs even during this period. "In the beginning of the problems, when I was about fifteen, he would promise to change. I would get all psyched up for it, and then nothing happened. We'd get beautiful letters from him about how he is crying over us, but then he wouldn't send child support. We are not stupid kids and we're nosy, and it got to the point that our mother couldn't hide from us the stuff that was happening. I get the mail most days, and I would look for a child support check and it wouldn't be there. So I know he wasn't sending it. The message from him was, 'I treat you like shit. I promise to change.' But then he wouldn't. It was hard on all of us."

His mother's new husband is great, according to Alan. He is responsible, verbally expressive, instead of physically abusive, and can be counted on to keep his word. "Until you live in a family where that does count, you don't realize what you missed. There used to be no boundaries, nothing was yours personally; my younger sister dealt with guilt a great deal about not wanting to see him, but now I think she sees how many times she was let down. I had to protect her a little bit when Dad was getting physical or when he was playing games with her head. But I was dealing with a lot of guilt myself and didn't want to try and influence her unfairly. My older brother was away at school and didn't have to deal with a lot of this except when he was home over break."

I asked about Alan's relationship with his grandparents. I wondered if he had also shut them out of his life as a means of survival. He explained they had a fight over the telephone because they would send gifts only to his younger sister. When Alan asked them why he was ignored, they would say they did not have enough money. He would counter that they had enough money to send a card if they cared about him. They accused him of acting childishly. As was the case in his dealings with his father, Alan found it easier to ignore them.

Alan sums up his relationship by saying that Mick had not been performing the role of father. "There was a role reversal. How long can you tell your dad to act like a dad? He played the guilt tactic, and there is only so long that works. Letting him go was the hardest thing I've ever done, but it was also the most necessary. It is still hard for me. But as you get healthy, you tend to attract healthy people and have healthier relationships. Enough is enough."

Norman, the eldest, has a much better relationship with Mick than Alan does, and is also closer with his father than with his mother. He blames his current schism with his mother on the divorce and his unwillingness to side with her. A quiet young man of twenty-three, he was not at home during much of the divorce battle and became drawn into the conflict only when he visited from college. "At first I was on my dad's side. Then when I came home I was on my mom's side, and then I went to my dad's side, depending upon what served me best! I think my dad was to blame for a lot of the stuff that happened... not paying child support, not going to court, sneaking into the house after he and my mom had split up..."

As is the case for many older children of divorce, when there is some distance from the family, the picture can take on a different perspective. There is an increased ability to separate, and a child may make the decision that it is easier to stay away from the family, "For me, there is no side now because it doesn't matter any more—I found it hard to take either side. I found myself being pulled into the battle because there was no escaping it. When I went to college I could turn off whatever I wanted, but at home I was being fed whatever they wanted."

Norman realizes that his younger brother and sister may not be as lucky in their ability to separate from the family. "They are on her side because they live in the house. I saw my dad was more to blame, but it wasn't much more. There wasn't as wide a gap as you might believe. I would have stayed with my dad if he stayed in the house, but my mom stayed, so I lived with her. There were things that my mom was doing that I figured out, though she didn't want anyone to know. I was hearing from everyone that he wasn't paying child support, for example, but I have no proof. It doesn't matter to me anyway because I wasn't getting any money."

For Alan and Norman, there are areas of agreement but also shadings of disagreement. Alan perceives his father as the last ruler of the evil empire. Perhaps he sees him this way because he had more experience with him during the hottest time of the separation. Alan is also younger and may be more prone to being influenced by Mick. Alan sees no wrong in his mother. For Norman, there is more of a balanced view of his parents. He acknowledges his father's significant problematic behavior but also does not exonerate his mother. He has most likely not been subjected to the disappointments that Alan experienced and thus has a more positive relationship with his father.

There is much to be learned from these two young men's reports (some of which we see again in chapter 6):

First, children's experiences and reactions differ vastly, even though their perceptions may be somewhat similar. Part of the differences may be due to personal makeup—the thickness of a person's skin or the ability to block out input from a parent. Part of the differences may be due to the age at which the child is subjected to the high conflict that so often accompanies divorce or the way a specific child is treated. Finally, a child may be able to leave the conflictual environment (in Norman's case by attending college), thereby avoiding many of the battles.

Second, we learn that children living in the same household may draw different conclusions from their perceptions. Norman can justify some of Mick's behavior based on what he believes his mother was doing. Alan sees his mother in only a positive light and thus cannot condone any of Mick's behavior.

Third, we see the importance of children learning when to escape what must have been an unbearably tense household. The older the child, of course, the greater the ability to do so.

Fourth, some siblings are going to play a protective role over their younger siblings. Alan was torn. On the one hand he wanted to protect his sister by pointing out to her when he thought Mick was overstepping the boundaries. On the other, he did not always trust his own instincts and wanted his sister to figure things out on her own. When children feel they have to protect their siblings from their parents, they are placed in an impossible dilemma.

Fifth, Alan referred to the role reversal he experienced with his father. This is not uncommon for children in single parent families. When the authority figure of the parent feels under attack or unsure of himself, he will sometimes resort to a childlike state in which he needs taking care of. Once a child steps in to be the caretaker, he is starting down a slippery slope toward assuming too much of an adult burden.

Sixth, children experience guilt when they do not see their parents. Both Norman and Alan mentioned this, and Alan referred to feeling continuous pressure from others to visit his father. He even cited the guilt that his younger sister was feeling. When we think about parents who lose contact, this becomes a key part of the experience for the children. Alan especially was in enormous pain and conflict for years because of the abuse he experienced and his decision to cut off contact. Objectively, his cutting Mick out of his life was the appropriate response for Alan, given his experiences. Many other children are not able to act as wisely.

Seventh, the role that child support can play as a representation of love and nurturance is a key one. Children are aware of the financial assistance their noncustodial parent is supposed to pay. How it is used in the relationship varies a great deal, but, in this family, it becomes one more bomb in the ongoing battle.[10]

Eighth, with the help of the children, we get a more balanced view of the games that parents can play with each other after the breakup. We also see how difficult it is to know what the "truth" is about a family.

Conclusion

Fathers who are inadequate and withdraw on their own, a common occurrence among this population of noncustodial fathers, and those that have been rejected by their children have been the focus here. Even though these are the less acrimonious post-divorce situations, we observe a significant degree of tension. A key theme introduced is that the "facts" are in the eye of the beholder. Do some of these fathers truly hold an impression of the events in their family that is so different from what was heard from their children? Or is this selective memory on the fathers' part? In other cases, particularly where court documents have been reviewed, the facts more obviously point up that the fathers may be denying the role they have played in how events have unfolded.

When the "facts" about certain situations are at odds, the best way to ensure that they are clarified is to strive for improved communication. We will return to this point at the conclusion of the next chapter, after we hear some of the more acrimonious situations, and in chapter 9.

Chapter 3

When Fathers and Children No Longer Visit

The More Acrimonious Cases

In this chapter we hear the stories that are more acrimonious. What makes them more conflict-laden in part is the more direct contact with the mother. The majority of fathers in the survey blame her for their loss of contact with their children.

Two patterns are represented here.

Pattern 3: Fathers Who Are Blocked by the Mother

The most common complaint of the fathers is that access to the child is being blocked by the mother. Some fathers have theories as to why the mother is acting that way (she wants revenge; she is part of a conspiracy against men), while others are at a complete loss to explain her behavior. The blockage comes in two forms: (1) The mother is making scheduling difficult and the children unavailable (for visits, phone contact, or written correspondence); and (2) the mother has poisoned the child against the father. (Richard Gardner's parental alienation syndrome[1] would include poisoning of the child, coupled with the child assuming some ownership of the rejection. A mother could be rejected using the same reasoning; see Chapter 5.)

With the first scenario, the father believes extreme efforts are being made to prevent his having contact with the children because the mother is acting on a vendetta. The children are often not aware of what is going on. In a less vindictive variation of this scenario, the father is not being blocked because of what he has specifically done. The mother may honestly believe it is not in the best interests of a young child to see the father because of the confusion that the child is experiencing. When visits are scheduled, competing plans are made for the children and the children are not encouraged (as opposed to being actively discouraged) from visiting the father.

In the second scenario, the children often refuse to see the father because of what they have been told about him or because their negative impressions have been reinforced by the mother. The impression here is that the mother is actively working to turn the children against the father.

Pattern 4: Fathers Who Are Accused

Frequently underpinning many of the situations in which fathers lose contact is the allegation of sexual or physical abuse. While this reason could be subsumed under the previous pattern, where the mother is blocking visitation, it is significant enough to discuss as a separate pattern. Fathers claim that mothers use this charge as a way of tipping the balance against the father when there is a custody battle or financial dispute. In reality, three possibilities exist: The mother knowingly falsely charges the father; the mother mistakenly charges the father; and the mother correctly charges the father.

The exact definition of abuse is also relevant here. While purposively touching or fondling a child in a sexual manner is obviously abusive, other behaviors are more difficult to define. A father who helps a young child bathe him- or herself may be doing so in an abusive manner or in a hygienic manner. The line between the two can be thin. When a charge is raised against the father, child protective services enters the fray. As a result of their initial involvement, and pending an investigation, a significant amount of time may elapse before a falsely accused father resumes contact with the child. The atmosphere between the parties involved may become so acrimonious that a resumption of consistent visitation is impossible to achieve.

Pattern 3: Fathers Who Are Blocked by the Mother

LEIF

A number of men believe there is a female culture whose members band together when necessary against men, as was seen in earlier patterns. Leif hints at this in his recounting of how his sons were turned against him by his ex-wife with the help of two female professionals.

Raised by two parents, Leif, a prep school and college graduate, married his wife, Elana, when both were twenty-three. He went into business and she found employment as a secretary. Their first son was born three years later and a second son shortly after that. The marriage was initially stable, though Leif reports that Elana was extremely close with her family and that her closeness to them often intruded on their marital relationship.

Over the next few years, trouble began brewing. According to Leif, "I believe it was a lot of things. My youngest son had asthma and my wife thought he should see doctor. They went to a female pediatrician and a psychological evaluation was recommended. Lo and behold, my son starts going for therapy with the psychologist. Then my oldest son goes, and then they all want me to go. I didn't think it was necessary."

Therapy was an unknown quantity for Leif. The more his family went, the less happy he was with the results. "I did go a few times and answered a lot of questions, but as my wife started to go she began to get distant and began feeling more independent. She didn't need me anymore, and the kids became her number one concern. The next thing I know, they thought that the marriage was bad because we were not communicating and that was causing the asthma. I didn't think therapy was needed and I was sensing they were ganging up on me. They were all women. Then I found out they were one big happy family, as the pediatrician was the mother of the psychologist my wife was seeing!"

Leif felt further isolated when he was told his negative attitude about therapy was hurting the marriage and, by extension, the whole family. He felt backed into a corner and tried to save them by building a pool in the back yard, something he and the children had always wanted. Once construction began, Elana asked him to fill the hole back up. He refused, had the pool finished on a sunny day in June, and was thrown out of the house and marriage the next day. "She called the cops, claiming I pushed her. I did push her down once in retaliation for being scratched by her. The more they went to the psychologist, the more the therapist convinced Elana I was a violent person and that she needed a cop to get me vacated. Elana and the boys had left the house, and she filed a restraining order. A court-appointed therapist was then recommended to us because the family was all screwed up. I was willing to go because I wanted to get back together, but the first psychologist convinced the judge that she should hang on to our case."

Now living out of the house, Leif began paying child support and visiting the children two hours a week. He wanted to see them more often. Elana and the psychologist tried to restrict his time, claiming he was dangerous. They fabricated stories about his hurting the children by roughhousing with them during visitation. A call to child protective services after

Elana alleged that Leif had been drunk during visitation, exacerbated the conflict. Leif invited the caseworker into his apartment upon notification of the charges and, when no alcohol was found, was exonerated. In fact, the worker became involved as an advocate for Leif having more visitation with the boys. Another court-appointed psychologist evaluated the family and also concurred that more visitation should be allowed, and the judge issued a new order.

"Things were not calm for the boys during all this," Leif told me. "They were getting worse. I asked them if they wanted to see me and they would say yes. Meanwhile, her lawyer was saying I was a menace to society. I couldn't get anywhere. I felt the kids were starting to go against me and because of what they had been told by my wife. During visitation, they would bring friends. I finally told the kids I didn't mind their friends coming, but I also wanted time with them alone. Then they started to want to stay with friends and not want to be with me alone. Finally, they didn't want to see me anymore. I believe they brought friends along because I was made out by the psychologist to be this violent person. I went back to court and was granted supervised visitation."

A supervisor was put in charge of the visits, but those failed when the boys first refused to show up, and then, when they did come, had to be carried kicking and screaming into the room with Leif. The supervisor recommended that the visits be made voluntary. Leif did not see them again except when he attended their sporting events. They never acknowledged his presence. He wrote them but was afraid to call, fearing their rejection. He sent a few gifts on holidays but, when they did not respond, decided to stop giving them things.

Copies of reports I received from Leif verified significant portions of these events. One social worker wrote that he could not verify any incident of abuse or neglect and that Leif had tried to reestablish a relationship with his children. The children had, the social worker added, refused to visit the father as ordered by the court.

A psychologist's report described Leif as overly critical and Elana as overly protective, with each blaming the other for the breakup of the marriage. Elana was also described as dependent on professionals to make decisions for her. Both were also described as caring deeply for the children, with Leif being particularly frustrated with his inability to establish a relationship with his sons.

In evaluating the children, the psychologist observed them with Leif and found that, after some initial reticence and resistance, they were able to interact with Leif fairly spontaneously. The cause of the split in the family is difficult to understand, the psychologist wrote, but added that the boys sometimes had trouble reading Leif's feelings and that he may have been unpredictable. Elana and the boys may have formed a protective shell around themselves out of fear of Leif. The source of the fear is unclear, according to the reports, and nothing in the past could be found to be at the root of the fear.

It was further noted that the children's uneasiness with their father made the father uneasy with them. The psychologist hypothesized that the boys blame Leif for the breakup, though Elana and Leif offered different versions of the divorce. The recommendation: supervised visitation that needs to be agreed upon and worked out carefully by the parents. A male therapist was also advised so that the boys can learn to relate to a man in preparation for restoring their relationship with their father. In essence, the reports supported much of what Leif told me. But still the boys will not visit.

Leif is not the only one who has suffered. Leif's parents also were cut off by Elana. They sent gifts that were returned in the mail. "Their grandchildren were turning their back on them. One year my father sent a check, which they cashed, and they never said thank you," Leif said. "That really devastated my parents.

"I feel deprived and sad, and I have missed the opportunity to be with my only sons for the past ten years. I have space for them in my condo and still hope that someday they will come. Friends say to wait until they get out of their mom's home and maybe they'll come back. I don't know. I feel that I will always try to communicate with them, but if they don't say thank you, I would not send them any money.

"I really think it was a conspiracy, where the psychologist built up the confidences of my ex-wife. I think my wife was protective and needed the children. The kids were home from school quite a bit. My argument was she was keeping them home to keep herself company. She pulled them back as she saw them drift away when they were with me. Eventually, I decided it was better to stop trying because they didn't want to see me."

Leif lives in a small town and, coincidentally, ran into his son in a store a month before I interviewed him. "I was with my brother and said to him that I recognized one of the sons working in the store. I didn't want to go over to him, but my brother said he wanted to see his nephew. Then he brought my son over to see me. He just looked down the whole time. He said he thought I didn't love him and hadn't been trying to see him. But I had, and, at the end of the discussion, I told him I hope he always knows I love him. I have not seen him since then."

This case has elements similar to the others. Leif feels cut off from his children after Elana forces him out of the house and takes custody of them. She wanted him involved in therapy earlier but he felt ganged up on and withdrew. There is at least one violent episode between the couple. Attempts at reconciliation, which Leif wanted, are turned aside. The battle escalates as Leif seeks more contact with his children. The children turn against him and eventually refuse to see him, perhaps encouraged by Elana and the psychologist. Leif feels he has to stop attempting to force the issue and steps back. The cruel dénouement happens when, ten years later, he runs into his son, now in his early twenties, who accuses Leif of abandoning him. Leif expresses his love for his son but to no avail. He is rejected once again.

DAVID

I first met David at a Fathers United for Equal Rights (FUER) meeting. After I lectured a group of twenty-five men and women about parental kidnapping and the negative toll it can take on children and parents, he approached me. An African-American in his early forties, he has worked for the federal government for the past twenty years. When he reported he had not seen his children for six years, I asked if I could interview him for this book. It was not until a year later that we finally arranged the time to talk. He is known as a frequent member of the FUER group and one whose opinions are valued.

Eager to talk, he provided, with few cues from me, a steady stream of family history. While I had questions I wanted to ask to clarify some of his points, he was difficult to interrupt. He was quite interested in me getting all of the information about his plight. When I did wedge in a question during short pauses, he answered forthrightly. It turns out that, unlike most of the other parents in this book, his children are in hiding from him, yet not from the child support enforcement office who sends them child support garnished from his paycheck. His case is one that has elements of a number of patterns. The mother, Tonya, is blocking his access to them, but he is also not receiving any help from the courts. He believes his daughters have been turned against him, and he also knows that he made an initial mistake by turning over custody to Tonya without a fight.

"I have been trying to see my daughters [ages nine and eleven] over the years, but every time I go through the courts I am thwarted by them. It made be bitter for a long while. Last year I found out where they were [in a different state] and spoke to the principal about coming to see them and arranged to visit during school hours. I sent the school the court papers saying I had the right to see them and the principal was very supportive. He called my ex-wife, and when she heard I was coming, she told the principal she was going to disappear, which she did. Right now I am going through the child support enforcement agency to try to find out where they are. But they haven't yet told me. My court order says I should always have their address and phone number. She's very erratic."

David's marriage had been marked by erratic behavior. He and Tonya met when both were in college and he was about to enlist in the Coast Guard. They lived together off and on, and then, after graduation and his enlistment, he was transferred to Washington and they married. Their first daughter was born soon afterwards. "We got along okay for a while. But we came from different backgrounds. Sometimes you are in a situation and you don't want to see things clearly. By the time our second child was born two years later, I had left the house and come back, filed a separation agreement, and I was even unsure if the second girl was mine. But she looked like her sister, so I figured she must be. We were drinking moderately at the time and were going through a lot of ups and downs. We had access to day care from the military, but she wanted to stay home and take care of the kids. But this was a luxury we couldn't afford. So we had arguments about that and things just escalated."

Tonya had children from a previous marriage whom she was not raising because of the intervention of child protective services, according to David. The children visited Tonya and David sporadically, and he began to take a fatherly interest in them. He continued to hold out hope that she would stop drinking and that her childrearing would improve because he still felt a strong physical attraction to her. They had heated arguments and occasional physical fights during which he would choke her or be attacked by her. By the mid-1980s, when the girls were two and six months old, David and Tonya permanently separated.

Despite their differences over childrearing (he held a traditional view and believed dinner should be served every night at the same time, and she was more laissez-faire) and his dislike for some of her friends, he turned custody over to her. "I believed at the time that daughters should be raised by their mother. I was also about to be transferred. I think that if I had fought, I would have won because I had the job and I had a better parenting history than she did. I wouldn't leave without a fight again if I had the chance."

He asked for frequent visitation, and the case languished in the courts because of the question of the jurisdiction in which it should be tried.

About this time he was discharged from the Coast Guard and began looking for work. He also began paying child support of five hundred dollars a month. "I have no problem paying support in general. The children are my responsibility. It is on both of us to give the best that we can give. I got a job with the government where they [Tonya and the children] lived and have been with the government for the past six years."

David tried to see the children as often as he could over the next year. During one attempt at visitation on his daughter's birthday, he went to the projects where they lived and tried to give her a gift. Tonya stepped in and threw the gift down the stairwell. David remembered at that point that he was dealing with someone who was very unpredictable, "I learned not to feed into that behavior," he told me. "I learned I just have to walk away from that kind of thing or I will make it worse. One time there was a look on my older daughter's face when my wife and I got physical, and that's a look I never want to see. In the end, my daughters would probably think I was the villain. To avoid that I had to decide to not get involved.

"My wife would tell me I could come over and then she would change her mind at the last minute. I never knew which way she would be. She made an accusation one time.... I was going to work and the police came to my door and said I had been accused of sexual abuse. The next day I went to their apartment and Tonya is smiling, and I asked my daughter what she had told her mother and she just put her head down. I had given them a bath but had asked them to wash themselves, and somehow my ex-wife twisted this all around. After an investigation by a social worker and a doctor, they reported nothing had happened. But all one has to do is put the specter of child abuse in the air, and the burden of proof is always on me."

Custody battles dragged through court over the next two years. David was having some visitation during this time. In early 1989 all four of them appeared for a hearing, and the girls' positive behavior toward their father apparently convinced the judge that Tonya's accusations about the girls' fear of David were false. After a recess Tonya disappeared with the children. He has not seen them since.

The frustrating aspect of this story for David is that while the children are in hiding from him, child support is still being removed from his wages. While the child support enforcement agency knows where the children live because they are receiving his support, the agency will not tell him their jurisdiction, so he cannot continue the battle for visitation and custody. "I have asked for help [from the courts] but they aren't doing anything. They drag their feet. She did call my house about a year ago and left a message on the answering machine from one of the children, but it seems that the children have been poisoned against me, and that can have a negative psychological effect."

To explain Tonya's behavior toward him, David gives two examples. "She had a bad relationship with her father, and I think she resented me trying to help parent her first children. Also, we would watch TV together and she would get involved in the show and start to take on the role of the woman and scream at me like I was the guy on the show. She told she hated men."

How does David cope? "I try to keep a diary and cards for each of their birthdays so that when I see them again they can know that I have been thinking about them all these years. My mother is dead, but my father only has one other grandchild and really misses out by not seeing his granddaughters. I have other people who are supportive of me in my family, while she comes from a very dysfunctional one. But I miss them terribly. Birthdays are especially hard for me. When I had them I wanted to grow up with them. My oldest one is eleven, and I have missed out on all these years with her. Daughters need to be involved with fathers so that they will know how to deal with men in life. And a father can give advice about things that a mother can't."

David views the courts as prejudiced against males, "I think the whole feminist thing gives women all the power. The courts think the mother should have the children. But women do not have a monopoly on caring." In his eyes, race was not a factor in how he was treated; that white fathers also get the same treatment. "All I can do," David said in parting, "is hope that one day they will remember all the good things I did with them before we stopped seeing each other."

David's case embodies many characteristics of other fathers' situations. First, he willingly stepped aside when the marriage fell apart and allowed his wife to be the full-time parent, believing daughters should be with their mothers. Second, his attempts to increase his involvement were blocked by false accusations of sexual molestation. Third, he believes the children have been turned against him. Fourth, his ex-wife and children are in hiding from him. Fifth, the courts have the ability to locate her through their child support enforcement arm but have not revealed her whereabouts to him so he can relitigate. David does not paint himself as a saint. Some mutual domestic violence did occur, and alcohol was abused by both partners. He remains an active member of the support group, where his involvement is spurred on as much by the pain of separation from his children as by his belief that he is being unfairly treated by the court system. In the meantime, his search goes on.

TERENCE

Sometimes parents have children from two (or more) marriages and must struggle to see any of them. Terence is one such parent. He has summer visitation with his first son who lives a thousand miles away but does not see or speak with his other son from a second marriage, even though he lives only a hundred miles away. Terence is being prohibited by his second son's mother from visiting, even though he has a court order. History is playing a part here in Terence's behavior. Experiences with court battles over his first child influence the lengths he is willing to go for visitation with the second.

When I reached Terence for our interview in Chicago, he was assisting new members at the indoor tennis club that he managed. Despite being busy, he was eager to be interviewed and had pursued me earlier to participate in the study.

Like many life stories, his turned out to be complicated but instructive. Terence, thirty-two, met his first wife, Laraine, while in college. Their marriage quickly disintegrated but produced one son, Jim. When Laraine wanted to relocate to a different city, she asked for sole custody of Jim. Terence, who was very attached to Jim, fought her vociferously. He won a lengthy and expensive court battle by arguing that Laraine should be required to stay in their city of origin to maintain joint custody; she left town, and Terence got custody. While proud of his victory, the father admits that the battle took its toll, which Terence wouldn't fully appreciate until years later.

Terence and Jim moved in with his parents, who helped raise their grandson while Terence worked overtime in the sports management business. It was at work, while demonstrating tennis equipment, that he met his future second wife, Berry. She was a born-again Christian and deeply involved in her church. He joined the church and soon became an active member. "I committed my life to Jesus and that was the basis for the marriage. Christianity got us together: the church, Bible study, and so on." Terence and Berry were married one year later and moved into their own apartment with Jim.

Just six weeks into the marriage, Terence confided, "Berry tapped me on the shoulder and said she was unhappy. She didn't want to raise Jim, and moved out three days later. He and I stayed in the apartment for about a month but it was hard for me. I had several sitters and I worked late at nights. My job was very demanding, and I was not home when he came home from school. Sometimes he'd be waiting for me after the bus dropped him off. He was only five. My parents were upset, but I couldn't move back in with them because my job had moved me too far away. I started to go for counseling. I got injured on the tennis courts and had my leg in a cast. Everything was falling apart.

"That's when I made the toughest decision of my life: I decided to send Jim back to Laraine." As Terence describes it, "It was incredibly hard for me. I felt like a part of me died when I let him go. Everyone wondered why I would give him up when I had fought so hard to get him. But I was very upset by Berry's leaving and in no state of mind to raise him." Jim's departure was with the understanding that he would visit his father over the summers and on occasional holidays.

With Jim out of the picture, Berry and Terence reconciled. They attended church-related counseling and were pressured by the church community to stay together. Nothing worked. They separated for the final time eighteen months later when Terence again was transferred to a new job position. Berry was four months' pregnant. When Lenny, Terence's second child was born, it was a struggle for the father and son to bond because they lived in different cities. "I did not try for joint custody because I was fed up with the battles and Berry was resisting. The fight in me was gone. I know that sounds like an excuse, but that is what I felt at the time. I did have occasional visitation with Lenny, but I did not feel close with him. Sometimes I would pick him up at his home in one city, drive to my parents' home in another city, and then take him to his home before I returned to my home in a third city. I'm a good person and went through the motions and felt like I couldn't fight for my child anymore."

Terence did win monthly visitation. But Berry blocks it. "She feels that Lenny is too young to be confused by seeing me on an occasional basis, and frankly, I am unsure what to do. I can't get him on the phone either. Berry is challenging me to take her to court, but I don't know what good it would do. Remember, I fought once to see Jim and that was very difficult. I don't know if I am willing to go through a fight again when I am not sure what good it would do anybody. I am, though, stuck paying a great deal of child support for both of my children.

"It has been a year since I have seen or talked to Lenny. One side of me says I am paying the money and should see him, and the other side of me is saying that it will only confuse him. My parents have no contact with Lenny, and that is bothering my mother. Berry has sent pictures of Lenny but has been discouraging contact. My mother is Catholic and feels guilty about not seeing her granddaughter. It is hard for my sixty-eight-year-old parents to drive there for a visit. My mother doesn't know if Berry would let her in if she did go.

"What is the most crazy is that my two ex-wives are now friends. They got together, found out how much I am making, and came after me. When I have Jim, he asks to see Lenny; I say he can't, and he doesn't understand why."

Most interesting to me were Terence's feelings about his sons. While he feels very dissatisfied not seeing Lenny at all, not having frequent contact with Jim is more difficult. It was Jim he initially fought for and won custody of, and it was Jim with whom he has always had the best relationship.

Since his divorce from Berry, Terence has moved away from their Church community. In fact, he is reinvolved with the Catholic church and recently married for a third time. His new wife does not resent the onerous child support payments he makes each month to his two ex-wives. "She has accepted it [the support payments] better than me. I have bitter feelings any time I write the check out." If he was able to see Lenny, he would not feel so angry.

Here we see how the battles over one child, with whom Terence still has visitation and frequent telephone contact, ultimately affected the desire to battle for the second child. Terence is out of contact with his four year old son. But he most likely would not be if he had not suffered so greatly in his fight for Jim. He also is caught in the common position many divorced parents are in, wondering how much enforcing rights for visitation with a young child will be disruptive to the child. Some child development experts believe that little contact between the noncustodial parent and child is preferable for the child because it reinforces the notion of the custodial parent as the single psychological parent. Having a second parent dropping in and out of a very young child's life can be confusing.

The other side of this argument is that it is usually the father who is the noncustodial parent, and this thinking contributes to the father's role becoming increasingly peripheral. It also leaves little room for the noncustodial parent to become involved in the future. At what age does the noncustodial parent get introduced to the child?

Terence is caught: He is being blocked by Berry even though he has a legal right to visitation, and he also is unclear about how helpful his own participation would be in Lenny's life. It is interesting to consider whether a mother without custody would have the same doubts about her participation.

Pattern 4: Fathers Who Are Accused

The most dangerous and upsetting of situations for parents, children, and professionals is when abuse has been alleged. In interviewing fathers who claimed they were falsely accused, I often wondered what the truth was. In some cases, I asked for court documents and they were forthcoming; in other cases, I asked but they were not shown me. Seeing someone exonerated in court does not necessarily mean they were not abusive, just as a father's refusal to share his highly personal court records with me does not mean he is guilty.

Many of the parents I interviewed raised the issue of false sexual allegations as being at the core of their not seeing their children. In order to resolve any of the specifics of these cases, I realized I would have to conduct extensive interviews with all the parties involved *and* review case records and court papers—in effect, do my own investigation. Obviously this is an impossibility (though, in two cases, I did review court documents). Rather, with the next few cases, I am presenting the accused's side of the story with the caveat that I have not investigated the veracity of their statements in most cases. Certainly false allegations of abuse do occur, as was discussed in the first chapter. Investigators do make mistakes in reaching conclusions about allegations, just as some molesters do escape the scrutiny of the law. I have included a few of these situations in this book because they are so prevalent among the population of parents and children who do not see each other anymore.

SYLVESTER

Sylvester's tale is unique here in that the two daughters he has lost contact with are adopted. His story is unfortunately not unique in that he claims, like many fathers, that false charges of sexual abuse were brought against him.

By his own description, the product of an idyllic two-parent family ("two loving parents, my mother didn't work, and I had loving grandparents"), Sylvester met his future wife, Sharon, in high school. They did not marry until he was in his mid-twenties, when he had finished a stint in the army and began working as a machine operator. Sharon was a schoolteacher. "The marriage was great at first. But after a year, I had a spinal cord injury that put pressure on the relationship. Then she discovered she had an infertility problem, which put further pressure on us. We decided to adopt, and the adoption process placed an even greater strain on the marriage because of the anxiety of waiting. There was also a problem with adoption fraud where we lost money."

They finally were able to adopt, and both bonded very easily with their first daughter. They were fortunate to adopt a second daughter a year later but experienced problems bonding with her. She was cranky, slept little, and cried a lot, which further stressed the relationship. Then Sylvester's health deteriorated once more. "I had another catastrophic injury, which required major surgery. I was unable to work much, and, while that permitted me time at home with the children, it was a financial strain on the family."

It was easy to see the ledger sheet of problems building up to the breaking point for the family. Counseling was attempted from time to time to resurrect the marriage. When their youngest was two, Sharon decided to make the move. "I came home from work," Sylvester told me, "and found a note from Sharon saying she had left with the children for her sister's house. Her brother was living with us and he moved out at the same time. Her parents just happened to be in town from California for a visit," he said sarcastically. "I got the feeling that this had been planned for a while and everyone knew about it except me."

Sylvester sounds like many divorced men I have met. He was unaware of the problems brewing or never took them seriously because he was focusing on the external issues of trying to support the family rather than the internal ones of trying to save the relationship. In a voice that was crackling with emotion, he told me, "In thinking back, I am not quite sure why we broke up. There were money problems, and the second child was very difficult after the first was so easy. Her older sister was very prosperous, which put a strain on us to measure up. I was too busy trying to make the bills and didn't know what was happening between us."

Sharon moved quickly. She immediately hired an attorney, removed money from the bank account, and began custody proceedings. Sylvester sought joint custody because his lawyer advised him he had no chance of winning sole custody. He won, began paying child support, but, despite the court order, had trouble arranging visitation. She complained that the children were having adjustment difficulties when they spent the night with him. Sylvester, who was still living in the family's original home, avoided taking the children there during visitation because he believed that would be too upsetting for them. "It was hard spending time with them in someone else's home, though at least at my parents' it wasn't too bad. It began to affect the closeness I had with my daughters. It became extremely upsetting for me. I would call every night, and then it was decreed I was calling too much, so it was reduced to three times a week. Sometimes Sharon would even block that."

With Sharon impeding Sylvester's contact with the children, things escalated. "In 1986 she accused me of sexually abusing the children. She had tried before to modify visitation—it was very in vogue at that time to do it—she had a medical background and it was easy for her to draw from this

with the false accusations. She tried a number of times until it was successful. I went for a long time without seeing them while the court straightened
things out. I finally got the abuse charge dismissed at the grand jury level.
By this time they needed to see a psychologist to figure out if it was okay
for them to see me after going for two years without us having contact. I
got to see them once before she moved to a new state and started new allegations of sexual abuse."

I questioned Sylvester about what the children were specifically saying
about abuse. He contended that she and a number of therapists had
planted the idea in the children that they had been abused by him and that
it was a complete fabrication. Why fabricate such a thing? I pushed. "I
don't know if she wanted to punish me or gain control. She always had issues of control. It was always a women-against-men kind of thing in her
family."

When Sharon moved out of state with the children and renewed the
charges, more time elapsed. Now, in the new jurisdiction, Sylvester has pe-
titioned the court for a *guardian ad litem,* a professional who becomes the
advocate for the children.

Sylvester knows that there is a long row to hoe before he will have contact with his children, even if he wins the court case. "My daughters have
had to go along with their mother on a lot of this because that is the only
love they have access to. I think they are just trying to survive. A number of
psychologists have testified that they were not abused."

Having heard about two separate allegations of abuse, I asked Sylvester
if I could have a copy of any of the reports on the children. I wanted independent verification. Sylvester agreed to mail them to me. One month later,
a thick packet arrived with reports from three different mental health evaluators. The dates ranged from 1987 to 1994, with the most recent evaluation including a review of previous records and interviews with both parents and children.

The most recent report was conducted at the request of the court and began with a review of the family's history, which included marital conflict,
the accusation of abuse against Sylvester, his denial of these accusations,
conflicting testimony from various specialists, and an accusation of parental alienation against Sharon by Sylvester. Sharon's mental status examination revealed no clinical diagnosis, and observation of her with the children
concluded that she had a strong bond with them. Sylvester was described as
using denial and repression to control his feelings, did not appear paranoid,
showed some hostility, and believed he was being unjustly blamed. He was
diagnosed as possibly having a dependent personality. The reports said he
seemed upset over not having contact with his children and clearly cared

for them. He did not present as violent or as having a sexual identity problem, according to the evaluation. Finally, no evidence was presented that
would make him incapable of parenting his children.

Evaluations with the children included a review of seventy-four separate
documents, projective tests, and interviews. Inconsistencies turned up in
their stories when the children described one of the daughters as being sexually abused by Sylvester. Those inconsistencies called into question whether
any abuse had occurred. The significant conclusions drawn from the reports
include two findings: (1) Both children are firmly convinced that their father
molested one of them; and (2) Sharon contributed intentionally or uninten-
tionally to their parental alienation toward Sylvester.

The recommendation was that Sylvester and the children, with the assistance of a therapist, begin supervised visitation for short periods of time and
that both parents receive counseling.

Despite this recommendation, Sylvester is still struggling, months later,
to begin the visitation process. He is optimistic that the guardian ad litem,
who has now become involved, will help resolve things in his favor finally.
In the meantime, he suffers. "Not seeing my children is devastating. It has
cost me health-wise: I now have limited feeling in my feet and have developed more infections. Personally, too, it is devastating. Holidays are especially painful. I become very lethargic, not interested in anything, not bothering dating. I became obsessed with my case. How come I could read the
laws about custody and they would make sense, and then they would be so
twisted around by her lawyer and the courts? I mailed my children plane
tickets and they never came up. I send them cards and gifts on their birthdays. I send them checks which never get cashed. I could never let them go
completely, as some parents in my situation have done. As girls, they are at
an age when they need me now more than ever. I don't want them going
through adolescence and dating thinking they were sexually abused—it is
hard enough for kids to establish their sexual identity without that baggage. I also want to get them away from a therapist who keeps breeding
these thoughts of sexual abuse into them. My parents wanted to have visitation, and within two months, they were being charged with abuse, too. I
know there are other fathers and mothers with the same problems with visitation; I know I am not alone."

Sylvester's story would appear to be substantiated, according to the vo-
luminous documents I reviewed. But the charges of abuse, never substantiated, have driven a potentially insurmountable wedge between Sylvester
and his daughters. Sharon may be acting out of what she considers a concern for the best interests of the child, especially if the children believe one
was abused, as the reports indicate. She may sincerely believe the children

were suffering from the visitation and moved to interrupt the process. As she battles, he battles with the court on his side for a resumption of visitation. Can the guardian ad litem help Sylvester in enforcing the recommendations? For the near future, that may be his only hope.

DAN

As in Sylvester's case, Dan also contends his children were brainwashed to believe they were abused. Israeli-born and living in the United States for twenty years, Dan still speaks with a thick accent. A forceful talker and slightly suspicious, he uses colorful descriptions to detail what he admits were mistakes in marriage. His second wife picked up another extension at their house when I was interviewing him by telephone, and she helped to explain some of the issues that Dan did not think his knowledge of English would enable him to explain.

Raised by both parents, Dan described his mother as emotionally abusive and his father as physically abusive. Dan couldn't wait to escape his family. After fighting in the 1967 Six-Day War at age eighteen, he came to the United States, leaving everyone behind. Capturing the mood at the time for immigrants, he said laughingly, "I came because money grows on trees here. But they were lying."

Meeting people in America was not easy for him. Cultural differences loomed large, which continued later when he sought legal assistance. After dating infrequently, he turned to a matchmaker for help in finding a Jewish wife. A marriage was "arranged" shortly thereafter, something not atypical in either the life of an immigrant or an Israeli. "We didn't know each other very well before we got married and the whole thing was a mistake. We moved in next door to her parents and I began working for her father as an equipment repairman. Her parents were very involved. I lived with two wives (my mother-in-law and my wife) and slept with one," he joked again.

Soon after, a son was born, and three years later a daughter. "I was a good father compared with most fathers. I spent a lot of time with the children. My wife had a housekeeper and stayed home and watched soap operas. I knew she wasn't good for me, and we were both unhappy in the marriage. We fought like cats and dogs and she blamed me for everything—not making enough money, no communication, everything!"

Dan displayed little patience in wanting to work things out within the marriage. He had suffered a slight heart attack, which forced a day of reckoning. In the hospital he talked to a counselor who told him the marriage was killing him. His choice was to stay in the marriage and die, or to leave.

He went home and told his wife he was leaving, apparently to her great relief.

His next move was typical of many men who lose contact. They believe children should be with their mothers. "I moved out and started visiting the children and paying child support. I never wanted custody, but I loved my children and wanted to see them. Then, when I became engaged awhile later, all hell broke loose. She threatened me. When I went to pick up the kids it was like fire hitting me in the face. Then she accused me of everything imaginable. I can't even say it. She stopped letting me see the children."

I questioned Dan further. "She planted in them the idea that I had abused them when they were younger, and now they believe it. Yet she never brought any of this up when we first divorced—only when I became engaged and remarried [a similar story to Bill's earlier in chapter 2, in that a new relationship further escalated the acrimony]. She called child protective services, and they investigated and found nothing. I hired three lawyers. They all shafted me and I didn't have enough money to hire anyone else. I still pay support because if I don't, I go to jail, even though I am not seeing them."

According to Dan, the children were brainwashed. He writes letters and sends them cards but has not seen them for four years. "I will not send any money to them other than child support. They do not speak to anyone in my family. My ex has remarried, and they have changed their name to her new name.

"I wanted to talk to you because fathers get a bad deal in these situations and we have to stick together. There is no justice for men in these cases. I am waiting for my kids to approach me and I will tell them the truth. When they are old enough I will explain to them about life. I felt horrible when this first happened. It was worse at the beginning, especially on holidays. But I can't do anything about it if they do not want to see me. I tell them in the letters I will always love them. I think they are afraid to come here because she will punish them if they do."

I asked for a copy of the relevant records, but he refused. It could have been that he did not trust me and that, as a foreigner, he had a heightened sense of vulnerability, having already been denied his rights by the courts. It could also have been that the contents of the reports would shed a new light on the information he gave me. He is not being denied custody by the courts. The refusal is coming from his ex-wife. He doesn't think the courts will help him, so he has never sought assistance from them.

"The kids are paying for all this divorce. They suffer the most. They miss the love of their parents, their family and religion. Without a mother and father, you cannot have fun. To other parents I say, Don't take out the divorce on the kids; get divorced in a clean way."

Like many others, Dan's situation raises the question of who is telling the truth. Was there abuse? Or was the abuse charge fabricated by his ex-wife in a fit of anger over his new relationship?

TOM

Abuse charges know no limits in terms of class, race, or education. An Ivy League graduate, Tom had been an English professor for a few years at a northeastern university when he met his future wife, Eileen, a graduate student in a neighboring department. Whereas Tom's early childhood and background were fairly typical, Eileen was the product of a highly charged, high-achieving family unfortunately plagued by alcoholism and incest. According to Tom, Eileen's mother was alcoholic into her late sixties and Eileen herself brought an "addictive" personality and a drinking problem into their marriage. In addition, shortly after Tom and Eileen married, Eileen recounted numerous instances of sexual abuse at the hands of her father. Later, Eileen learned that her sisters had also been abused by him. Both themes played key roles in Tom and Eileen's marriage and divorce.

They married two years after they met, and, as newlyweds, both in their late twenties, moved to the Midwest, where they both had teaching jobs waiting. With the birth of their first child, a daughter, Eileen reduced her hours at work and became the primary caretaker, as she had always desired. The division of labor was fairly traditional, according to Tom. The marriage was strong for the first twelve years. "People looked upon us as the ideal marriage. I didn't know this was bad until later, but we never fought for the first nine years of the marriage. As I read later about alcoholism and the personality problems that go along with it, I see now that we were hiding a lot of problems."

Two other daughters were born within the next five years. Tom began to notice signs of trouble in the marriage when "Eileen converted to fundamentalist Christianity and then became like a counselor to women in abusive relationships. She got involved with various support groups and started to change. She also became aware of her own problems with drinking and those of her mother. We began to have arguments over the children and TV time. My middle daughter began acting out a lot. She wet her bed and went to the bathroom in her pants.

"We saw a series of therapists. Eileen became more involved in the ACOA movement [Adult Children of Alcoholics]. We went to one therapist who was a real charlatan. After eight sessions, he had a private session with me to get my side of the story and reported that he had heard from Eileen that my youngest daughter accused me of molesting her. He said he had to report me to social services. That is when the shit hit the fan. I never molested my daughter and I never understood if what she was raising with me was an issue that came from her own family or what."

The children were twelve, ten, and eight at the time. Social services ordered that Tom was to leave the house, or Eileen and the children would leave. Not wanting to upset the children, he left, expecting to have this resolved after the children were interviewed and be back home within a few days. It never was resolved, and two weeks later Eileen filed for divorce.

This began a long process of court battles, custody fights, and eventual estrangement between Tom and his children. "The first mistake I made was in moving out of my house. Once you abandon your property, it is tantamount to admitting guilt. I had no contact with my children after that. My lawyer and I tried for supervised visitation. She refused. The social worker ignored statements of support from our friends and, on the basis of an interview with my wife, decided I was a sick person."

Following a court trial on charges of molestation, Tom was found not guilty. At one point during the trial proceedings, his daughter was placed on the stand and was vague about the allegations. "She was asked to talk about good, bad, and funny touching, and said that I had tickled her on the chest at one point and that one day she would have breasts and that would be a problem. When she was asked specifically if I had ever touched certain parts of her body, she said no. I was acquitted in two hours.

"Things were pretty hot then between my ex-wife and me. I was living in the neighborhood, and one time when I happened to run into my eldest daughter, she called me a pervert and a creep. My lawyer and I decided it was best to not see the children for a while so that things could cool off. My lawyer also advised that I try and resolve the property issues from the divorce before getting into custody so that money couldn't be used as a weapon against me."

Six months later Eileen died in a commuter plane crash. She had legal custody at the time of her death. A new custody battle began, pitting Tom against Eileen's brother and sister-in-law. In order to resolve that dispute, Tom agreed to be evaluated by a psychologist, who spent a great deal of time interviewing friends of Eileen while giving short shrift to Tom's side of the story. The psychologist concluded from her tests of Tom that he was not deviant and that some slight molestation may have occurred. Her recommendation was that the children were so traumatized by the court battles that they should be placed in custody with the in-laws and have contact with Tom only when they wanted it. Tom was allowed to write and send gifts but not have personal contact. That was the last time Tom saw them, six years ago.

"I was willing to continue to fight, but my lawyer said that because of the unique qualities of the case it would take an enormous amount of money and time. In the end, the children would end up penniless and the lawyers would be wealthy. [The children won a settlement from the commuter plane company and inherited Eileen's life insurance.] So in the interests of the children and preserving some money, I agreed to let it go, hoping that with time things would be settled. They have not."

According to Tom, the children have not fared well. "My second daughter has suffered the most out of this and has gone to special schools, has an alcohol problem, and is now attending a psychiatric boarding school. During the years, I have sent them cards, gifts, letters, audiotapes, and have received nothing in response. I get the children's grades. On her eighteenth birthday my oldest daughter's lawyer wrote and said she wants no more contact with me. I know she is in college."

While I did not get a sense from Tom that he was experiencing a great deal of loss, a research assistant who had interviewed him for me two years before reported that he was grieving a great deal at that time. Perhaps time (six years) has helped him to cope. "I do miss the children," he told me when asked, "but I don't know what I would do if they were suddenly thrust in my company. They will need therapy for a long time."

I asked what he told people who asked about his children. "I say that I have three children but do not go into depth about it unless I know the person pretty well. I tell them I am a widower and all the children are in school in a different state. My friends and associates know most of the story. Being trained as a researcher, I have the failing of being able to detach myself. I look on it more as a personal tragedy for my wife than myself. Her family are all Ivy league types, yet they were also molesters and drinkers. What I have learned is that the children in my wife's family are high achievers as an effort to cover up or to lay insurance against any revelation of the family's terrible secret. I was told by one therapist that, in a way, I was an innocent by stander. There was a strong history of self-destruction on Eileen's part. It was a history of repressed rage that is the result of molestation, the 'don't talk about things' school. That has affected everything."

Here the abuse charge lay the groundwork for the later cutoff. Rather than charge ahead and force contact when he could have, Tom elected to step aside for the benefit of the children. It may have been a serious mistake, though it is hard to know how upsetting it would be for the children if he had attempted to gain visitation.

Conclusion

Critical points emerge from the eleven interviews in these two chapters. We can frame these points with a return to one of the earlier questions: Whose perspective is the correct one? Fathers' views sometimes do not fit with the perspectives offered by the children. Most likely, if I had interviewed the mothers, a third view would have emerged. Yet this does not mean the fathers' perspectives are incorrect. Short of an act of abuse, there often is no single truth to any event or to the motivations that underpin actions. This must be kept in mind as we consider the teachings from the fathers' stories.

First, many of the fathers are in great pain because of the separation from their children, whether they caused the separation or not. The loss for some men is greater than others. If this is the only fact that is remembered, it alone will help to change how we understand these fathers. No longer do we need believe, when deadbeat dads are lambasted, that all of them are uncaring. If we treat them as if they are, we lose a very important opportunity for change.

Second, fathers often feel beaten down by a court system they view as unresponsive to men. In a nutshell, courts and fathers do not mix in most of their eyes. This is the experience even of men who have won custody in court.[2] The winners often feel they have been lucky or that they have gone to greater lengths than a mother would to win custody. The losers, interviewed here, are unshakable in their beliefs about this treatment. It is nearly impossible for men to believe at the outset of a custody, visitation, or child support dispute that they will be treated fairly despite the growing numbers of fathers who do receive favorable judgements.

Third, unmistakable commonalities appear among the cases. The typical paths these fathers follow:

- The father withdraws from parenting at the time of breakup because he believes a mother should raise the children or because his legal counsel is pessimistic.
- Having stepped aside, the father faces an uphill battle. Ill feelings come to permeate the relationships and a charge of abuse may be leveled.
- Attempts to maintain contact are rebuffed.
- The father is left feeling powerless and frustrated.

Fourth, the children provide revealing commentary about the role of conflict in the home, child support, and visitation. They also highlight the different reactions that children in the same home can have to a father. This teaches us that we must consider each child unique in the family and not talk of the children as a generalized group. It should not be said that "they" (the children) feel a certain way until we are convinced that, say, Suzie and Billy actually do feel the same way. We diminish their individuality and restrict oppportunities for change if children in any one family are considered monolithically.

Fifth, contact sometimes varies by child. As discussed, this means the picture of the out-of-contact father is more variegated. It may mean the father is capable of sustaining a relationship with one child and not another, that particular factors come together in a unique way to stop contact with a particular child, or that one child's ability to maintain a relationship is different than another's.

Sixth, and finally, the fathers often feel disenfranchised, like pariahs. They have often lost their positions in the community in relation to their children. They reveal flashes of anger mixed with hurt. They feel wronged and, as a result, may forever become a worse parent, a less trusting parent and person, because of it. Some indicate feelings of shame about their situation (and this from fathers who volunteered to be interviewed). It can be difficult for them to reconnect with their children if they are, at the core, embarrassed about who they are. Will they ever be able to rebuild a relationship with their child if there is a reconciliation? Will they ever be able to talk reasonably with their ex-wives if an important decision needs to be made related to the child? The concluding chapter sheds some light on this.

Chapter 4

When Mothers and Children No Longer Visit
Feelings of Rejection and Betrayal

Enormous attention has been paid to fathers who leave. What happens to mothers in the same situation? We know mothers are stigmatized if they do not have custody. The response to them is even more dramatic if they are not in contact with their children. Consider the reaction to a father in this situation. Then, consider if a mother is held to a higher, or at least a different standard. Gender differences come into play. Fathers (men) can leave relationships and, until recently, still be seen as masculine, though perhaps irresponsible. (New definitions are afoot: One recent billboard in Baltimore designed to keep fathers involved with their families shows a picture of a chicken with a caption indicating this represented men who father children and leave.) Mothers leave relationships and are seen as uncaring, unloving, mentally incompetent, licentious, selfish, and "unfeminine." The playing field for our consideration of these two groups of parents is clearly not level.

Given the obstacles these mothers face, we must consider how they came to lose contact in order to shed needed light on the aftermath of divorce. Yet despite the growing number of these mothers, as discussed in chapter 1, our understanding of this population of mothers is particularly meager. It has been suggested that noncustodial mothers are less likely than noncustodial fathers to cease contact with their children after the breakup.[1] Mothers may make a greater attempt to stay in touch with their children because they believe they are more important to the children's well-being.[2] It can be, on the other hand, that moms are not encouraged by society to stay involved as are dads because the *financial* cost to society of a mother stopping contact, and potentially not paying child support, is not as great as when a father drops out and does not pay. Discussions about deadbeat fathers have come to include mothers, too, for political correctness, but the burden on the welfare system is vastly different. The emotional cost to family members is less easy to quantify.

I interviewed the president of Mothers without Custody[3] (a national advocacy and support group for women) to gain her perspective on why some mothers do not stay in touch. In her many years of working with noncustodial mothers, she believes that a variety of factors combine to make continued contact between mother and child difficult.

"The issue about women not being good mothers [when they become noncustodial] is built into their heads. They begin to believe that there must be something wrong with their parenting skills. It becomes a self-fulfilling prophecy: 'If I do not have custody, then of course I must be a bad person. If I am a bad person, then I should not spend time with my children.' She sees a recent change in this perception, though, and believes that now, not having custody has more to do with fathers becoming involved with their children than with maternal incompetence. "As women demanded that fathers become more involved in family situations, it naturally evolved that, as that happened, they continued to want to be involved when a marriage broke up. This helped set the stage for fathers gaining custody and for the mother eventually losing contact."

She makes four other points about mothers and custody.

"I think that the issue of child support is a large bone of contention with mothers. They don't believe that they should have to pay support because so often the fathers are better off financially, which is why they have custody in the first place." This belief starts an adversarial process between the mother and father, which she contends the legal system fuels, her second point. "The legal community mucks up the waters. If the relationship was not adversarial to begin with, it becomes adversarial very quickly."

Third, she blames the fathers themselves. "Many of the issues are reversed when it becomes the mother who does not have custody. The fathers indicate that mothers don't foster contact. Well, mothers say the same thing, that fathers with custody also do not foster contact."

Her final point is that mothers withdraw from the battle for the good of their children. "Because we deal with moms going through an emotional process, we encourage them to pull themselves out of the middle. Sometimes that means the moms won't fight for custody or fight for hours of visitation. Instead, they will try to build a relationship. The result of their pull-ing out may be that they lose a legal opportunity for involvement in their child's life, which can eventually lead to a loss of contact."

She believes that ultimately we need to have a different perspective on gender and parenting. "It is time for us to let go of our gender expectations and to look at parenting in a more equitable light."

Much of what she says is congruent with earlier research on noncustodial mothers I conducted.[4] She identifies a pattern of the inadequate mother, a pattern of parenting I also observed. When some of these mothers lose cus-tody, their feelings of low self-esteem are confirmed, and little attempt is made to stay in contact if there is any sign that they are not wanted. With custody going to fathers more frequently now, there is an increasing poten-tial for mothers to feel inadequate and drop out. Mothers often claim they lose custody because their financial situation is weaker than the father's. But they also lose it because the children choose the father over the mother when offered a choice. A mother who feels incompetent, an impoverished mother, or a mother who has been rejected will have a psychologically diffi-cult time fighting to maintain contact if there is objection to visiting from any of the family members.

As she notes, I also found some mothers who willingly give up custody when they believe it is in the best interests of the child to live with the father. These mothers are often acting altruistically, without hostility, though with sadness. As there is often less animosity involved with these custody deci-sions, mothers in this situation are more apt to remain in active contact with the children,[5] although losing custody sets the stage for a lack of contact be-cause it suggests possible significant relationship problems. This is not the case when the father loses custody. A father without custody is more the norm, and no statement about his capacity as a parent is suggested.

I do not agree that attitudes about women have changed that much (though it is a matter of degree). A recent national survey of women re-ported that 88 percent of the respondents felt it was their responsibility to take care of the people in their family. An even higher percentage of women who did not work outside of the home felt this way.[6] Mothers in the 1990s who are not fulfilling such roles still would suffer greatly.

The Survey and the Interviews

Interviews with eleven mothers (over 20 were interviewed) are presented here. Some I interviewed a number of times over the course of three years, while others I had contact with only once. Before I present the interviews and describe four patterns that emerged from them, the findings from the research with the seventy-six mothers who are out of contact are offered. These provide a broad perspective and an opportunity to draw some tentative comparisons with the fathers' survey results.

Like the fathers, the seventy-six mothers were drawn from Parents without Partners, and, additionally, Mothers without Custody. This almost exclusively white group had an average age of forty-four, and tended to be employed as secretaries or technicians, business and salespeople, and occasionally professionals. Their average income at the time of the survey was twenty-six thousand dollars, comparable to that of white working women in this age group in the United States.[7]

The mothers were living away from 142 children, 44 percent of whom were daughters. More than half had children age eighteen and under, most of whom were living with their father. The typical mother had been separated for seven years at the time of the survey.

The patterns of contact between mother and children sometimes varied by child (if she had mothered more than one). Like the fathers, the mothers were asked to indicate their level of contact and whether it was in person, by telephone, or by letter. Slightly over a quarter said they either had absolutely no contact or spoke by telephone or saw their child only once or twice a year. The remainder had contact that varied up to a few times over the past year, yet had gone without contact within the previous six months. As a group the mothers had not been out of contact with their children for as long as the fathers had been.

In about half the cases, the courts were involved in resolving custody disputes, and in 41 percent of all cases mothers were required to pay child support payments (a significantly smaller percent than of the fathers). Eighty-six percent of the mothers claimed they "always" paid the support they owed. In sum, these are women who are generally employed, some in beginning or mid-career though at low-level jobs, with an average income and a good amount of life experience as a separated or divorced parent. They are not teen or young adult mothers.

Why did contact cease? The mothers could select from four choices or write in a reason. Fifty-eight percent answered that the other parent was preventing contact, 30 percent contributed it to distance, 16 percent cited their own issues were interfering, and 16 percent said that the children's issues are stopping contact, with no consistent write-in reason given. Their answers were remarkably similar to the fathers'. But when queried in an open-ended question that sought the same information, differences appeared. Mothers were much more likely to indicate the children did not want contact (34 percent) than were fathers (which may be a realistic appraisal or could be a reflection of a tendency toward self-doubt not seen in the fathers). Mothers were slightly more apt to blame distance (18 percent) than were fathers but were about equally likely (62 percent) to describe the other parent as blocking visitation or poisoning the child against them. A few mentioned money as the reason.

Other notable differences between the mothers and fathers appear in table 1 (see page 83) and are worth considering.

It was also learned that mothers reported more stress-like symptoms in connection with the separation from their children than fathers. Fathers felt less supported by their friends and the community than the mothers did.

It was hypothesized that the pain the parents suffered being apart from their children was similar to a form of post-traumatic stress. One way of thinking about stress related to any event is to consider to what extent intrusive thoughts about a particular trauma pop into the traumatized person's mind. In other words, unpleasant associations about the traumatization would all of a sudden appear, which would affect the person's everyday activities. A second way to think about post-traumatic stress is related to the extent avoidant behavior is necessary. For example, does someone avoid going to certain places that serve as reminders of the traumatic event? Is someone purposely not dealing with feelings related to the trauma? The parents were administered a standardized scale that was adapted to pertain to separation from a child. The answers suggest that half of the mothers and about one-quarter of the fathers scored in a range indicating they were experiencing some form of post-traumatic stress, with intrusive thoughts being the most common form of reaction.[9] As a result, it would appear that being separated from one's child could be, for many of these parents, akin to feelings of being traumatized.[10]

The responses to these questions point out some of the potential differences between mothers and fathers in what happens to them, why they think it happens, and how they feel about it. (I say "potential" to remind the reader that this is not a representative sample but one drawn from volunteers who were members of self-help groups). Many mothers went from a situation with a lot of contact with their children (as they tended to initially have custody after a breakup) to a no-contact situation. Fathers did not tend to have the same experiences in the shift in their contact with their children. This alone could prove very traumatic for the mothers. But this is not the only key difference. The mothers, according to self-reports, were more likely to have been abused and to have lived with a substance abuser before the breakup. Obviously, this could have an emotional impact on them. They most likely were more apt to suffer financially in the transition to a single-parent family. Thus their entrance into a situation of no contact

TABLE 1. Differences between Mothers and Fathers without Contact

Who was more apt to first have custody after the breakup? (27% of the mothers versus 17% of the fathers)	Mothers
Who was less apt to be court-ordered to pay child support? (40% of the mothers versus 66% of the fathers)	Mothers
Who was less apt to feel the amount of court-order support was fair? (33% of the mothers versus 46% of the fathers) (Mothers who provided support gave an average of $532 a month vs. $583 a month for fathers).	Mothers
Who was more apt to report a history of domestic violence in the marital relationship? (47% for mothers vs. 34% for fathers)	Mothers
Who was more apt to identify the other parent as the perpetrator of the violence? (30% of the mothers versus 17% of the fathers)	Mothers
Who was more apt to report a history of substance abuse in the other spouse? (23% of mothers vs. 12% of fathers)	Mothers
Who was more apt to indicate that accusations of child abuse had been directed at that parent? (22% of fathers vs. 8% of mothers)	Fathers
Who was more apt to express contentment at not having contact with the child? (Almost 1 in 7 fathers was content,[8] as compared with 1 in 16 mothers)	Fathers
Who rated the other parent more favorably as a parent? (Less than one-third of the fathers gave mothers a poor rating, while almost half the mothers gave the fathers that rating.)	Fathers

single parenting follows a path that could be exponentially more difficult than that of the fathers.

The stories of the eleven mothers reflect many of the same issues raised by the larger sample of seventy-six. To some extent, their stories highlight what others have experienced. They are a more diverse group of women, racially, culturally, and economically, and more closely match the general population demographically. Like the fathers, they were drawn from the survey as well as from government programs, social contacts, and word of mouth. Four patterns were found that tend to encompass the experiences of mothers losing contact with their children after divorce. As is true with the patterns offered for the fathers, these patterns do not account for every mother's situation and some overlap is noted. In fact, these interviews were harder to classify than the fathers'. The reasons for this could be many: Mothers' situations could be more complicated than fathers; their situations may be comparable but the fathers may present issues in more black and white terms; or, as a male interviewer, I could have elicited different types of information from women than from men.

The overarching theme that seems to touch on every mother's story is the extent of the pain she feels being out of touch with her child. To a greater extent than for the fathers, I am left with the impression that these mothers feel victimized by the father, whereas the fathers feel victimized not as much personally as by a system that generally demeans their importance. Two patterns are presented in this chapter and two in the next. While some mothers do walk away from their children, refuse to visit when invited, and do not look back, the stories of mothers who claim to have behaved in this way are not captured here. Those mothers exist and, like fathers who act the same way, are not fit to parent. Their actions stem from significant feelings of inadequacy. They absent themselves, not fully appreciating the value that they still could hold for their children. They make the mistake of deciding for their children that there should be no contact with them. If they are abusive to the children and unwilling to change, then their absence is necessary. If they have no desire to see their children and are not interested in change, attempts to reconcile with them will most likely be futile.

The mothers in these chapters wanted more contact with their children than they were having. For various reasons, they do not have it. The first two patterns presented here represent those where the mothers feel rejected by the children. In the first pattern, the sense is that the children have come to their own conclusion to reject the mother, though they possibly have been influenced by other adults. With the second pattern, there is a sense that the children are rejecting the mother because they have been brainwashed, usually by the father. These two patterns are different only by degree.

The remaining two patterns, discussed in chapter 5, include situations where the mother is seen as incompetent or has been accused of abuse, and where the mother sought out the involvement of the father and eventually lost custody because of her own efforts to involve him. The courts play a part in many of these cases. As we heard from the fathers, and as would be expected from a group of parents who have lost in court, their perception is that the system has worked to their disadvantage and is biased against them.

Pattern 1: Mothers Who Are Unwanted by Their Children

This is the least easy pattern to compartmentalize and overlaps with some of the other patterns. Essentially, the mothers lose contact because of relationship problems that develop with their children either before they become noncustodial or afterwards. As their relationship sours, it may be affected by the father's interference or by the mere presence of a stepmother. But the failure of the mother–child relationship opens the door for such interference, rather than the reverse, as is seen in the second pattern.

Some parents and children, of course, develop serious relationship problems whether they are living together or not. Adolescence in particular is a time in which this is most likely to happen. Children and parents living together fight, and one storms out of the room. A few hours (or days) later, they are communicating again. Living under the same roof, they find it difficult to avoid each other. When there has been a family breakup, it is easier to have these relationship problems spiral out of control because the opportunities to mend fences are fewer and the chances of the other parent interfering are greater. What is captured here in these stories is relationship-driven rejection that leaves the mother feeling partially or completely at fault.

Pattern 2: Mothers Whose Children Are Brainwashed

In this pattern, the mother has often ended the marriage and is confronted by a father (or another family member) bent on retaliation. The father, for a variety of reasons, is perceived as turning the child against the mother. He may believe the mother is ill suited to raise the child. He may want the mother out of the picture because he has emotional needs he believes the child can meet. Or, he may want revenge and uses the child as a pawn. In this situation, according to the mothers, the children are fed a continuous stream of negatives and lies about the mother. The children reach the point at which they do not want anything to do with the mother. The mother, in turn, feels betrayed and powerless to change the relationship with the child because she is often blocked from continued contact. Whereas aspects of this are similar to the first pattern, in which the mother and child have difficulty sustaining a relationship, here the implication is that the father (or another family member) is initiating and sustaining an alienation process.

Pattern 1: Mothers Who Are Unwanted by Their Children

BETTY

Very soon into my interview with Betty, we talked about grief and loss. This is a central theme of many of these parents' lives, and it is certainly central to her life. Her father was killed in a car accident when Betty was six, leaving her mother to raise her and her younger sister. Betty and I discussed that mourning used to be considered a short-term event, a passage that one should get through within six months or a year after a tragedy. Now it is believed that the mourning process can go on for years and that a person may grieve throughout life and still be productive and happy. Betty said she has never fully gotten over the death of her father and wished she knew as a child what she now knows as a forty-four-year-old adult about giving herself permission to grieve. This may, in part, explain her view of what has happened with her current parenting situation.

Following her father's death, Betty's mother went to work outside of the home. Betty was immediately forced into service around the house and was the main source of child care for her younger sister until Betty left for college to become a nurse. She believes that her early caretaking experiences paved the way for her later choice of profession. There may have been some early caretaking of her mother, too, even before her father's death. In adulthood, while in therapy, Betty remembered that her father had abused alcohol. He would often come home late from work, skip dinner, and withdraw from the family for most of the evening. She suspects that alcohol was involved in his accidental death.

Betty met her future husband, Greg, in college. They married after three years of dating. He enlisted in the Air Force during the Vietnam era, and the couple moved around a great deal. Married life was not happy from the start for Betty. When asked specifically about domestic violence between them, she admitted that she had been beaten enough times to require treatment from an orthopedist. "He would be angry at me and lash out physically. I never struck him first, only near the end and in response to his hitting me. From the beginning he was abusive in a nonphysical way, and then it became physical."

Despite the state of the marriage, a daughter, Julie, was born on their eighth wedding anniversary. Greg retired from the Air Force and began civilian life and Betty worked part-time as a nurse. "It must be surprising to learn that we had a planned child, after hearing how bad the marriage was. But I thought it would help and I wanted a child. When she was born I was a very open responsive mother, and I thought it was the most wonderful thing in the world. I feel like I bonded to her very quickly. That was a problem for Greg, though, and that is what precipitated the end of the marriage. It was shocking to me when I realized that my closeness to Julie was a problem for him. It was even more shocking when I saw him do to her what he had been doing to me. I saw him losing patience, shaking her. He had no rational idea that babies are the way they are and you can't control them. He felt I should be able to control her behavior and I couldn't. It was scary, so I left."

It is not uncommon for abused women to have a baby in the hope of saving their marriage or changing the behavior of their husbands. Often the target of verbal abuse also, women develop a false hope that if they can make their husbands happier by changing their own behavior, everything will be better. It rarely happens, though.

Betty was so concerned about Greg's irrational and odious behavior that she told his parents that the marriage was over because she was fearful that he would harm himself or her and wanted to put his parents on guard. There was never a discussion about where Julie would live. Both agreed she belonged with Betty, and Greg agreed to visit weekly and pay $180 a month in child support.

Because Julie was very young at the time, she did not appear to miss her father, and, when older and more verbal, never mentioned wanting to see him. Betty reported that for a five-year period, between when Julie was five and ten, she often had to *encourage* Julie to see him. Betty and Greg continued to have a stormy relationship. She consulted him about child-care-related issues and found him to be totally illogical and unreliable.

When Julie was eleven, a sea change occurred. "I don't know why," Betty says. "It became an adolescent mother-daughter hostility thing. I took her to the pediatrician and asked for advice about what was going on with her. She was not happy, and I was told she was just acting like a little kid. I know now that plans were being made with her father and that is why she was uncomfortable. She was living a life of contradictions. She was keeping up her every-other-week visitation, and what finally happened was I got a letter from the court discussing a change of custody. She had made up her mind at some point and I didn't know about it. But now I understand why she was so happy to turn twelve. She had been told she could have a voice as to where she wanted to live at that age, and that is when the petition showed up. I was my usual blind self. I tried to figure out what was going on, but she was totally secretive; she had been planning it for the whole year."

As a result of the court visit, custody was reversed. Betty became the visitor and was required to pay monthly child support of $325. In the previous year Greg had remarried, so the thought of living in his home had become more attractive to Julie. Also, Betty's mother had been living with Julie and Betty for years. She was critical of both of them, and a great deal of tension had roiled up in the family. Even though Betty finally moved her mother out of the home before Julie turned twelve, Betty thinks it was too late for Julie to back out of the plans she and her father had been making.

The influence of a stepmother or the attractiveness of a remarried family is frequently cited as a reason for custody to be reversed. A deteriorating living situation at Betty's house opened the door for Greg and his new wife.

As soon as Julie began living with Greg, she refused to visit Betty. Betty seems totally bewildered by it all. "She just doesn't want to see me, spend any kind of time with me, write me, or phone me. In the three years now that she has been gone, I have received one letter from her and a couple of phone calls. I last saw her up close at a joint counseling session twenty months ago. [Julie sought therapeutic help after the change in custody.] I went to some of her basketball games but have not seen her since then. I quit going because she would ignore me. She was unable to be comfortable with any relations with me."

I asked Betty if she thought Julie knew that Betty loved her. "Yes. We had an excellent relationship her whole life. I have been told that I did too much for her in terms of what I gave up of myself, that she wanted space from me and that is in part why she left. I think she has been manipulated by her father and that they probably deserve each other."

As Betty talked further, she expressed increasing amounts of hurt and anger. Like some parents I interviewed, she places the responsibility for the future relationship firmly in her daughter's court. "It has been the worst hurt that I have ever had to deal with, including being without a father. There will never be anything as traumatic in my life as this. Knowing this, I have enthusiasm for life, as I know that compared with this the rest of life will be a piece of cake. I can't think of anything that will be as bad. Her death would not bother me that much. She is just a child support bill that I pay now. There is very little emotional attachment."

Betty has not always felt this way. When Julie last called Betty on a Christmas Eve six months before our interview, they had excellent communication. They talked for two hours, and then Julie cut short the discussion because, Betty believes, Greg came home. Betty has not heard from her since. "I told her at that time, 'Don't expect me to call you.' I told her the ball was in her court.

"My only regret is that when she first started to act upset and was having problems I didn't go to a counselor. I used friends and her pediatrician instead."

Betty believes she has tried everything and feels that it is now up to Julie to reconnect with her. Their relationship went sour, her ex-husband interfered, and nothing could be done. Had there been a stronger mother–child relationship, it might have weathered some of the storm. Had she continued to keep open communication despite getting nothing back, she may have learned more about why contact ceased. She refuses to open herself up again and assumes a posture of distancing herself and insisting that Julie reconnect with her on Betty's terms.

Judy's situation is one in which a mother tried to maintain a relationship despite her daughter's enormous emotional problems. As the daughter reached her teens she continually pushed Judy away. An acrimonious custody situation coupled with restricted career opportunities for both parents in the same geographic area made it difficult for them to work as a team during the daughter's emotional turmoil.

JUDY

Judy, now forty-seven, was the youngest of three children. Raised in a religious household, her father was a minister and her mother helped in the parish. While her home life looked happy on the outside, she realized much later that her father had wanted to leave her mother for years, but would not because of his strong church ties and the rarity of divorce at that time. When she finished high school, Judy went to a small college and majored in anthropology. Upon graduation, she enrolled in the Peace Corps and was stationed in Turkey, where she met her future husband, Nelson. After they left the Peace Corps, she began graduate training and they eventually married.

Judy offers a great deal of insight into the marital relationship. "The marriage was happy at first. But in thinking about it, [I realize] it was a traditional marriage like my parents', where the man is supposed to be the boss and the woman is supposed to cater to him and be responsible for the relationship. We would fight because Nelson would get angry if I did not agree with him. I wasn't playing my part right. We replicated my parents with self-esteem problems. I have problems with self-esteem, as does my mother. We both struggle to fit into the woman's role and have underneath a lot of intelligence. In a relationship we feel we should have some input and don't know quite how to deal with problems of negotiation, gender roles, and self-esteem. I've started reading books about codependency, and now I know where I fit in with my mother. Feeling guilty about everything and feeling susceptible to manipulation, I feel inadequate if things aren't right because I feel it is my fault.

"During the marriage, if I had my own views, Nelson would get angry; he was similar to my father, which is why I think I married him. He demonstrates that he is competent in managing and I play the role of dependent person, but it doesn't work well and then we both resent each other."

Their only child, a daughter named Rose, was born after five years. Both parents were very close to Rose. In fact, one month after her birth, Nelson insisted that Rose and Judy go with him to Turkey (where he was conducting field research) because he could not bear the thought of being away from Rose. During the trip, the marriage began to unravel.

"My confidence was being eroded by his treatment of me. He was withdrawing and getting angry more and more. Several times he would hit me (though never hard enough to require a doctor's care), and several times I would hurt him back. Once, he insisted we go to New York. I shouldn't have gone, and we were both really upset and weren't talking. I ran behind him and kicked him."

The marriage continued to unravel, yet Judy could never quite understand what was at the root of the problem. In retrospect, she admits to seeing characteristics of the battered wife syndrome in herself—she thought the fault for the failure of marriage was all hers. Like many people suffering from low self-esteem and dependence on a partner (and like Betty), she would struggle to make things better but would fail hopelessly as her self-esteem plummeted further.

"Finally it all came out. He told me he was falling in love with my brother and that he was having sexual feelings for other men. I realized this wasn't going to change." As shocking as this revelation was, it was not the only significant impediment to their staying together; violence was also an issue. "During this time, my daughter would shout, 'Daddy, don't hit my mommy.' Even though he never did hit me in front of her, she somehow just knew I was getting hit. With all of this going on, I decided to leave, even though he had really already left emotionally."

Judy and Rose moved into Judy's brother's home. Nearly finished with her doctoral course work, she furiously tried to wrap up her dissertation so that she could enter the job market at a decent salary. An arrangement was worked out where Rose, then four, visited Nelson on weekends. After a year of visitation, and with Judy's dissertation defense scheduled, Nelson insisted on increasing his time with Rose. He threatened to abduct her if Judy did not agree to an alternating-week schedule and shared custody.

"I felt terrible; I did not know what to do. I was advised to file a petition for custody. Until that point, everything had been done without the court's involvement. Nelson fought it in court [the first of more than forty trial dates they would have], and his lawyer tore me apart. The judge decided on shared custody."

The new visitation schedule was initiated, but after a year, Judy became concerned about Rose's behavior. "She began acting weird. She had always been a very active, assertive child, and she started to change. Her personality metamorphosed, and she got quieter and started to get scared being out of my sight. I told Nelson she needed some help, but he kept refusing to go along with therapy. I blame myself for not pushing it, but finally he agreed to let her go to a therapist. It turned out he was showering with her and sleeping with her on a regular basis. When the therapist expressed her concern, he got mad and said that there was nothing wrong with his behavior and that in Turkey fathers are much closer with their children."

According to Judy, Rose's behavior continued to deteriorate and she became suicidal, injuring herself, talking about wanting to die, scratching pictures of herself, and experiencing nightmares. She was constantly masturbating, was scared to go to sleep, wet her bed, and started stealing.

"It became clear she was being sexually abused. We went to court to try to reduce visitation, and even though the therapist and a consulting psychiatrist testified, we didn't win. The opposing therapist convinced the judge the behavior was related to the divorce."

A few months later, Nelson remarried and Rose's behavior showed a marked improvement. No mention of Nelson's homosexual tendencies were made again. Visitation continued on a weekly basis.

A year later, when Rose was nine, Judy (with her newly finished doctorate) accepted her first teaching position. It was in a different state. She wanted to take Rose with her and have her visit Nelson once a month, instead of sharing her every other week. Nelson balked and postponed court dates until after Judy and Rose had moved to their new location. The court saw no compelling reason for Rose to move with Judy because she was coping well with shared visitation. It was Judy who had left the state of origin. The court ruled in Nelson's favor, and Rose returned to him. Rose had a good relationship with both parents at that time, according to Judy, and most likely was happy to avoid making a choice.

For the first time, Rose began living with Nelson a majority of time. Judy tried to cope with a new job, a new home and city, and separation from Rose for long periods of times. The plans for visitation often went awry. The seeds of a loss of contact were sown.

"It became a real fight to get her there. It was very far. Nelson would drag his feet about making plane reservations for visits. It was always a struggle. I was devastated living without her. I saw her the next summer and then moved to New Jersey, which was closer to her. But each visit was a big fight. She was not interested. I would set rules for her. [Differences in households often cause children to strongly favor the more permissive parent.] Then she started stealing stuff from my brother. [Rose was eleven at the time.] I got really upset when I heard that."

This began another long series of negotiations between Judy and Nelson, Judy asking that Rose start therapy and Nelson denying that it was needed, a pattern similar to one in their marriage. Judy then was hired for a permanent position in California. Rose visited only occasionally, and

Judy saw her whenever she traveled east on business. Court battles over custody continued. Judy had previously been exempted by Nelson from paying child support because she had not held a steady job. Now that she was employed full-time, he demanded it. He also began to argue with her about the seven weeks of summer vacation she had with Rose.

Judy invited Rose on some of her overseas research trips to France and Saudi Arabia. Rose refused. "I would call her all the time to talk and she was very unresponsive," Judy reports. Then, Rose finally agreed to a two-week visit. Judy was ecstatic. "But when she arrived, she began to act funny. I finally became concerned enough to go through her things the day before she was to fly home. I found underwear of mine that she had stolen, and I also found new, very expensive underwear that she had shoplifted. I confronted her about it, and she cried and begged me not to tell her father. I said I'd take the underwear back to the store for her because she was about to leave. I didn't know at first whether to tell Nelson and I consulted a psychologist who said he should be told. I was probably not as sensitive to her as I should have been, though. I'm not sure I understood what she was going through."

Judy's actions unleashed a torrent. "I wrote Nelson and received a furious letter in return. 'I can no longer hold my peace,' he wrote. 'You are mentally unstable and this is all your fault because you were ranting and raving at her, and she doesn't want to come out to see you and it is not safe for her to visit.' She has not come out since then. We rarely speak."

The mother-daughter relationship has not stopped completely, though. It is just impossible for Judy to predict when contact will resume on a regular basis. "I visited her back east once after the disastrous visit. She said she would be happy to see me, but as the date got closer she sounded less excited. Her father drove her to where I was staying, and we only visited for two hours. She did bring me a gift but that has been about it. She did call after the California earthquake to see if I was okay. Yet, if I call, it is impossible to get her on the phone, and we'll go for months without talking. I keep calling her. Her father will block calls and say she doesn't want to talk to me, and then she'll get on the phone and say the same thing. Or she'll cut me off during a conversation and tell me to shut up. I tell myself not to call her because it just makes trouble. In retrospect, I wonder why I kept going to court all those years for this result."

Judy is trying to make sense of everything that has happened to her and to the relationship that is hanging by a thread. She not only is struggling with that loss but also with the concerns she has about Rose. Whereas some parents can take comfort in knowing their child is growing up well without contact with them, Judy does not have that luxury. "I'm worried about Rose because her grades are terrible. The school counselor whom I speak to occasionally says Rose is extremely manipulative. The legal system did not protect my daughter. I still believe she was abused. My life has been devastated. For years I tortured myself, I hated myself, wondering what I did wrong.

"A therapist helped me by telling me I had the responsibility of parenthood without the power. We have the image in our society that mothers have the power and are completely able to take care of their children, but it is not true. I try not to torture myself."

Despite being rejected by Rose, Judy holds on to a shred of optimism. "Parents like me should try everything to get along with the spouse. Keep up contact. Tell your child they can call collect anytime. Tell them you will always love them. I think underneath all that, they will know you love them. I think back to the good times that we had. I think somewhere somehow she loves me and trusts me. People tell me to just wait. I keep thinking that later things will change."

In this situation, it can be argued that the relationship was spoiled by Nelson, that his behavior started the whole alienation process. But it also could be that once Judy left to pursue her career, the die was cast. It was fair for Judy to lose custody, though not contact, when she moved away. What happened next is more confusing. Nelson would probably argue that Judy was unbalanced, an emotional state that Judy hinted at herself in the early stages of the marriage. But Judy would argue that Nelson so manipulated everything that any relationship between mother and daughter was impossible. When Judy confronted Rose with her illegal behavior, Rose may have sought support from Nelson, perhaps lying about her own behavior. Nelson was quick to accept Rose's framing of the problem being Judy's fault. Such a depiction would have fit his own view of her. It was painful for Rose to maintain a relationship with Judy, given the history of conflicts and potential abuse, and she sought to sever it. Rose was ambivalent, though; she occasionally did call Judy. Judy and Rose had an adequate relationship at the time of the custody decision but events that *later* transpired, that included Nelson, caused the relationship to unravel.

Finally, Judy feels rejected and wonders what she did wrong and why she went to court so often, given the outcome. Her feeling, perhaps an outgrowth of her low self-esteem, is that she made some mistake. For these reasons, this is best represented as a mother who feels unwanted.

In some cases, parents lose contact with adopted children. In Ethel's case, conflict with a biological daughter from a first marriage was the deciding factor in her losing custody of and eventually contact with an adopted son from a second marriage. The question Ethel and other parents like her consider is this: How much should she continue to try to see a son who is rejecting her?

ETHEL

Raised by two parents and the oldest of five, Ethel married a man she met in college. "I didn't know him very well," she admitted, "but in a month he became abusive." She endured, but eight years later, and with her two daughters and one son in tow, she walked out following a particularly severe battering incident. The children ranged in age from ten months to eight years old at the time. "I had a choice of going to a woman's shelter or staying in another state with a friend, and I chose the friend. We went on welfare because I had health problems [a number of the mothers in these chapters experienced health problems or accidents], couldn't work, and my first husband refused to pay child support. Three years later I met Ted [who would become her second husband] on a blind date." He seemed to be the answer to her dreams. He was older than she was, had a stable income, had never been married, and wanted to build Ethel and her children a new house. There were two problems that quickly emerged after the marriage, though. First, the house was near Ted's parents. Second, Ted's mother was very critical and interfered with all Ethel's decisions about childrearing. Ted would support his mother instead of Ethel when they came to loggerheads. "I only wanted happiness and peace but she was meddling and very angry at me because I was Catholic. She also resented my close ties with my family."

Ethel was happy with her situation otherwise. Ted was supportive of her staying home and taking care of the children. They were involved in their church and decided that they could be helpful to others by providing foster care. Over the course of the next few years, they were foster parents to four children. One day, they received an emergency call about accepting a fifth child, a boy, who needed immediate placement after being abused by his mother's boyfriend. They again opened their home and decided, after being foster parents for one year, to adopt Peter.

But marital problems arose. Despite her dream house and the chance to stay home with children, Ethel became increasingly dissatisfied as Ted became more distant.

"I had a husband who did not want to be intimate in his marriage," Ethel admitted to me. "In fact, we went for four years without any intimacy. Also, Ted was weak in relation to his mother. She continued to find fault and was critical of me for having foster children; she even accused me of exposing our family to AIDS when we had a child from a cross-cultural family living with us. It got to be too much and I ended the marriage."

Ethel, then forty-one, planned to raise all four children (her own three and Peter) by herself. (The other foster children had moved out.) She loathed the prospect of telling the children they were going to have to move out of their comfortable home and transfer from their private schools. When she finally marshaled the courage to tell them, two of her children took the news with equanimity. But her youngest daughter was very distraught and considered leaving Ethel and going to live with her father. The negotiations around living arrangements dragged on. During a particularly messy mother-daughter fight, Ethel slapped her and told her she did not want to be her mother anymore. The daughter as well as the other two biological children left for a few days to stay with their father. The eldest daughter and the other son returned but the younger daughter elected to stay with her father. She had told her father that Ethel had been abusing her for many years.

At this time, Peter, who was now the adopted child of both parents, became the focus of an intense custody battle. Ted's lawyers got wind of the animosity between Ethel and her daughter and used the information against her in court. Ethel was granted visitation and compelled to pay child support of $315 a month, even though her earnings were a pittance compared with Ted's. (She was earning $7 an hour.) "When I first read the custody decree, I thought there had been a typo and the names had been reversed, the decision was so outrageous. Ted had never shown great interest in Peter, and I was obviously a good parent, or I never would have been licensed as a foster parent. Ted just did not want to pay me child support. I wonder if my ex-father-in-law bought off my attorney. We live in a small town, and it was an old boys' network."

Even though Ethel won liberal visitation, she said she found it hard to exercise it. "I was supposed to pick Peter up on Fridays at five but couldn't get out of work until six. So I was called a bad person. By this time, Peter did not want to see me. His dad was buying him all these things that I couldn't afford. My other children were resentful because he was going on vacations and we could barely put food on the table. The lawyers on his dad's side were so vicious toward me, they questioned my character even though I had been doing good with foster children. They said I had adopted Peter to do something with a foster child that would bring me money because I knew I was getting divorced—that I was going to hold Ted up for money, with Peter as a child support chip."

Other problems emerged that made visitation with Peter difficult and have led to her not seeing him now for more than a year. For example,

Ethel wanted to recover her personal items from their former house, where Ted and Peter were living. But Ted convinced the judge this was harassment, that Ethel considered coming to the house to be a game. Ethel has serious concerns that Peter has undergone a personality change and become a con artist. (He is now seven.) She says he twists whatever he and she would do together during their visitation. In touching on the issue of sexual abuse, something many parents raise when they say they wonder about hugging their children, she reported, "I fear if I see my son or hug him too much, that he'll say Mommy hugged me and Mommy touched me. I don't trust him. My daughters are devastated by this. They have seen the change in Peter's behavior and are aware that other things are going on, like he was taking showers with his father. They worry about abuse."

Ethel grew reflective during the interview and said, "It is funny that your research would come up now because I have been grieving the last few months and feeling so bad that I don't have children around anymore except for my other son. But I don't even want to call anymore because Ted will say I am putting thoughts into Peter's head. I feel so guilty sometimes, not seeing him. This is what happens in a divorce: Any good intentions are called bad intentions. The court system is very vicious. Judges don't take the time to really assess what is happening in families. You would have thought, the way they talked about me, that I was the worst mother in the world, and it has taken a long time to heal from this." Talking again about the slapping incident with her daughter, Ethel added, "People who raise teens know how hard it can be, and these kinds of fights are not that unusual. My daughter and I are on speaking terms now, though we aren't as close as we were. Some of my reluctance to see Peter may be related to some of the shame and guilt about the thing with my daughter."

For Ethel, striving to see Peter brings up the bad feelings she has about her actions toward her daughter. As noted earlier in the book, a mirroring effect can occur where parents see their worst selves in others, particularly their children. Ethel has weighed everything and decided that, given the effort and the lack of success involved in seeing Peter, she will not try to see someone who is uninterested in her and causes her more heartache with her own children. "He is not one of the things I can fight for. When he is older, he may come back to see me on his own. If he was my natural son, I would feel like it wasn't so hopeless, but this is different. I am sure he will survive...."

Patty: A Daughter's Perspective. I interviewed Ethel's middle child, Patty, who is fifteen and again living with her. She confirms much of Ethel's story. "I didn't see my mom for a few months, and my sister went for over a year without seeing her. Mom and her had a fight, and Mom slapped her because she was being really rude. My sister got mad and left, and we left, too, so we would all stay together. I don't know really why I left.

"I decided after three months that I missed my mom very much. I was really depressed [Patty was twelve at the time] and decided I had to leave my dad's and go back with her. I had to do what was best for me and not for my brother and sister. My brother stayed with Dad for a year and then left because he couldn't take Dad anymore. Dad was being a jerk. He didn't approve of who my brother was dating. He was very mean to my brother's girlfriend. He was also very manipulative. My brother and mother didn't talk for that whole time, but they are talking a little now. My sister [whom Ethel slapped] stayed. My sister blames Mom for everything."

Patty was forthcoming about the relationship between her, her mother, and Peter. "I guess we last saw him a year ago. I would like to see him but, ever since he lived with Dad, he has become spoiled and hard to deal with. He doesn't listen to you. He manipulates things."

Patty is a high achiever and quite proud of her sports accomplishments, having made an all-state team in soccer. Part of her desire for perfection overflows into her relationship with her father. She needs to have everything in its place, but their relationship is an ambivalent one. "I didn't see my dad for a while and then I thought I better start to see him because if anything happened to either of us, I would want things to be resolved. So we talk now but not much. I saw him a month ago, and it's weird because I don't feel like there is any bond there. He doesn't seem like he cares. It doesn't make me want to come back and keep trying."

Patty also wanted to talk about divorce in general. "I have a lot of feelings about divorce, but I know the only good thing that comes out of this is that I am a stronger person. I have always felt stuck in the middle and not knowing which parent to go with. It feels terrible, and I have always felt that if I need something, I will make the other parent feel bad and that makes me feel bad. [These themes are also seen in chapter 6.] I know if I get married that I will try very hard to make it work so that my kids won't have to go through this."

Ethel's relationships with Peter and one daughter are poor. Ethel feels her slap was the straw that changed the relationship with her daughter and that it was justified to some extent, a sentiment with which Patty agrees. After divorce, such conflicts are more likely to escalate. Here it left Ethel out in the cold.

The last case in this pattern involves a mother who was separated from, reconciled with, and then separated from her daughter again, while resolving a difficult relationship with her son. It is representative of one of the highly public manifestations of divorce that has been captured in news reports—a child wishing to divorce a parent. In Kate's case, her sixteen-year-old daughter tried to divorce her but failed.

KATE

Kate was never close with her own mother, who was distant and unreachable. Her mother's emotional unavailability bothered Kate a great deal, but she did feel close to her father.

Kate, forty, met her future husband, Steve, one year after high school. "It was on the rebound. I was throwing off my boyfriend, who was into drugs. Steve was two years older than me and pursued me, which I liked. We got engaged, became pregnant, and married, so we had our first child, a son, right away.

Both Steve and Kate brought difficult histories to their new family, which may have contributed to the marriage being weak from the beginning. Steve's father, an alcoholic, was still married to Steve's mother but was having an open affair and living with another woman. Steve had not spoken to his father for years and, like his father, would later become an alcoholic. Steve's mother was bitter and hard to handle. While there was no violence, Steve would get totally out of control when he drank.

Kate recounted to me during our interview, "I considered divorce but thought I should stay in because of the kids [a daughter, Anna, was born two years after their son, George]. Finally, I figured out Steve was fooling around. Women would call the house looking for him and send him gifts. I ended the marriage."

They agreed Kate would have custody. As she prepared to move out on her own with the children, she asked him to watch them for a few weeks while she went house-hunting in a rural area. When she returned, the terrain had changed dramatically. The children decided they did not want to move. Kate is convinced they wanted the stability of their house, friends, neighborhood, and schools and were not choosing Steve over her. (Yet later in our interview she began to doubt this). In fact, Steve offered to move out and give her the house. But Kate was afraid of him and felt that if she stayed in the house, he would never leave her alone and would feel he had carte blanche to drop in whenever he wanted. It was fear of him when he drank that drove her away from the family home in the first place. As a result she was left with little.

Money was never an issue, Kate told me, and she was not looking to "hurt him" with a hefty divorce settlement. Rather, she wanted him to stay away from her. What she meant by that was typical of what I have heard from other women: If I don't hassle my ex-husband about anything, like money, hopefully he will not hassle me. It is born out of a desire to end the relationship with no strings attached, even though such an ending might leave them at a financial disadvantage.

Despite being able to rationalize it, Kate was devastated by the children's decision. She had been particularly close with Anna and thought that Steve had only a bare-bones relationship with both of them. "I got some bad legal advice and ended up with liberal visitation. I don't know if I should have pushed for joint custody or not. I decided to accept [the children's] decision. Maybe they were too young to know what they were doing? It also made me question how close to Anna I had really been."

The next two years were harrowing for her. She was seeing Anna and George fairly frequently, but problems with Steve escalated. "He would call and pester me. He would call my mother and my friends and beg them to convince me to come back to the marriage. At the same time he brought me into court and got child support out of me. Then things got even messier. He met a woman and remarried, and she became very involved in the kids' lives. She got down to the nitty-gritty in terms of when I could visit and when I could call. She tried to take control of my kids because she did not have any of her own."

Kate began seeing her children less and less. They were also hitting adolescence and were less interested in spending time with their mother. "I didn't get to see them all the time but it was nothing really terrible. I would call and Anna would have other plans. Then things fell apart. I was making plans with Anna to join my boyfriend and his daughter, who was Anna's age, for a trip east. Steve started asking a lot of personal questions about the sleeping arrangements, which were going to be quite proper. Anna was about to leave for swimming camp for a few days before the vacation and heard us fighting and freaked out. She went to see a psychologist, and Steve decided she should stop seeing me for a while, that her problems centered around me. They thought she shouldn't have to see me until she was ready. What was supposed to be a few months turned out to be a year."

George was more interested in hanging out with his girlfriend than his mother but continued to see Kate every few weeks. Kate brought Steve to court for not helping her maintain contact with Anna, and Steve countersued in his home state (Kate had moved) for increased child support. Suits and countersuits involving different states of residence were filed, and, at one point, Kate was almost jailed for failure to pay support, even though she had been paying it through another state.

As the acrimony over visitation grew, Kate was supposed to have spring break with Anna. Anna made plans to go skiing with friends, and Kate said Anna could not go, that she had to follow through with the visit. Kate called the police when she showed up for visitation, and Anna refused to leave the house. Anna told the police she did not want to go and, being fourteen, was released from the obligation.

Anna then sued Kate for divorce. The judge threw the case out of court because it was capricious, but the emotional damage was inflicted. "I stopped seeing Anna for six months, hoping she would have a different attitude. I called her on her birthday, and she was distant. I decided I had done enough to not be divorced by my daughter. It was becoming more painful than I could bear, and that is when I decided I wouldn't pursue her anymore. I deserved more respect than that."

But children can be fickle. For reasons unknown to Kate, Anna decided she wanted to spend Christmas with her. "It was nice. She called me. I then asked her about Easter and Anna agreed to come, and then at the last minute she said she had to work, and she works for her father. So I haven't talked to her since. I don't even send letters."

While the relationship with Anna has ceased, Kate has become closer to George. He is in the service and phones her regularly. Like many other children in high-conflict divorces, he kept to himself and avoided conflict as long as he was living with his father. Once on his own, he felt freer to see her.

The lack of contact with Anna haunts her. "I have a hard time explaining to people what has happened. They assume the worst, that I did something wrong to lose custody of my daughter. I know a lot of people who have been driven crazy trying to keep it together, and it drives a lot of mothers nuts. Even my mother is upset that she doesn't see the children, and for someone who is as distant as she is, that's unusual!"

Kate gave me permission to call both her children, though she was unsure if Anna would agree to be interviewed.

George: A Son's Perspective. Now twenty-one, George is married and has a small child. When I asked for an interview he hesitated and said he needed to think about it. I called him again the following week and he agreed.

"I stopped seeing my mom for different periods of time, once for three months, and then for six months. I think we only saw each other then because she would see my sister and I would be around during the visits. She and I had kind of something between us that made the relationship not so great. We didn't see each other because I did not care if I saw her. I don't know how she felt at the time."

I asked about George's relationship with his father and how he came to live with him instead with her. "I remember even when young, my mother would ask me if she left, would I want to stay with her or with my father. I said I would stay with my dad. I had my mind made up even then. I think with my sister, though, she chose to stay with me because she looked up to me. It was more that than anything specifically about our mother."

After the breakup, George felt that his father encouraged contact between him and his mother. Despite this encouragement, when Steve remarried, his new wife came to be more of a mother to George than Kate. This might be because George believes that the difficulties between his two parents were engendered by Kate. He did not wish to go into more detail than that.

I inquired about his grandmother, who Kate had said was experiencing such pain from not seeing her grandchildren. He offered a different view. "I stopped seeing her. I moved out four years ago. She would talk to me when she called to speak with Anna when we visited my mother, but with me now out, we have less contact. I called my grandmother twice in the past four years, but, while we were at my dad's house, she never called us. Anna and I wondered why she never called us. It was not until two years ago I got up nerve to call her. She was fairly responsive. I expected to hear from her and never asked her why she didn't call. She would send a card once in a while. It was not hard being out of touch with her because we had not seen that much of her."

As parents who have lost contact hope, George and Kate were able to reestablish ties and build a relationship. "It wasn't until recently that we've been on better terms. My son being born and my getting married had to do with us getting back together. My being more mature and her feeling she missed out on some things with me have also played a part."

George also suggested I call Anna, as Kate had agreed to let me do. Anna had recently turned eighteen. I spoke to her father, Steve, who said she was not at home. When I explained I was calling because of research I was doing on the aftermath of divorce, he told me he had not seen her for a while because she had run away!

First George and then Anna had a difficult relationship with Kate. George was never close with her when young and offers an unflattering portrait of his mother and grandmother, starting with Kate quizzing George about who he would choose to live with if there was a divorce. George freely admits to not wanting to see Kate for many years—the classic rejection. Problems between Anna and Kate developed, or became more acute, as a result of the divorce. Anna initially followed George after the divorce and never reestablished a bond with Kate. Anna's running away remains unexplained.

Pattern 2: Mothers Whose Children Are Brainwashed

These next three cases involve a much higher degree of interparental conflict, which resulted in the children rejecting the mothers. As was discussed with respect to the fathers, sometimes children from the same family are affected quite differently by a breakup. In the first case, following an explosive divorce and a series of threats and actions by other parties, Darlene's son refused to see her, while Darlene maintained a strong relationship with her daughter.

DARLENE

Darlene describes her own upbringing as unremarkable. "It was the suburban two-parent thing of the 1960s." She graduated high school and college in typical fashion, met her husband, Jon, at a college town bar, and married him one year later. Both worked for the university she had attended and were initially happy. Problems did not surface until her pregnancy with Adam, when Darlene had to stop working during the last few months before the birth. With the temporary loss of her income, the family experienced financial hardship, which deepened when Darlene could not return to work because Adam became ill shortly after his birth. A daughter was born two years later and their financial struggles increased.

Marital difficulties escalated over the years, according to Darlene, when Jon became sexually and verbally abusive. "I pleaded with him to go for counseling. I was in counseling because of the way I felt from the abuse. In addition, Jon had a hard time not having a perfect child. That is how most arguments started—what to do for Adam, who needed a lot, while our daughter did not. My husband was very controlling.

"I asked him to leave. He refused and said if I tried to take the children, he would kill me. They were scared to death, so we talked, and I agreed I should leave and they would stay with him. [They were twelve and ten at the time, and she was thirty-six.] Even though they were scared of him, they did not want to leave school, their home and friends, and come with me.

"After I moved out we got divorced, and I was to get a share of the house with its sale. Jon used that as a tool to turn the kids against me [the brainwashing action]. He told them that if he had to pay me off, he and the kids would have to move. The children thought I was going to take the house from them, and they wouldn't talk to me for a long time. What could I do? I relented and gave up my share of the house. He kept the money, and the kids started seeing me again."

As is often the case, couples accustomed to fighting will continue to find things to fight over. With the house settled, visitation was the next battleground. "Jon would get incensed about my seeing the children. They eventually said not to make waves and that I should stop calling so much. I was paying child support during this time, so I should have been able to see them more than occasionally."

A new ingredient was introduced into the mix when Adam was trying out for the fall production at his high school and Darlene was dating one of the two directors of the play. The second director was very harsh on Adam, which Adam interpreted as being due to Darlene's dating the first director. He did not get the part he wanted and resented Darlene greatly because of it. At one point he screamed at Darlene about being abandoned by her and about her now causing this new rejection. Adam was in therapy at the time, and Darlene asked the therapist to intervene. The therapist refused, saying that he had a precarious relationship with both Adam and Jon and that any intervention that looked favorably on Darlene might result in Jon withdrawing Adam from treatment. The therapist advised her to write every few weeks, which Darlene has done faithfully. But she has not seen Adam. Her relationship with her daughter has survived, despite the daughter hearing Jon disparage Darlene.

"Now I see my daughter every day and she keeps me up to date on Adam. She wants to live with me, she said, but she also likes her high school. I don't know if she is trying to appease me. She is loyal to her father. It is sad, though, about Adam. I remarried eighteen months ago, and he has yet to meet my new husband. I feel terrible about not seeing him because we once were very close."

I asked Darlene to step back from the relationship and give her impression as to how this evolved. "I do know Jon is extremely angry that I left him. And I know my son was very upset about the divorce. Jon turned Adam against me. After the incident with the school production, Adam refused to see me anymore. I don't know if it is brainwashing, his own bad feelings, or both. I can only hope that at some time in the future he will get rid of these feelings and we can get together.

"I have a wonderful relationship with my daughter and she says it is because she can block out her father when he talks about me. Adam can't, though, and is afraid to speak up."

Darlene suffers in a situation in which she feels powerless. Jon's anger at her inspired him to turn the children against her. He made them think she was to blame for their impending change in lifestyle with the sale of the house. The animosity between mother and father was so great that Adam, susceptible to his father's opinion, elected to avoid his mother by turning off their relationship. For Adam, each new failure in his own life was viewed as being his mother's fault.

A number of other parents I interviewed also believe they are not seeing their children because the children have been poisoned against them. In Kerry's case, differences in culture have complicated her situation. One half Japanese and raised in a Japanese-American culture that placed a high value on integrity and honesty, she assumed everyone told the truth. She felt ill prepared to cope with lies told by her ex-husband, Philip, who maintained what Kerry claimed was a double life.

KERRY

Kerry lived with her Japanese mother after her parents separated when she was two. Her father, a Caucasian, suffered from post-traumatic stress disorder related to a World War II injury and could not work. Kerry's mother was forced to seek work as a nurse outside of their small hometown and grew disinterested in staying in the marriage. An amicable separation was arranged. Neither of Kerry's parents remarried, and her mother continued to visit her ex-husband on holidays so Kerry could have a sense of family.

Kerry was a popular student in high school, strong academically, and won a music scholarship to college, where she met Philip. They married shortly thereafter. "I had always wanted to wait until I had my master's degree to get married, but he was very persuasive. He set his mind on something and kept on pushing."

While the first five years of the marriage were happy ones, Kerry noticed a change in Philip. "He became distant. Our sexual relationship had never been great and he blamed me, calling me frigid. He was verbally abusive and would keep putting me down, and I became more dependent on him. After he became withdrawn, I had a brief affair while I was traveling on business. That really opened up my eyes to what a relationship could be. I came back and told him, and we went through a rocky period for a while. We went into counseling and he promised to change."

It was not until many years later, during the heat of a custody battle, that Kerry learned the reason for his distancing himself from her: he was homosexual. "I found out he had been gay even before college. He became inactive when we were first married, but then he began sleeping around. He went into treatment and didn't tell me for a year. He was very busy as an aide to the governor, so he was out a lot and was quite secretive. Apparently he had been abused as a child and had a somewhat seductive relationship with his mother, though it was not physical. He learned about deception as a child and continued to deceive me. I had been raised in a home and culture where honesty was sacred and people never lied."

Despite the problems in their marriage, they decided to have children. Three girls were born over the next six years—Andrea, Doris, and Mary. As we have heard from other parents, children are often conceived with the hope that they will save the marriage.

"My staying in the marriage was a mistake. But I felt I should follow through with my commitments, and he was nicer. When I conceived the children I was committed to having each one. Looking back, we had more of a platonic relationship. Later I learned he was having affairs with men during this time. I immersed myself in work, and I nurtured the children a great deal. I was able to arrange my work schedule, which involved music, around them. Philip was also quite involved with the kids. He worked long days but would see them when he could."

The marriage staggered through the early years of childrearing but took a turn for the worse following a boating accident in which Philip was severely injured. A long recuperation period and painkillers made him moody and more verbally abusive. Fights were common, and after one particularly ugly incident, Kerry announced she was leaving. Philip persuaded her to stay, but the reconciliation was short-lived and she left for a final time.

"Custody was to be shared. Because I worked in the home, I thought the children should be with me most of the time and not with a sitter at Philip's house. I filed for full custody and he countersued. He was running scared and worried about not having been the primary caregiver and that he would lose. The children were doing fine with me and visiting him, but he systematically turned the oldest two against me and that is how the real problems started. He also broke nearly everything in our mediation agreement. One time, I wanted to take all three on a vacation, but the oldest two refused to go. He had told them that if they went with me on vacation, I was going to kidnap them. When I got back with Mary, Andrea and Doris were like pit bulls against me. He had three straight weeks to work on them, and Andrea has been angry and distant ever since. Doris was caught in the middle. The girls wouldn't talk to me and did not want to visit me. Philip had told them that I had broken up the family and that everything was my fault, and they, being children, believed him."

At a hearing with a custody evaluator, the oldest two children said they wanted to live with Philip. Both parents were evaluated to be competent, but some false portrayals of Kerry (coupled with the children's stated preferences) resulted in the recommendation that Philip and Kerry share custody. Life returned to normal over the next few months, and the children and Kerry began spending time together. Philip became concerned that he was losing ground and used a series of manipulative tactics, according to Kerry, to gain court-ordered custody of all three children. Again, it was the children's wishes, more than anything else, that seemed to prevail. Despite having the right to visit while final custody decisions were in flux, Kerry often went to the house and found the children were not home.

Like most of the parents interviewed in the book, Kerry found the loss of daily contact terribly painful. "Knowing what was going on and what they were saying about me was very difficult. [She starts to cry.] What saved me was my mother. She was very supportive and told me not to hold any revenge and anger in my heart. She had visited them all along but I couldn't."

The pain of not seeing them was not all that Kerry suffered. Like Rachel, who is described in the first chapter, public humiliation followed. "The children would totally ignore me in public and hang on to Philip when I went to watch them at a school play. People would draw their own conclusions, seeing how they ignored me. The majority would not take sides, but even now I go to school events and everyone gets quiet when I arrive. They don't talk to me and it is very hard. I feel like an outsider."

Accompanying this pain, and perhaps exacerbating it, was the ongoing emotional battle with her ex-husband. This led her to a momentous decision eight months later. She decided that, faced with mounting legal fees and after intensive counseling, she should relinquish full legal custody of the children to Philip. "I realized that Philip knew no limits in his desire to win custody and beat me in this battle. Philip would never stop fighting me until he had won. He told people if I went through the divorce, he was going to destroy me financially and emotionally. I concluded that if there is a war going on and someone stops fighting, the war stops. The children were the bullets in this war. If I had fought and won in court, he would still try and poison the kids against me. He has turned Andrea against me so much that I have barely seen her in a year. Doris has begun to visit with Mary, but Andrea may be a lost cause. I sent them letters and gave her a birthday gift, and she wrote back once asking for a bunch of her stuff, like her dolls. But I can't give them back to her. It is too painful."

When the conflict was at its worst, Kerry felt suicidal. Since then a glimmer of hope has appeared. The children are in therapy and are slightly more accepting of her, though Andrea still keeps her distance. As Kerry puts it, "It is hard for her being caught between us. If Daddy is right, I must be wrong."

As with many mothers, the role of mother and "person of value" are tightly connected. Kerry said to me, "What value do I have as a person if my children don't want me? For a long time I believed the answer was zero.

I have been helped with therapy to see that I am still my own person without my children. I have learned that I can still be worthwhile without seeing them. I thought I couldn't stand not knowing if my children are being treated well or are being fed. I have learned that I cannot be involved with these things. I tell people who ask about my children that I have a very angry and vindictive ex-husband and that is why I don't see them."

Kerry has tried to find something positive in the experience. "I have grown a lot as a person and am much more compassionate. I have learned there are certain things you can fix and certain things you cannot fix. That must come with being forty-five. Mothers are used to fixing things and making them right, so it has been hard to not do that. I am able to cope with it much more than before. When I came back from vacation with the two youngest, I realized I had spent the whole week being detached and that if I had opened myself to relating to the children, it would be too painful. So I have this buffer that I have learned to live with. I have learned that I don't have much impact on the children anymore. I would never have expected after being such a totally involved wife and mother that I would be thrown out and have no say at all in their lives. It is a miserable way to be a parent, and it is barbaric when a good mother like me has her children removed from her life."

Finally, like many parents, Kerry expresses hope for the future. But it is tinged with a dose of reality. "I am looking forward to seeing Andrea at some point. I can't hope it will be a great relationship, though. It is almost like she died."

Philip's anger at the divorce and at being exposed as being gay contributed to his need to form a strong bond with his children at the expense of the relationship Kerry and the children needed. His consistent attacks and the children feeling caught in the middle persuaded the children they were better off not seeing her.

Sometimes it is not only the father but other family members as well who are working against the mother. A mother-in-law, for instance, may be involved, as happened in Marge's situation.

MARGE

Marge was one of five children (as well as being a twin), raised by both parents. She readily admitted to having an unhappy childhood and, as the interview wore on, became increasingly explicit about it. At an early age Marge learned that she and her twin sister, the two youngest children, were unwanted, and always felt terrible about it. Her parents quarreled incessantly. There was no escape for Marge because her parents tried to solicit the support of the children in their battles. Marge believes her parents stayed together for the children. In fact, Marge's mother felt so put-upon by her father and trapped by the need to maintain a family that she became suicidal, her feelings of victimization exacerbated in part in response to his continual philandering.

There is more. Marge revealed that her older brother sexually abused Marge and her sister while they were still living in the home. Marge is very angry at her mother (who is now deceased) for not protecting them from him. As adults in their forties, all the other siblings deny this ever happened. Her twin sister, though, has suffered greatly. Marge describes her as having significant emotional problems, psychiatric hospitalizations, and periods during which she was hanging out with gangs and prostituting. Marge is now out of contact with all of her family members.

After high school, she attended a nearby college where she met her future husband, Jack, who was a few years older than she was. They married two years later despite cultural and class differences. By Marge's description, her family was upper middle class and Jewish, and Jack's was lower class and Italian. Her parents were vehemently opposed to the marriage on those grounds, which made Marge even more resolved to go ahead with it. "I knew the night we married that I had made a mistake in marrying him, but I wanted to get out of the house. I became pregnant three months later and had my second daughter one year after that. We would have had more children, but I had an abortion. I wanted to have my tubes tied but he blocked that."

Marge described the marriage as totally unsatisfactory and vowed she would leave when her youngest child was ten. She says Jack had bad values, placed his relationship with his friends ahead of theirs, gambled, never helped out with the children, and put her down constantly. "I felt like a dishrag, and toward the end I wanted to kill myself. I became severely depressed and developed an alcohol problem. Part of it was due to my remembering some of the early incest I had suffered at the hands of my brother. In the end our marriage became just like that of my parents."

Two weeks after her youngest daughter's tenth birthday, she kept her promise to herself and left. Marge was thirty. Another man was involved, someone who treated her "like a lady." He was her crutch, Marge reports, and made the transition much easier.

Until the marriage ended, Marge had a good relationship with her daughters. With the breakup, there was an initial agreement for joint custody: The children split time between Marge and Jack, who was living with his mother in her home. But trouble was brewing. Marge believes it was her mother-in-law's influence that eventually played such a destructive role in her relationship with her daughters.

"His mother used to watch the kids. She had them so brainwashed that five months after I left, the children were spitting at me. They took a broom and trashed their bedrooms. They began to abuse me in every way they could. One time my ex stole money from me and I threatened to call the police. He said if I did, I would never see the children again. I couldn't take it anymore. At one point during a really rough time, I asked them what they wanted, and they said they didn't want to see me anymore, and they asked to be dropped off at Grandma's, so I did. Since then, I have hardly seen them and it has been four years."

Jack dragged Marge into court for child support, but because she was abandoned by the children (whom the judge interviewed), the judge exonerated her of that responsibility. "Even though they didn't want to see me, I still tried to stay in touch. I would call and Grandma would be shouting in the background, and the kids would say, 'Please don't call because all you do is start trouble.' They were supposed to see me under a court order but they refused."

Little has changed in the relationship over time. What has shifted is Marge's attitude. She refuses to beg to see them. "For years I would cry about not seeing them. I would approach them on the street to talk with me, but they would tell their father, who would call the police and say I threatened to kill them. I live in the same town as them and hear from acquaintances that they are nice girls and doing well. The older one is about to graduate from high school. I think I'll leave town for a while. It is easier if I am away from them, less painful. I am thinking about moving away for good [the avoidant behavior that can be associated with post-traumatic stress disorder]. They have essentially disowned me. They say on their school forms their stepmother is their mother. I am out of their lives."

Does Marge hope to see them in the future? "They have been totally brainwashed against me by their grandmother. If they come back and treat me with respect, that's fine. But if they are abusive, I don't want to see them."

A few points can be made here that apply to these mothers. Marge feels totally justified in her actions. She is taking a harder stance than Darlene and Kerry. She demands respect from her children before she will reestablish a relationship with them and is unwilling to be a supplicant. Elements of their situation can be seen in other patterns. When the children plead with Marge to not call because it just starts trouble, we see a pattern described by fathers whose children withdraw from them to avoid escalating conflict. Also seen is a glimpse of the relationship problems that can develop between a parent and child. Marge believes, though, that brainwashing is at the core of the conflict and the cause of the rejection. I wonder if the knowledge that her children are "doing well" is a further thorn in her side. To some extent, parents whose children are having problems after not having contact with them may feel a bittersweet sense of vindication. Of course a parent wants her children to be happy. But if Marge's children are happy not seeing her, she must feel less needed.

Divorce makes children vulnerable to choosing sides and to outside influences. They are likely to believe that one parent has been responsible for ending the marriage and blame that parent if there is a scintilla of evidence to support that position. With these three mothers we see how such eventualities could take place and lead to the mother being rejected.

There is also an element in some of these situations of the children avoiding conflict by siding with their father or by allowing themselves to be persuaded by a stepmother or grandparent. Some of the children have developed emotional problems, perhaps as a result of their being dragged into their parents' conflict. Avoiding conflict by not seeing the mother may be the healthiest position for many of these children.

Perhaps most harrowing, the mothers here are forced to take positions on how much to continue to pursue their children who show no interest in them. Most will not pursue them, saying the ball is in their children's court and that they are not going to prostrate themselves further in their attempts at visitation. A few choose to keep the door open by expressing a willingness to talk at anytime and by writing constantly.

It is not surprising that mothers would come to varied conclusions about this issue. Each is responding to different family situations both past and present. But more important, each also has to construct a self-image that answers the critical question of when, if ever, parenting (particularly of a younger child) stops. Does it stop when a child no longer wants involvement and when the pain of pursuing it is too great for the mother? Or does it continue from the mother's perspective despite the child's behavior? The construction of the answer requires the mother to take stock of her situation and determine how she wants to view herself and be viewed in the future.

Conclusion

These two patterns focus on different ways of understanding parent-child loss of contact from the mothers' perspectives. In essence we are looking at mother rejection on a continuum, with the first pattern rooted more in the mother–child relationship, while in the second the interference of another adult is sparking relationship problems. In the next chapter we examine loss of contact that leaves the mother with the belief that other people have interfered.

Chapter 5

When Mothers and Children No Longer Visit
When Others Raise Concerns

The previous chapter examines seven mothers who believe they lost contact due to their children rejecting them, either because of relationship problems or the active involvement of another adult turning the children against them. In this chapter we examine two other patterns, those having to do less with rejection of the mother by the child and more with the quality of the mother's parenting being called into question.

Pattern 3: Mothers Who Are Accused of Abuse and Neglect

As with fathers, mothers also lose contact because of allegations of sexual, emotional, or physical abuse, or neglect.[1] In the situations presented here, mothers claim the allegations are being raised to prevent them from gaining custody or even having visitation with the children. Often the charges first lead to a loss of custody and then, over time, to a marked reduction in contact. One mother, for example, admitted to displaying emotional problems, which opened the door for a neglect charge.[2] In some cases, the loss of custody and contact occur at the same time. Another mother I interviewed who denies the allegations believes her children are convinced they were abused after false memories were planted.

Pattern 4: Mothers Who Seek Greater Involvement
from the Ex-Husbands and Then Lose Custody and Contact

In this pattern, the mother seeks out the noncustodial father. She wants his involvement, feeling he is not admitting his paternity or that she needs his financial or emotional support in raising the children. Fathers here are pursued because they are seen as trying to shirk their responsibilities toward their children. As a result of the mothers' pursuits, the fathers become involved with the children and eventually gain custody. The mother's need for the father's involvement is used against her later if the father and children wish to cut off contact with her.

In sum, the mothers in this pattern are dealing with fathers who are initially reluctant and then get drawn into parenting. The end result is a loss of contact. There may be the suspicion of child neglect in this pattern, which may be what enables the father to cut off contact.

Pattern 3: Mothers Who Are Accused of Abuse or Neglect

Some parents will go to great lengths to see their children, even if they have been denied access by the courts because of charges of abuse. Being jailed because of her attempts to see them has not dampened this next mother's desires for visitation.

EVA

Born in Cuba, Eva emigrated with her two brothers and without her parents to the United States in 1962 during the height of the Cuban missile crisis. Her parents had been well-to-do and politically connected with the anti-Castro forces. Despite the family's financial solvency in Cuba, the children were penniless when they arrived. The three children, ages eight, ten, and twelve, were placed in foster care for two years before their parents arrived and the family was reunited.

Aside from the separation, Eva reports she had an unremarkable childhood for an immigrant family. Her parents were hardworking, and the children struggled initially with English before mastering it and graduating from high school.

Eva went to work at a large Miami restaurant where she met her future husband, Jack, who was also working there. Jack was an American by birth, but their differences over the years turned out to be more of class than of culture. Three children, two sons and a daughter, were born in quick succession. "The marriage was good at the beginning. We decided I should stay home with the children and he should pursue his career. He was born with a silver spoon in his mouth and was spoiled rotten. When he couldn't have his way he got upset. The business he was in gave him a lot of time to fool around. I suspected his being unfaithful but there was never any proof; I would press him about lipstick on his shirt collar and he said it was crayon marks from the kids. If we ever got into an argument, he would twist it around, and I would apologize and feel bad for having accused him. I wanted the marriage to survive for the children's sake."

By the late 1980s, Jack tired of the marriage and left for someone else. Eva was awarded custody and child support in addition to Jack's having to pay the mortgage and medical bills. With his large salary, Eva believed money would not be an issue. By contrast, she was making "peanuts." One year later Jack sued for sole custody and lost. He stopped seeing the children for seven months. Until then, he had been only peripherally involved with them, even though he had always said he had wanted to be a more "hands-on" father than his own father had been with him. His visitation, when it resumed, remained inconsistent.

A year later he sued again and won joint custody, with the children remaining a majority of the time with Eva. The court appointed psychiatrist described both parents as competent to parent, Eva recounted. "Then, just when the kids and I were getting our act together, he filed for sole custody, charging me with mental abuse. He had barely had contact with them and couldn't know anything. He was getting information from other people, including the woman he was living with, who was making calls to schools and reporting me to child protective services."

Following evaluation by a new slew of experts, Eva lost custody. "They said I was emotionally abusing them and was overinvolved, and if they stayed with me, the children would not grow up to be independent adults. One psychologist my ex hired tested the kids and supported me, but that was thrown out of court, even though it was his psychologist.

"I wasn't even allowed visitation because they decided I had abused them, which I had not. I had to go for therapy, and their therapist had to agree it was okay to visit. The children are now starting to remember me sexually abusing them, even though it is not true. I am afraid for their well-being. I don't know if my kids have been brainwashed—they have to be so confused."

Eva became desperate. The children were living in a different state by now with their father and did not want to see her, believing she was a sexual and psychological abuser. She was not supposed to visit but went to see them anyway and was thrown in jail for two days for contempt charges. Then a restraining order was issued against her coming near or calling the children.

"Two months ago I had to appear in court and, with the help of a good lawyer, beat back two warrants for my arrest. I got released on my own recognizance. My ex and his wife alleged that I threatened to kidnap and kill my children and that I threatened to kill the judge. They also said I was constantly making harassing phone calls. None of this is true.

"After being unsuccessful in setting up a custody hearing, I decided to start writing my children. Every letter was dated, with copies sent to judges. All I wanted to do was write. I believe I will be put in jail for that. They have continued to allege so many horrible things. Because of that I am facing two and a half to five years in prison if I am found guilty."

I asked Eva how her children felt, had they tried to contact her. "No. I believe they are deathly afraid of me. I saw one son last year at a baseball game he was playing in. I approached him and he said I was not supposed to be there. I said I loved him and told him to tell his brother and sister the same thing. He whispered he loved me, too. I did not want to traumatize him. They are alleging that the contact was traumatic, and they sought a new restraining order. I now have thirteen or fourteen violations."

During the years, Eva has started a support group for parents' rights. She wants to change visitation laws. "But the bottom line is that, and putting aside that I am a political activist, I want to see my children. That is all I want. I wouldn't be doing all of this if that is not what I wanted as a mother."

Eva has lost contact because she is accused of abusing them, a charge with which the courts concur but which Eva believes the children falsely remember. Accusations of abuse during custody battles do occur, though they are rare. They are upheld more often than denied,[3] an issue explored further in chapter 7. False memories do occur, though their prevalence is hotly debated.[4] This is a classic example of the parent claiming one set of circumstances and the children and custodial parent claiming another. Who do we believe? Is Eva forging ahead with attempting to see her children to prove to the world that she is innocent when, in reality, she is guilty? Or is this the same attempt that any parent who was falsely accused would make? At what point does one stop trying if the children do not want to see her and believe she is guilty?

Whereas mental and sexual abuse were at issue for Eva, neglect, physical and sexual abuse allegations appear in the history of the next woman. Diane, whom I met through a child support collection program that had dunned her for failure to pay support for her youngest son, was a teenage unmarried mother who did not see her own father for many years. She has seen her son only twice in the last two years. The irony and pain of the generational repetition do not escape her.

DIANE

I interviewed Diane in a private office at the child support collection program. A slight woman of twenty-four with light brown hair and blue eyes, she proudly stated that she had recently passed her GED exam and was eagerly anticipating matriculating in a community college where she would begin her training to become a teacher.

When she was a toddler, her own parents split up, following a stormy marriage. She spent her childhood with her mother and stepfather as the breakup led to an even more acrimonious post-divorce relationship. She remembers one scene when she was seven and her biological father came to visit her. A fight broke out, and her stepfather threatened to kill her father if he ever returned. While Diane vividly remembers the fight, she did not know until she was ten that the loser in the fight was her actual father. Thus, Diane grew up without having any consistent contact with her biological father. No one even talked about him, and it was not until she left home at seventeen, after she was molested by her stepfather, that she found out her father had attempted to see her during the previous seven years.

By seventeen, she had already given birth to her first child, a son. When she was molested she ran impetuously out of the house and left custody of him with her mother. Her mother and stepfather were about to throw her out of the house anyway because she refused to terminate her relationship with the child's father, whom they despised. It took her three years and many court battles before she regained custody. Her mother fought Diane for custody, Diane believes, because she saw her as being too irresponsible to raise a child alone and also because her mother needed to defend her husband against the molestation allegation.

At about the same time that Diane regained custody of her first child, a second son, Jerry, was born, and the brief marriage that produced him broke up. "My husband at that time was an alcoholic, physically abused me, and I couldn't take it. I got him to leave. Jerry continued to visit my in-laws who became very attached to him. One day when Jerry was visiting my in-laws, I got a call from protective services that I had been abusing and neglecting my child. My in-laws had filed charges. I was shocked. I called Jerry's pediatrician, who didn't know anything about it. Protective services told me he was going to be adopted by my in-laws or by someone else. I called Jerry's father and told him to keep custody so that Jerry wouldn't be adopted, and that I would take care of him and we wouldn't have to get protective services involved. They had me over a barrel, though it was all untrue. We agreed to an arrangement where custody would be with Jerry's paternal grandparents and I would visit. They said my visitation would have to be supervised. But Jerry really wanted to be with me. What happened was that every time I visited my son, he would scream and not want me to leave."

At this point in the interview, Diane started to cry. "It was very hard for me to leave him with his grandmother. She was jealous of my relationship with him, and she started to make it hard for me to see him. Then they moved to a different home and I didn't know where they were. I stopped paying child support because I wasn't seeing him, but I didn't have any money anyway. I am supposed to have visitation and they keep moving. I get on Jerry's father, and he tells me where his parents are sometimes; other times he won't. I recently turned him in to child support enforcement because, now that he's working, they should come after him, too.

"Not seeing my son is a bitter pill to swallow. I can't bring them into court because I can't afford it. The one good thing about being in this [child support collection] program is they are going to help me get visitation again. My other child wants to see his brother and doesn't understand why he can't. I don't understand why they are doing this because I was not abusing him."

As with many parents who do not see their children, there are specific times that the pain is greatest. "When it gets near his birthday, it is especially hard, or when I am getting his brother ready for bed. I wonder what Jerry is doing and it is hard to not watch him grow up. Maybe talking to you will help: If the system or other people see how much it hurts parents, maybe it will help others when they see how painful it is that a parent isn't seeing her child."

Ironically, one key part of Diane's life has fallen into place. Her own paternal grandmother helped her to reconnect with her father. He served time in prison for income tax evasion and has been released. Her advice to other parents in similar situations? "Hang on and eventually things can work out, as they have between me and my father. I see him twice a year now. He lives three hundred miles away, but I talk to him on the phone every week."

Diane was a teen mother who first lost and then regained custody of one child. Because of an allegation of abuse, she was forced to turn over custody of a second child to her ex-in-laws. Her lack of trust in the system precipitated such a move. Now that she has been enrolled in a child support program, she may get the help she needs in straightening out her visitation. Depending upon when one met her, she could come across as "just another teen mom" who maltreated her children and had them taken away. The interview, though, presents a more multifaceted picture, much of which is confirmed by the personnel at the child support enforcement agency who referred her to me. Yet again, because of the charge of abuse, a wedge was driven between her and her son. It is important to note that most jurisdictions, even if abuse has occurred, will allow some supervised visitation at a future point if a parent is showing attempts at self-improvement. This has not occurred for these mothers. Either their cases are so horrific that they should not have it, or they are being denied their rights.

Some parents claim they lose custody because, while they have problems, the "system" is not there to help them. Whereas these feelings cut across gender and race, they may be especially prevalent in African-Americans, who historically have been disenfranchised from the system. Wanda, an African-American twenty-seven-year-old who was participating in a job training program when I interviewed her, believes that custody was unfairly given to her ex-boyfriend, though she admitted to her own shortcomings. She needs a lawyer, she told me, to help fight for custody. Yet she cannot afford one and feels that on her own, she will have no chance of getting custody of her daughter.

WANDA

Wanda's early life was anything but placid. The product of a two-parent family, Wanda describes a childhood marked by alcohol abuse on the part of both parents and domestic violence perpetrated by her father. She dropped out of high school in the mid-1980s when she was seventeen and pregnant. Following the birth of her child, she moved in with her boyfriend, with whom she lived for the next five years. He was a construction worker whom she knew from the neighborhood.

Wanda's parents helped out occasionally in the early rearing of her daughter and even tried to talk Wanda into moving back into their home so that she could finish high school. She refused for a number of years. Her relationship with her boyfriend was never especially strong, and, when she became pregnant with a second child four years later, they separated. After a few months, they reunited. It did not last. He shocked her one day by marrying someone else. When Wanda's new daughter was born, she moved back into her parents' home. She was then too old to go back to high school and, instead, enrolled in a GED program.

Wanda's boyfriend was never interested in their first daughter and only marginally so in the second. He visited both daughters occasionally and sent money or brought over Pampers at his convenience, rather than when Wanda needed them.

Then, one year later, tragedy struck. Their first daughter died suddenly, probably from a seizure. She was not with Wanda at the time, and Wanda is noncommittal about the details, describing the death as accidental. This loss, by her own account, sent her into a deep depression, which most likely precipitated neglectful behavior that concerned her ex-boyfriend. He sued for and won custody of the baby. At that time there was no legal agreement, and Wanda had been letting him visit whenever he wanted.

"I was told I lost custody because I had not recovered from the death of my first daughter. I should have had a better lawyer, as I disagreed with that. The father had not been close to her when she was young and wanted custody only to hurt me. He knows the only way he can get to me is through her." His marital status and job security all worked in his favor, Wanda believes.

She was granted visitation every other weekend. After a year, though, her attempts to visit were denied by him. She went for almost two years without seeing her daughter. "If he decides I can't see her, I don't. There is nothing I can do at this time but accept it. He is in violation of a court decree. The courts tell me I need a lawyer, so I don't go back to court because I can't afford one. The court system in my eyes is nothing. I am paying child support but that doesn't help me. He feels I shouldn't see her because one time he brought her here and she stayed with my parents and not with me. Yet the court order says she can stay with anyone in my family."

Coincidentally, a week before our interview, Wanda saw her daughter. "He decided I could see her for the weekend. She's now six. She knows who I am. She kicked and screamed when she had to leave. We both cried."

Wanda is a little more optimistic about the future than she was before she saw her daughter. She is banking on her daughter choosing to live with her when she is twelve and can request her own living situation. While there is some comfort in knowing her daughter has a good relationship with her father and stepmother, it does not ease her own sense of loss. "To say that I buried one child one week, and then went and fought in court to keep the other one I had, tears me up emotionally. I don't know in what direction to go. My tubes are tied, so I can't have any more children. When I look around and see her toys but can't reach out and touch her, it is terrible.

"Losing them both in different ways was the hardest thing I ever experienced. I lost my first child to death and then my second one in court. I don't understand why I had her taken from me if I haven't abused her. All the judge had to do was put her at the end of the hall and see who she went to. Then he would know. Every day I wonder where she is, what she is doing, how her hair looks, what she is wearing, does she look nice?

"With my first child I didn't drink. I drink now to ease the pain. I try to do things for myself to make the day go faster. My self-esteem is down, whereas when I had my daughter in my care my self-esteem was high. There was no telling how far I was going to go. Now I sometimes don't care. I am in an NA [Narcotics Anonymous] program. My next goals are to get my GED, go to training, and build myself a nice house and have my daughter come home.

"As far as the deadbeat parent and the court system, I totally disagree with that. I feel as though all people who have children who are not in their custody are not deadbeats; sometimes it can be on the other parent's end. I have no problem paying support, but I can't get more time with my daughter and that is not fair. Putting parents in jail is a big waste of the taxpayers' money. You have people in jail who refuse to pay child support, but everyone is not that type of person. All mothers who have lost custody and want them back should stand up and fight for their children, but it is really hard when you don't have money and the man and his wife do. But I have the time and I will get my child back. She might be twelve but I will get her back."

It was most likely Wanda's initial bout with depression that alarmed her ex-boyfriend and put her custody status in jeopardy. Then, she believes it was the court system refusing to help that led to her not being supported in attempts at visitation. Her drinking and the potential effect that could have had on her court appearance may have also been an impediment. Ultimately, she felt disenfranchised from everyone who was supposed to help her be a mother. In view of the nature of the case, the loss of custody (depending on her behavior) may have been in the best interests of her child. But, according to her, she is also being blocked unfairly from contact. (See chapter 7 for more on the legal implications of denial of contact.) Her behavior, by her own admission, opened the door for what was to follow.

Pattern 4: Mothers Who Seek Greater Involvement from the Ex-Husbands and Then Lose Custody and Contact

This case reflects the attempts of a mother to involve a father in their children's lives.[5] As a result, she lost custody. Some situations are incredibly sad both in the path they take and in the outcome. In Ferne's case, it might have been possible to predict that with the life choices she made and misfortune never more than a step away, an unhappy conclusion was inevitable.

FERNE

Ferne's childhood was difficult. Raised in an ultra-religious family in Kansas, the second of three children, her father was very punitive. If one child misbehaved, all were punished, often physically. High expectations were the norm. In fact, Ferne finished high school with a near-perfect academic record and was succeeding in college with an A average when she received her first grade of B. Her parents were so angry, they cut her off financially. She dropped out and waited tables to support herself. For the next six years she attended college on and off whenever she had amassed enough money to pay tuition.

Ferne moved in and out of romantic relationships during those years and, after one particularly traumatic breakup, had a brief fling with a good friend. She became pregnant and had her first child, a son. Her parents were horrified, but she decided to raise the child on her own. Three years later she was involved with another man, this time a married salesman. When he moved to Denver, he asked Ferne and her son to join him and provided an apartment and job for her with his company. She loved the city and jumped at the chance to move from Kansas.

When she arrived in Denver, she became pregnant once more and decided to keep the baby. Meanwhile, her relationship with the salesman was deteriorating. "I felt trapped because of the pregnancy. I realized he was not going to marry me. He was verbally abusive. I gave birth to his baby, another son, and began plotting how to get out of the situation. He was transferred, and I decided to stay in Denver and get my own apartment. To minimize the stigma of having a baby, I took his name in common-law marriage. That meant I could say I was married and assume that persona."

Back on her own, Ferne, then thirty-one, worked while trying to complete her education. She and her two sons shared a one bedroom apartment. Then, while crossing the street one day on her way to work, she was struck by a car and ended up in the hospital needing reconstructive surgery. "A specialist, Ed, gets called in to treat me. He is drop-dead handsome and charming. He is very personable and helpful as the complications of the accident are worked out. I was very concerned because I had reconstructive breast surgery and I worried that no one was going to love me. I was materialistic and obsessed with how I looked, and in a matter of seconds with the crash it was taken away from me. This guy is saying all the right things. He started to call me when he was stressed out and developed a crush on me. He starts visiting, and an affair begins, even though he is married. I allowed it to happen because I needed the affirmation that I was still attractive. It was unethical for him, though.

"I have a pattern of hooking up with men who have a power relationship with me. I look for men that I can look up to and who are emotionally unavailable. I'm playing out something with my father, who was so unavailable. I get involved with people who are verbally abusive and control freaks. It is so predictable with them because I know what to expect."

The relationship continued for a year until one day he dropped into the conversation that his wife was pregnant. It was an epiphany for Ferne, who realized that Ed was never going to marry her and their relationship had to end.

"Then I found out I was pregnant. Ed told me I *will* have an abortion. I said, 'No I won't.' I went home and had a meeting with my children [they were four and eight] and said, 'Okay, I'm a three-time loser now, and we are going to decide if I will keep the baby or give it up for adoption.' I said if I keep the baby, we will all have to make sacrifices."

Clearly, asking children to make these types of decisions and calling their conceptions mistakes is not the best parenting practice. Yet the children agreed to help with raising the new baby and Ferne made plans for its arrival. As part of the preparation, she sued Ed for child support. Attorneys battled back and forth. Ed claimed the child was not his. When a prenatal blood test indicated it was, he argued he did not have to pay anything until the child was born. Ferne went on welfare to support herself and her children. When she was about to give birth, she received another letter from Ed's attorney again contesting paternity. She hit the roof.

"I went and told his wife. I can get very impulsive. I knocked on her door and she had just had her baby, and I was overdue and showed her all the letters from the attorneys. I said, I think you may find this interesting reading, and she asked me who I was and I told her to read the papers. She filed for divorce from Ed the next day.

"The baby was born a month later. We went to court to get child support, and he agreed to pay with the condition he did not want anything to do with our son. He was so angry at me. For the next seventeen months, he would withhold child support by a few weeks each time until it was a financial problem. I had a job but was let go because the case became known in the area and no one wanted to hire me."

Once again, Ferne acted impulsively. Fed up with the lack of consistent financial support and interest Ed had shown, she dropped the baby off at his office on a Friday and demanded that he take care of him for a few hours while she interviewed for a job. (This is the point at which, consistent with the pattern represented here, she forced the child on Ed.) When she returned, Ed and the baby had left.

What happened next is every divorced parent's nightmare. Over the course of the next few months, Ed was able to retain legal possession pending a final custody hearing in which his attorney was able to convince a judge that Ferne had a criminal record, was mentally incompetent, and recklessly endangered the baby (Ferne disagreed with all three points). She was allowed visitation but was blocked by Ed from actively seeing her son. Ferne returned to court, and they began participating in a system in the county that allowed divorced parents to drop off a child with a neutral party for visitation so that neither parent has to see the other. There was one problem: It cost money that Ferne did not have. She won a ruling that required Ed to help with the cost (Ferne was paying him child support at this point.) But when she did have the money she was frequently late because she had to pick up another child at a special-education program across town. As Ferne stated, she was caught between the needs of two children and decided to try and meet the needs of the oldest one, who was living with her. The presumption when she did not show up on time was that she did not care. By the time of our interview, it had been six months since mother and son had seen each other.

"I can't even talk to him on the phone. Ed has remarried and is telling our son to call his new wife Mommy. I am going before the legislature because they are so appalled by what happened to me. I have lost time that I am never going to recover. I am very emotional about this. The court-appointed psychologist said I was a good mother but Ed's lawyer put on a better show than my pro bono attorney, who made me look crazy. How do I prove I am not crazy? I couldn't win; he just had so much money. I would visit my son at first at his school, and he was so confused by all this, I decided to not visit part-time because it would make him worse.

"I have to believe I was a good mother, and that even though he had only seventeen months with me, that would carry him through the rest of his life. I think when he is an adult he will seek me out. He has good memories he can draw from."

Ferne showed poor judgment throughout her children's early years. Highly insecure, she followed an unobtainable man across country and was constantly in need of reassurance about her appearance. She forced Ed into the picture after he refused to take responsibility. As a result, he turned the tables on her and she lost not only custody but contact. It is easy to see how she could have presented a less attractive alternative to the court than Ed and his new wife. Like Wanda, Ferne could easily have been depicted as a danger to her child and unfit to parent.

Conclusion

The road to a mother becoming *noncustodial* is different from that taken by a father. It is a more unusual road. It is often tainted with extreme behaviors on the part of both the mother and the father and questions about the mother's competence as a parent. From this unusual foundation, the path to losing contact grows. It is more unusual for mothers to lose custody and contact with their children than for fathers; when mother–child contact is lost, the cases are bound to appear more fraught with problems. I believe that is the case with the eleven cited here.

A few words about the four patterns presented. We have learned from the reports of these mothers as well as from those in the survey that mothers are rejected by their children, that ex-husbands block visitation for a variety of reasons, and that their own behavior can set the loss of contact in motion. New wives or ex-mothers-in-law are replacing the mother in ten of the eleven case studies. The eleven mothers to various degrees see themselves as being ignored by the courts and victimized by the fathers. As with the fathers' stories, this has to be taken with a grain of salt. In some of the cases victimization certainly occurred, while in others the history is much less clear and may have been engendered by the mothers' behavior.

Depending on one's perspective, the playing field for the mothers may not be level. It can be covered with financial hurdles, fears about safety, their own low sense of self-worth (which is diminished further when they lose custody), and society's negative attitude toward them. Fathers, as we have heard, lay claim to other impediments.

Some mothers lost custody and eventually contact with their children when they appeared weak. What is a mother to do who needs help? The broader social message here is that, if you are a mother and cannot take care of your children, someone else will—that there are people waiting in the wings to take over. This is a dangerous precedent if it precludes help being sought. It is also dangerous if the mother's "weakness" is not confirmed on a continuous basis. It is not sufficient to say a mother is incompetent and should not have custody or visitation. She must be proved unfit over time, or else custody and contact should resume. Parents do change. The thorny questions to consider are whether the acquisition of custody from the mother was preemptory and whether it occurred at the appropriate time in these cases. Should more be done to keep the primary custodian and child together? Are broad-based attempts by societal institutions to get the father more involved taking the place of attempts to maintain a child's relationship with the mother who has custody if those bonds are tenuous? Encouraging father involvement may, in some cases, have the unintended consequence of hurting the mother–child bond. We need to carefully assess its impact. Both further involvement and strengthening the mother–child bond should be undertaken, otherwise the relationships may become unbalanced.

Key points can be drawn from these interviews. First, these patterns are not representative of all mother–child cutoffs. We do not hear about mothers who leave and have no interest in staying involved. The mothers who drop out of sight or did not wish to be interviewed are not here. The ones who are invested in their children and want contact are.

Some of the cutoffs occur because the child decided to withdraw from the mother to avoid parental conflict. The mother may have been the easier one to disengage from: some children are less intimidated by their mothers than their fathers. Or, the child may have felt the mother would be more accepting in the long run if he disengaged from her temporarily. If we consider the prevailing view of mothers' abilities to nurture and be accepting, it is possible this perception played a part. At the same time, if she were not nurturing, she may also have been the easier one to withdraw from, as she was clearly not fulfilling her role.

I believe the mothers described themselves as personally having more problems than fathers. They present themselves with more self-doubts and admit to more problems, a pattern unfortunately typical of women in general. Women also tend to be more forthcoming in discussing their self-doubts. These mothers, when compared with the fathers, were no exception.

The shift that these mothers underwent in ultimately losing contact is noteworthy when compared with the fathers. Most did have full custody initially and then lost it. The fathers, by comparison, often had contact as a visitor first and then faded further away. The fathers' fading involvement began with the breakup, whereas the intensity of the mothers' involvement actually increased in most cases with the breakup before it eventually subsided.

While the fathers react with anger and pain and externalize blame, the mothers feel hurt, and internalize what has happened to them. A few attest to the terribly difficult position women find themselves in when they seek custody. If they appear upset when fighting for it in court, they can be seen as hysterical. If they seem rational and calm, they can be depicted as distant and cold, a catch-22.

The mothers who were interviewed have suffered enormously. They are in great pain, though a few have tried to shield themselves from it. It is obvious from their stories that many mothers who are not seeing their children have been pushed out, have been misunderstood in their attempts to parent, or have unconsciously and unhappily colluded in being pushed out.

Our society has a fixed view of the dad who drops out and heaps scorn on him for financially and emotionally abandoning his family. He is the bad guy, irresponsible and uncaring. No clear picture has developed of the mother except to perhaps imply that she is maladjusted. But from hearing these stories, a clearer perception may develop that shows that much of what happens is a self-fulfilling prophecy. Do women, more accustomed than men to blaming themselves for mistakes and for internalizing what they hear, accept more easily the negative depictions that their ex-husbands and children throw at them? Do these mothers find it harder to shake off the attacks because, when custody is threatened, they internalize the negative connotations attached to being noncustodial? If so, they are battling a double whammy.

Chapter **6**

The Children's Views

My life died when my mom first left. I died at four. My protector left.
I didn't totally die, of course, I just went into a coma and the new person who came out was a mask, and I have just learned now to take
the mask off and let the world see my colors. I feel better with no parents around because I can be myself.

> POLLY, *a young woman in her early twenties, whose story*
> *is described later in this chapter*

I don't believe because you gave birth to a child, that makes you
a parent.   TOM, *age twenty-seven, also interviewed here*

Why do children stop seeing a parent after divorce? What is the
child's reaction to this loss of contact? In previous chapters I have focused
on the actions of the parent in this relationship. Here the emphasis shifts.
Typically in discussions of divorce, the passive nature of the child is empha-
sized: He or she is left by the parent. But in some cases, the child, particularly when older, is both victim and an active participant in the post-divorce process. He or she helps decide what will happen in the relationship
with parents. In this chapter we hear from children who had no control
over the lack of contact with their parents as well as those who actively refused contact.

To understand the potential experiences of these children, we must begin
with some of the common reactions children have to divorce. On a very basic level, these children are apt to feel sadness and loss, betrayal, and anger.
(The degree and extent of reactions vary by age.) Sadness derives from the
loss of the family they had. Their home life will never be the same. With the
loss of that family frequently comes disruption in their routine and a reduction in contact with a parent. Schools, neighborhoods, friends, and their
home, once permanent fixtures, may all end up like scattered pickup sticks
as their parents consider the need for relocation. These are not all the losses
at separation. Their financial situation tends to worsen. They may be separated from one of their siblings. If there is joint physical custody, they may

begin shuffling back and forth between residences and have less contact with each parent. This is almost always "done to" the children: they are the victims.

The feeling of betrayal children experience with the breakup stems from a loss of trust in family members. Perhaps a mother indicated she would "always be there" for the child and now has left the home. Maybe a father is caught in a lie about his behavior. In order to grow and develop happily, children need to rely on consistency in adults. If children experience a lot of parental transitions, they do not function as well.[1] When their sense of trust and consistency is challenged by the breakup and departure of one parent, they learn to distrust people. If they internalize the experience, take it inside themselves, they may feel that they are not trustworthy either and start acting that way. They too may make promises they will not keep. They become unreliable. Feeling they have been lied to, they in turn twist the truth.

A third common feeling is anger. This is a natural outgrowth if the child feels loss or feels betrayed by a parent, or believes that decisions are being foisted on him. Anger can be expressed in a wealth of ways but is commonly shared with the parent who is available, the custodial parent. Many single mothers and fathers have complained to me that their children are angry at them and not at the other parent who rarely visits. Why is it, they ask, they bear the brunt of the anger and pain and not the visiting parent? One of the reasons, and there can be many, is that it is safer for a child to be angry at a trusted parent rather than one who is unpredictable. The child may correctly discern that sharing anger with the absent parent may scare him or her away even more. The child may also vent anger at the custodial parent to test whether that parent will also leave, as a way to test the parent's love. (See Candy's story, for example.)

Anger, like betrayal and sadness, may be a feeling a child generates or a feeling he learns from a parent. This is especially likely when the separation has been acrimonious and emotions are flowing freely. If the child sees the father as depressed and furious at the mother, it will be easy to feel the same way, as we see in many children in this book. Anger can be debilitating to the child. He or she may blame one or both parents for the breakup, be furious at them, and feel guilty because of that reaction. Few children feel comfortable being angry at their parents over a long period. If a parent is in a fragile state because he or she has been buffeted by the breakup, things may be exacerbated further if the expression of anger at the parent has a significant impact on the parent. A parent's fragility can also take a different turn. He or she may identify with the child's vulnerabilities, feel uncomfortable with such an identification, and attack the child when the vulnerabilities are manifest. Such action further results in the parent and, in turn, the child feeling upset.[2]

Children are also likely to blame themselves for the divorce. Already vulnerable after being exposed to months of parental fighting before the breakup, a child may be unable to objectively determine what his behavior has caused. Imagine being four years old, spilling your milk for the umpteenth time at the dinner table, having your father scream at you, and then having him move out the next day. An eight-year-old may hear her parents arguing over a punishment for not keeping her room clean and then have her mother vanish in the morning. The child (depending on the age) easily connects herself to the parent's departure in these cases. If only, the child thinks, I had cleaned my room, they would not have fought and Mom would still be here. Reassurances from parents usually do not help here, even though the reality is that the parents would have found something else to fight about if the room had been clean.

Children do not always distort events and place themselves at the root of the breakup. In the worst cases, parents do blame the children for their marital problems rather than accept responsibility for their own actions.

The result of parental abandonment can be devastating, particularly when it happens in traumatic fashion. The early life of the late Beatle John Lennon provides such an example. Freddy, John's father and a merchant seaman, was at sea when John was born and remained there for most of the next few years. Julia, John's mother, lived a devil-may-care life during Freddy's absence, and the couple eventually separated. Freddy returned from sea one day and forced John to choose between life with his father or life with his mother. John first opted for Freddy, but when he saw his mother's tears, he ran after her and did not see his father again for almost twenty years.[3] It can be argued that the angst that John felt from making such a choice, coupled with his mother's untimely death, was reflected in the angry edge and longing of much of his music.

Herein lies the classic struggle that is replayed in many divorcing families. Children are forced to choose an all or nothing situation, though usually in more subtle ways. And in so deciding, they end up with half, when what they most need is a whole.

Early abandonment can lead to other problems. One thirty-five-year-old mother whose parents divorced when she was seven went for eleven years without seeing her father. Since that one meeting she has not seen him again. Now she has a daughter of her own and has terrible dreams and flashbacks that her daughter will be abandoned just as she was at that age. This issue did not arise until her own daughter was the age that she was at the time of the abandonment. She describes herself as a non-nurturing type of person who married a steady, dependable man (unlike her father), who is also not very nurturing. It is not, she says, that she does not love her daughter. It is just that nurturing is hard for her because of her own experiences.

In another case, that of a young man named Sid, abandonment left a hole he tried to fill, sometimes adaptively, sometimes not. Sid's Jewish mother divorced his non-Jewish father and remarried an Orthodox Jew. Sid was ten at the time and was sent for Jewish education and training following the remarriage. Sid's biological father, a criminal, was incarcerated in another state at the time of the new marriage. Sid never felt he fit in with the children at his new school because he was a product of a mixed marriage. When Sid was thirteen, his father, finished with his time in prison, came for a short visit before moving to Maine. Contact between Sid and his father stopped again.

When Sid graduated from high school, he picked up and went to Maine in search of his father, having only a vague idea where he was. Like other children in his situation, Sid felt as if he had a puzzle inside of him and he was trying to find the missing piece to get a fuller understanding of his life. He did not necessarily buy the picture of his father he had gotten from his mother. He needed to find it out for himself. In that way, he would be in control of it, he thought, not his mother. He is still searching for his father and for himself.

Complicating matters further after a separation, children may be placed in the middle of warring parents, as we saw in the previous chapters, and have a range of reactions. Some experts, in studying children of highly conflictual divorces, find that exposure to heated battles causes the children to constrict their reactions and become defensive. At the same time, parents involved in these incidents may deny their own roles in them. A situation is then set up where the children cannot work through such problems by discussing them with their parents.[4]

Information from a series of clinical interviews with children in the six-to-twelve-year-old range who were at the center of high-conflict divorces offers another way of thinking about children's reactions. The children's reactions could be placed on a continuum from strong alliance with one parent, to shifting allegiances between parents, to outright rejection of both parents. Some children maneuvered between their warring parents by distancing themselves. This withdrawal gave them an air of mastery as opposed to their feeling like a Ping-Pong ball. By comparison, other children responded to conflict by either appearing passively calm and composed or by appearing joyless and withdrawn. On the extreme end, a few children exhibited marked behavioral problems, including self-destructive and out of control behavior.[5]

Some research also indicates that the more children of high-conflict couples have contact with both parents after divorce, the worse they fare.[6] What is unclear, though, is how those same children would fare if their contact with restricted: Would they have an easier adjustment or would it be even worse, with some symptoms showing up months or years later? In general, but with some exceptions, recent research does conclude that children who have ongoing contact with both parents are best served.[7]

Sometimes they are forced to grow up overnight by being expected to assume the caretaker role for an emotionally incapacitated parent or by assuming a parental role with a younger sibling. Many children, of course, are in great need themselves and are left bereft of either parent being able to nurture them. Needing help sifting through personal feelings, a child may find his parents emotionally unavailable as they nurse their own wounds. The child might be left wondering, "Who will take care of me?" Reactions of depression, anxiety, fearfulness and clinging behavior, social withdrawal, sleep and eating disruptions, and cessation of schoolwork and home responsibilities frequently follow. Finally, it should be noted that these *reactions* to divorce often follow a highly disruptive period in the family during which parents have been fighting actively or withdrawing from each other. The children are exposed to an extended period of family disruption beginning with the initial marital instability through the time of the breakup and ending, ideally, with a period of post-divorce stabilization. The post-divorce period of stabilization, when all matters have been settled from the divorce and the parents are no longer warring, may take years or never be accomplished. Thus as children move into life after the breakup, they have been suffering and may continue to suffer. As children of divorce, they are "at risk" for a host of emotions that children of two parent families are often not exposed to.

Once the separation occurs, the contacts with the visiting parent can go smoothly or can be problematic. How the child understands the nature of the contact with the noncustodial parent and how that contact fits into the family context will help determine how the child feels about contact being pursued. To some extent, the child goes through a cost-benefit analysis. The age of the child can play a significant part here. The work of Janet Johnston and her colleagues at the Center for the Family in Transition is instructive here. For example, early preschoolers (two to four years old), being egocentric, often believe that others feel the same as they do and that they cause the actions of others. They may cling to an angry parent one moment during a parental fight and avoid the other parent completely. But when alone with that other parent, they may return to an accepting mode and form an attachment. This normal reaction can be confusing to the parents, each of whom may be searching for a sign of favoritism. Children this age are the most likely to believe they are the cause of the anger between the parents and, as a result, are highly vulnerable to conflict.

By the ages of four to seven, they can see another person's viewpoint, though often cannot accept conflicting perspectives. They take the side of one parent when with that parent and then shift next to the other parent when in that parent's presence. They are switching cognitively while the younger children switch emotionally. One way to view it is through the child who says after a visit with his mother, "Mommy doesn't get enough money from Daddy." The next week, after seeing his father, the child says, "Mommy wastes the money she gets from Daddy." He is cognitively taking on two perspectives.

At the next developmental stage, seven to nine years of age (and there is always some overlap), children can observe inconsistencies between parents' statements and their actions. They also become acutely aware that parents may not approve of their behavior with the other parent and have the ability to consider the consequences. For example, they are able to wonder, "If I say I want to stay with Daddy, will that make Mommy unhappy?" When children reach the next stage (nine to thirteen years old), they start to form alliances with parents and may sustain these alliances to an extreme extent. In fact, in many of the case studies discussed in the previous chapters, we see children form intense bonds with custodial parents that seem to be irrational. Yet developmentally, they may be "on time." Finally, in the middle teen years, children are able to take on both parents' perspectives and react to conflict by strategically removing themselves from the battle.[8]

By age eleven or twelve, children also become increasingly interested in their own friends. The peer group becomes important to their sense of self, while the impact of parents, whether there are one or two in the home, diminishes. Noncustodial parents often mistake this normal stage of individuation as rejection. Yet if the parent was in the home, the child in all likelihood would still be avoiding contact with the parent. When the parent does not see the child every day, though, such dismissal from the child's life is difficult to swallow or to interpret as developmentally appropriate. This pattern continues through the teen years.

A brief mention is needed of young adults, eighteen to twenty-three years old, whose parents have divorced within the recent past. This population, according to one study, also experiences a great deal of stress associated with their parents' breakup, with daughters feeling more vulnerable than sons. The stress was frequently linked to loyalty conflicts. Over time, the young adults did adjust. It is interesting to note that in many cases the divorce was much more likely to bring the young adults closer to their mothers than their fathers, and that the young adults worried more about their mothers' well-being than their fathers.[9]

After eighteen, when the children are no longer under the care or living in the house of the custodial parent, reconciliation with the noncustodial parent is most easily effected. No longer will the child worry as much about offending one parent by seeing the other because the child no longer has to account for his or her whereabouts. He can be more secretive. High school and college graduation, engagements, the purchase of a first house, and a pregnancy are all rites of passage when young adults want to straighten out relationships with distant parents. Rapprochements often occur at such points, according to a longitudinal survey a colleague and I conducted of noncustodial mothers.[10] This was recently confirmed by follow-up interviews with parents who participated in the survey for this book. (See chapter 8.)

Rapprochements can occur between adult children and elderly parents. In one remarkable case, two postal workers discovered they were siblings who had been separated thirty years prior to their landing jobs in the same post office. Following a breakup, the father had left with the son, while the daughter stayed with the mother. The parents and siblings never saw each other again, but a savvy coworker figured out from conversations with each of the siblings that they were related. The father had died during the thirty-year absence, but the son was able to reunite with his mother.[11]

When Contact Ebbs

Having discussed issues generally surrounding children of divorce, we move to a thornier question: How does a child adjust to the separation from a parent when it is not clear whether the child and parent will have contact in the future? While the descriptions of the children that follow begin to answer this, the short response is that no established models exist for understanding children in these often-changing "out of contact" situations. Clearly they are more complicated than a separation due to death.[12]

When thinking about how a child will cope with a loss of contact with one parent after divorce, some issues to consider include (1) what the nature of the attachment or relationship with the absent parent was; (2) whether a child needs to detach from and mourn the loss of the absent parent before emotional growth and development can continue; and (3) whether a healthy bond with the remaining parent, can be sustained which will overcome any sense of loss.[13] Losing contact with a loved parent, being unable to mourn that loss when it is unclear how "lost" the other parent is, and feeling unattached to the custodial parent will clearly take its toll on the child.

It is also important to note, in considering how well a child copes, that the child may cut off the relationship. Changes in families naturally erode the ability of the parent and child to stay in touch. But children, as mentioned, do intervene in this process. For example, the child may not like the noncustodial parent's new spouse or lover or vice versa and skip visitation. The child may become attached to the custodial parent's new spouse, which often causes the child to feel disloyal when visiting the noncustodial parent. Avoiding such a conflictual feeling may be preferred. In addition, the child's friends and growing involvement in school activities often loom as attractive distractions. Finally, the child, particularly during preadolescence and adolescence, may just be oppositional.[14] Johnston adds that children frequently resist or refuse contact because of (1) anxiety about leaving the custodial parent (2) an inability to separate his or her own feelings from the custodial parent's and (3) intense acrimony between the parents.[15]

Parental alienation syndrome (PAS), a term coined by Richard Gardner and referred to in chapter 3, bears comment here. Gardner uses it to mean not only programming ('brainwashing') of the child by one parent to denigrate the other parent, but self-created contributions by the child in support of the preferred parent's campaign of denigration against the nonpreferred parent."[16] He goes on to say that such denigration results from almost an environmental backlash against the outside parent as a confluence of factors conspire to unfairly tar that parent's relationship with the child.[17]

The PAS and Gardner's work are well known within the legal system. As such they are part of the collective conscience of parents' seeking changes in custody. The refusal of a child to visit a parent can be considered part of the PAS or have nothing to do with such a syndrome. As with many family issues, an assessment has to be made with an awareness of the various possibilities before a decision can be made about how to interpret and act on the information. Application of the PAS to the myriad cases that include some rejection of a parent by a child involves the eye of the beholder.[18]

These issues are basic to understanding both how children cope and the nature of the situations where children are closing off the noncustodial parent. In fact, as will be discussed in chapter 9, an appreciation of them may prevent parents losing contact or feeling hurt by the loss of contact. Imagine if parents in these situations believed that their children's exclusion of them from their lives was a *normal* developmental stage or a way to avoid pain rather than a sign of an unhealthy alliance with a custodial parent or a rejection?

If the contact is painful for the child or if the child understands it is painful for either parent, the child may be loathe to seek it. If schedules are hard to keep, if parents are screaming at each other and hanging the phone up each time there is contact, the child will not want to see that parent. That may make the lack of contact easy to handle in some ways.

The natural ebb and flow of divorce pushes people away from contact with each other rather than toward it. A better way to ask the question is "What is there to keep a child and a noncustodial parent in touch?" With all a child goes through, the sense of loss, betrayal, and anger that accompanies divorce, it is no surprise that a child becomes an active participant in deciding how much contact to have with the visiting parent.

Whereas the previous four chapters have focused primarily on parents' stories with occasional interviews with children, here the focus is on the children. Ten of them, ranging in age from six to forty-six (the six-year-old, now sixteen, was interviewed over the course of ten years), are interviewed. In some cases, interviews have included parents; in others, parents were not interviewed either because the child interviewed is now an adult or because the parent was unavailable.

Mark and Ellen's Children: A Decade's Perspective

I have been following one family of four children for more than a decade and have written about them in a previous book.[19] I have interviewed them more than ten times, often on videotape, so I have been able to document their growing-up years. Now ranging in age from late teens to early twenties, their experiences with divorce in terms of shifting loyalties between parents seemed extreme when we first met. Today we can see the impact.

When children move back and forth between parents, as with this family, all may become seemingly inured to the process as they construct a protective shell around themselves. A false sense of bravado is affected that breaks down under scrutiny. Relationships as adults become more dependent, less adaptive, perhaps in an attempt to make up for a past inability to rely on a parent to provide nurturance.

Mark, a post office employee in his mid forties, met Ellen while he was a college student at the University of Georgia. After a short courtship, they married and moved to northern Virginia to be near her family. Despite the fact that the marriage was shaky, the couple gave birth to four children—

Sally, Polly, Tommy, and Lee—within the next six years. Whether the root of the marital problems rested in Mark's marrying to escape the responsibility of taking care of his widowed mother or Ellen's overly close ties with her parents is hard to say. But one day, when Mark came home from work, he found Ellen had abandoned the family and run off with one of his close friends. The children ranged in age from six years to six weeks old.

Mark was furious. Intrusive relatives wanted to take the children, but he was driven to prove to them he could handle the responsibility. When Ellen returned alone six months later and sued for custody of the children, the judge, after a prolonged court battle, ruled in Mark's favor.

Matters were not settled. They continued to fight over every aspect of childrearing. It was as if the children were shuttling back and forth between armed camps. The children's birthdays and holidays were celebrated in each home. Vacations were taken separately. As Sally reached puberty, she became increasingly uncomfortable living the majority of the time with her father. She told me, "I have to decide [where I want to live] because I can't keep thinking about it. If I go with my mom, my dad will be angry and my grandmother won't like it. I don't know what I am going to do. They are always fighting over me. I am starting to develop. I wear a bra sometimes, and I don't know what else will happen. I need my privacy sometimes, and Mom would be better about that." We see two themes in her statements to me: first, the problem of jeopardizing one parent's love when there is a custody battle, a developmentally appropriate consideration; second, the budding-sexuality issue which often separates children from the opposite-sex parent.

Sally finally decided she wanted to leave, but Mark balked. After more months of wrangling, he finally acceded to her wishes. Living with her was becoming unpleasant and was negatively affecting her siblings as well as Mark's relationship with his other children. Her departure marked the initial crumblings of the family that Mark had so fiercely fought to hold together for ten years.

In families where animosity between divorced parents is so great, it is hard to imagine children *not* being used as pawns in an escalating game of "who can hurt the other parent the most?" Mark and Ellen are no exceptions. Once Sally left, she rarely returned to Mark's house. She would see her siblings only when they visited her and their mother. Months went by when Sally and Mark did not speak. Mark felt stung by rejection after having worked so hard to raise Sally during Ellen's absence and the initial custody battles. Next, Polly left for a taste of life at Mom's house. Twelve months later she returned. Feeling unneeded and unloved in Ellen's house, she returned home, believing she would fit in there as the only female. As she explained to me, "They need me here. I want to get a job, earn some money, and fix this place up so that it is more cheerful. They need a woman's touch." (She was fifteen at the time.) Mark, Tommy, and Lee protested that they could get along without her, an ominous prophecy.

They were right. Six months later, Polly returned to her mother's home. Ellen had remarried (Bill), and Polly wanted to be part of the new family. She went for six months without speaking to Mark. At an interview I conducted with them during this period, Mark stated, "Polly was missing her mother, and her mother was working on her to come back after school was out. [She] told me that I was trying to run her life and that I did not know how to love. Now Tommy is talking about going to live with them. If he goes, that is his decision."

Tommy did leave for a few months, in 1990, but, unlike his sisters, continued to communicate with Mark. One reason for the attraction of the mother's home, Mark prides himself in believing, is the lack of rule setting. Mark runs a tight ship, expects the children to be home at a certain hour, while Ellen is more lax. For a teen struggling to find an identity and separate from a parent, the greater freedom can be exhilarating.

By the fall of 1992, Mark reported that Ellen was again divorced (she vanished, according to the children) and had left her children from the new marriage with Bill, as she had done almost a generation earlier with Mark. Since then, Sally has moved out on her own and is working in a pet store. Polly has found a job and is living with her stepfather, as is Tommy. Mark sees them two or three times a month on a fairly regular basis, after going through lengthy periods of no contact.

Mark talks about the reconciliation with Sally and Polly. "After Ellen left this guy, the kids realized what she was like. Sally came back and said, 'All those years of living with Mom, she told me how lousy you were, and now I know the truth.' Her mother wanted to come to her high school graduation, and she [Sally] told her not to bother."

I recently interviewed Polly, Tommy, and Lee, now ages nineteen, seventeen, and sixteen. (An interview with Sally could not be arranged despite numerous attempts.) Polly, who always was outgoing and possessed a winning personality, has not lost any of her spunk. She chose to live with her stepfather rather than her father because her stepfather is more liberal. In fact, he allows her boyfriend to live with them. "A little while ago my boyfriend asked me to marry him when he can afford it. I said yes, so he is really more like a fiancé. My father likes my fiancé but does not like the fact that we are having sex." A high school graduate, Polly works in a jewelry store on a full-time basis. She has become accustomed to taking care of herself financially and emotionally, but does not enjoy the responsibility. As part of her attempts to establish independence, she has experienced extended periods in her life when she has not seen her mother or her father. To some extent, like all the children, she had a very short childhood.

I asked her about the previous few years. "First I stopped seeing my dad. He scared the heck out of me one day when we were having a fight, and, instead of kicking me, he kicked the wall when he was angry at me. I said, 'Okay, I'm moving to Mom's house.' I guess he didn't get enough sleep, and my running around got on everyone's nerves. I moved in with Mom and lived there for a year, and then I moved back because I couldn't hack it because Sally beat the hell out of me. My mom said I march to the beat of a different drummer, and Sally would put me down, so I said, 'I love you, Mom, but I'm going back in with Dad.'"

When Ellen vanished, she left no forwarding address. Since then she is like a shadow, showing up occasionally but never being available to be hugged or even touched. This pattern has continued for almost two years. "She screwed me royally. She dicked me over. She left me hanging in my boyfriend's arms, and it has taken me eighteen months to stop crying over it. I was close to suicidal, and it has taken me this long to get over it. She's stopped by three times since then, and I asked her when she was going to stay with us. Her new boyfriend likes to beat people, so I wanted her to get out of there. She threatens me. She said, 'I'm your mother and I can take you out because I brought you in.' During all this, my boyfriend was my only support."

Things were not much better between Polly and Mark. "I didn't see my dad the entire time I was living with Mom. He and I have a personality conflict: I would try to act like his daughter and have him proud of me, but then he retaliates. He won't call but he'll send a message to see how I am doing. Bill respects me more than my dad; he respects me as a person. I got used to my dad not calling. It would be nice to have him call, but he would have to talk to Bill. My dad was real proud of me when I graduated high school. I had dinner with my grandfather, and that was great."

Polly provides one of the few opportunities to learn about children who have gone back and forth between parents *and* been out of contact with both. For her, it was harder being out of touch with her mother because she and her father were never particularly close, even though she feels he was more consistently supportive of her. "My mom broadened my horizons to the point where I wanted more for myself. I felt closer to my mom."

I wondered what Mark and Ellen's divorce had meant to Polly. This is when the harrowing statement that opens this chapter was delivered. "My life died when my mom first left. I died at four. My protector left."

Tommy also has had an on-again, off-again relationship with both Ellen and Mark. Now working in a fast-food restaurant in a mall after dropping out of high school, he lives with his girlfriend in their own apartment. "I got thrown out of school for getting into a fight. My dad's real upset that I've quit, but I'd go back if the kids weren't such dicks and if the teachers cared!" Having moved in and out of his father's house, he stopped seeing his mother after a huge blowup. The way Tommy describes it, "After the fight my mother left, and we don't know where she is. She calls whenever she wants to, but we don't know how to reach her." Was this fight any different from the others? I asked. "We had fights like that before. It was about me being a teenager and things I do. Being a normal teenager. We don't fight about curfew. That's with my dad."

That particular fight resulted in Tommy moving back temporarily with Mark. Tommy also provides some important insight into situations involving children separated from first one and then the other parent. "It was hard not seeing her for eighteen months; it bothered me. She'll call whenever she feels she has to hear our voices; she called yesterday but wouldn't say where she lives. We hide things from her because I feel she doesn't have the right to know where I live, now that I have moved out again and am on my own."

What do you tell your friends about her? "I tell them she died or I don't have a mom. Not really. I'll say, though, for me, she has died. I saw her once in the past year for ten minutes. I got upset because I haven't seen her in a long time and I worry about her. You worry that she'll get into trouble with drugs or whoring." This is the first reference the adult children have made to her illicit behavior. Mark had depicted her for years in these terms, but the children never agreed. Now, there has been a shift in their willingness to see her without rose-colored glasses.

Like Polly, Tommy also spent some time with his stepfather after his mother moved out, but the young children from her mother's second marriage were too much to handle. "They got on my nerves, and everyone was fighting all the time." Bill's home had been a haven until that time. It was the one place he could go, even when he and Mark were not on speaking terms. "I stopped seeing Dad because we got into a fight. I used to go out at night, and I got my butt reamed out by him."

Most instructive are Tommy's feelings about the differences in not seeing his mother as compared with his father. "It hasn't been hard not seeing him because I lived with him for twelve years. He was always there. I know he's going to be there, and I usually call or see him three times a month. Being away from her is much harder. All my life I did not see my mom that much. I was not allowed to see her all the time, and now that I can see her of my own free will and she is not around, it is especially hard." Again we see how children take the available parent for granted, and how Mark was the easier target.

Lee is sixteen and still resides with Mark. He is friendly and down-to-earth. A high school junior, he works part-time at a restaurant.

"We aren't really sure where my mom is. I last saw her about two years ago and have not spoken to her since. From what I have heard from a friend's father, she is a prostitute." Before she dropped out of sight, he saw her as often as he could, though she was hard to reach. Apparently, he had wanted to live with her from time to time, but Mark, while allowing his oldest children to leave, had refused Lee's request, despite telling him earlier he could leave if he wanted to. "I wanted to leave for a change of scenery. Did my mother ask to have me come with her? No, it came more from me. I could visit her whenever I wanted, I just couldn't live there." I asked if he thought his father was being protective of him by not letting him go. He admitted that might have been the situation.

I asked Lee, as I had his older siblings, if the lack of contact with his mother had been a hardship. "I got used to it," he said, "so it's not all that hard. It was hard when I was younger. I went upstairs and cried. My dad was helpful at certain points in dealing with not seeing her. After a while, I got so used to not seeing her, it is like she wasn't there anymore. When friends ask where she is, I say she is dead [a recurring theme for these children]. It is like she is dead to the family because she is not in contact with anybody anymore. If I knew where she was, I don't know if I would see her."

Hearing such negative comments from all three children, I asked for any other characterizations of her. Lee's response was typical of a child who has been exposed to two different households and looks on the bright side: There is an attempt to find a unique quality in each one. "She taught me something. I think she taught me how to be my own person and not be my father's person. She made me into me and not into him." Clearly she offered an option for how he could view himself, though just as clearly he is unhappy with certain aspects of that view.

This family is emblematic of what can happen when parents continue to fight over children and never resolve their differences. The children struggle with boundary issues wherever they live, testing limits at home and, in some cases, at school. They have difficulty managing intimate relationships. As a result, they become intensely involved in them at a younger age than is typical. (Other children of high conflict divorces may have the opposite reaction and forestall becoming intimately involved for a longer period of time because of fears about such involvements.) In addition, the children have some difficulty managing feelings, as did their parents. Mark has adapted to his situation and has become more comfortable with himself over the years, but he was also clinically depressed for a long time. The old wounds take at least a generation to heal, it seems.

Further, we see issues of conflictual loyalties. The children initially are protective of their mother in the face of Mark's verbal attacks. With time, they come to see his definition of her as correct and are left feeling upset and angry at her, ambivalent about where to go from here. We see the pain associated with abandonment by a parent. Mark seems to get the brunt of the children's anger over the years. For example, Polly blames him when she moves out of the house but blames Sally, rather than her mother, when she moves out of Ellen's house. Finally, the children's stories shed light on the potential long-term impact of an acrimonious divorce on children. The emotional ups and downs, the problems with school and behavior that the children have experienced, and the large number of relocations, all take their toll on the children's sense of self. They develop an attitude that reflects the marginalization they have experienced, never having been fully appreciated for who they are in their mother's home.

When a Father Vanishes, Reappears, and Vanishes

Nicole was referred to me by a friend who knew her living situation and my interests. After meeting her, and on one brief occasion her mother, I interviewed her when she was twelve and again at fourteen years old. At the time of our first meeting, Nicole had not seen her father, Allen, for three years. By the second interview, Allen had reentered her life.

When thinking about my interview with Nicole, I am reminded of Alice in Wonderland. She is exploring a new world, a place few have been. She is acutely aware of her feelings about the loss and reappearance of her father. If we think of Alice as being at the mercy of characters she cannot quite fathom, we see a similar reaction in Nicole. She is trying to avoid the corresponding growth and shrinking that Alice went through in response to others by keeping herself slightly apart and safe from involvement with Allen. It is not always easy. Just as Alice wanted only to find her way home but was distracted, Nicole tries to keep her eye on one thing, not getting hurt again. Yet, like most people, she is ambivalent about a goal that shuts out her father when there may be a great deal to be gained from contact with him.

Allen and Nicole's mother divorced when Nicole was two. Allen stayed active in her life for many years and then, almost without warning, dropped out of sight, communicating only by phone and by letter. Nicole was left with little from her father to ease her pain. She brought pictures of

Allen and herself when she was young to our interview. She tried very consciously to hold on to the good parts of her relationship with him. Both father and daughter are writers, and she has connected to him through that avenue. Nicole credits him with her own interest in writing skills.

The First Interview with Nicole (Age 12)

"He's living in Indiana, as far as I know," Nicole told me, not 100 percent certain. "How long since you and he have seen each other?" I asked. Nicole thought for a minute and told me three years, also not entirely certain. "We used to talk regularly but I stopped doing that, and so it has been a year. I wanted us to write instead because it was pretty superficial on the phone, sort of like 'What did you do today?' and so on. So I asked that we write because I write from the heart and so does he. He has called my mom just to make sure I'm okay. I sent him a letter recently because I was kind of angry that he hadn't tried to reach me. I did not want to make the first move [by writing] because he's known for saying he's going to do something and then not following through. I wrote a letter, which I never sent because it was really angry, but I got my mother to talk to him about it."

Allen was described to me by the friend who arranged the interview as a talented writer who never found a venue for his work. An eventual house-husband, he had hoped to support the family through writing. When he promised to help out the family financially and did not, his wife left him.

I asked Nicole why she believed there was no longer contact. "I saw him when they first split up, and then he moved to another city, and then I saw him on holidays, and then he moved even further away and I saw him once a year, and then he sort of dropped out."

"What would get you two to communicate again?" I wondered. "I sent him some of my writings because he's a writer and I thought he would appreciate that, and I asked for some of his writings, and I don't know what will happen but at least maybe we'll write to each other," Nicole answered, then paused. But I don't want to see him right now. So I'm waiting to see what his response will be."

There is some obvious ambivalence in this. She wants to communicate with him but she wishes he would seek her out, rather than her always starting the communication. There are also, as in the next statement, some contradictions, which she acknowledges.

"I want to see him because something is missing. When I see him, I understand people and myself better. I decided I have nothing to lose, inconsistent as that sounds. I didn't really set myself up for hoping he would come back in the picture, but if he does, I'll be happy.

"I had a dream that he had died—he's not a very healthy person—and

I've been very angry at him, so I decided I didn't want to part on bad terms. . . but if he doesn't answer [my letter], that's okay." A few minutes later, she said, "I remember one thing about him when I was six. We went to a fair once when he was visiting, and I saw a big teddy bear I really wanted. He promised me it would be back at home when my mom and I got home from a long trip. I was really excited about getting it when I came back from the trip, and it wasn't there."

"Was that the first major disappointment with him?" I asked. "I think that was the one that I really remember. Another time he did not know my age and he forgot my birthday, but that was it." As if to fill in the gap left by Allen, Nicole added, "My mom is very supportive of my having as much contact with him as possible. If it weren't for her, I probably wouldn't have any contact with him. And she is always telling me good stuff about him. She didn't push me but wanted me to still have his address, so in case anything happened to her I could contact him."

Finally, I wanted to know how she discusses her father with her friends. Her response was similar to some of the adults and other children I have interviewed. She gives partial information. "I say I don't know him very well."

Nicole did not object to my interviewing Allen about their relationship. But she did not want to talk with him herself. I made an initial contact with him, but it was two years before I tried to reach him again for an interview.

The Second Interview with Nicole (Age 14)

When I interviewed Nicole two years later, Allen had come back into the picture in much the same way he had dropped out—unexpectedly. He appeared at the house with little warning. They had been communicating sporadically by letter. I reviewed the transcript of the first interview to see what questions had been asked. I decided to repeat many of them to check for consistency. The responses were painfully similar, though from the perspective of a slightly older adolescent. "We wrote back and forth, but it was on his terms only, in that he wrote me when he wanted to. I did not want to talk to him on the phone." This was a continuation of a theme that Nicole had mentioned in our first interview—the struggle for control of their communication.

Would Allen call and request to speak with you? I asked. "He would call when I was in school because I requested that. But if I was home I would talk to him for a minute and ask if he wanted to talk to Mom. I avoided him more or less."

I asked her again, as I had at the first interview, why contact had stopped. "I didn't want to talk to him on the phone. It was artificial and he didn't write letters, so we just kind of stopped. Our terms didn't meet. I guess I didn't want to talk because it was so sporadic. He'd call me every day for weeks, and then he would stop for a year, and then he'd send me a birthday card or gift. I just couldn't depend on it. I don't like things I can't depend on.

"The phone conversations and the contact did not work because when you can't trust someone the relationship just doesn't really grow. So I closed off. I guess I closed down when there was a pattern where he would say he would come on Christmas or to my next play and he didn't come. After a while I became a pessimist and hoped for the worst—that he wouldn't be there, so I wouldn't be disappointed. And it always happened that way. I got hurt a whole bunch of times, and, after that, you just stop believing in someone and then it ends the relationship. The first big hurt I remember was when he was supposed to come for Christmas, and he wrote and said he wouldn't come—it was one of the few times he wrote—and he sent me a silver star and I was supposed to put it on top of the tree, and that would be his presence. I was just so sad because I wanted him to be there for Christmas, and that was like the first pain. That was the beginning of my starting to give up on him."

I wondered if Nicole had found support elsewhere. "Has the decision to close off to him made you get closer to your mother?" I asked. "Yes," she answered. "We have become very close. I used to be closer to my dad when he took care of me and Mom worked. My mom is a real serious type. She's become both of them, and I accepted that after a while. I would hang out with her male friends, but that didn't work out too well. But yes, it has made us closer. I know she'll be there."

"What happened when your dad came back?" I asked. "He called from Missouri one night, and then he showed up on our doorstep and I was in shock. He didn't see me see him, so I had a few seconds to prepare myself because I saw him through the screen. I didn't know who he was at first because he'd gotten older and grayer, and I went into total shock. He stayed for dinner, and my mother saw I was very nervous and suggested I leave the room for a few minutes to call a friend, to give me an out. I had a really strong reaction. It was like I was on drugs. I was really freaked out. My dad came back in the room after going outside to smoke and saw me crying and having an hysterical fit, and my mom said to him, 'You know, it is really hard on her to have you walk back in.'

"I've seen him a few times. He came on my birthday, but I haven't really talked to him. We're taking it really slowly, and I am afraid to be alone with him because I don't want to open up to him again. I'm just not ready for that. My first reaction was anger because he needs my family now, since he just broke up with his girlfriend, and it's like 'Where were you when I needed you?' I'm sure I need him, a part of me needs to have a father figure, but I have filled in all of my holes myself now, and I was starting to pick back up and had accepted where it was, and now all of a sudden he needs me."

I wanted to know how Allen expressed his need for Nicole. "Just by showing up. And I'm sure he needs my mom's friendship because she is a very stable influence and a good friend to him." "Have you told him that you have to take things slowly?" I inquired. "He came to visit me just before I went away to camp, and I told him we had to take it slowly now, and I think he understands that. You can't just pick up a relationship you stopped.

"He dropped out the same way he dropped in. One day he just left, and that is how he showed up. He didn't tell us he was coming, and so that is the way the cycle seems to be going."

Here Nicole is saying that he was unpredictable when he left and the manner in which he returned makes him unpredictable still. His pattern with her affects how she views relationships with others. "Do you think he may drop out again?" I questioned. "Yeah, I can't trust him. I don't trust a lot of people because of my lack of trust in him. I wouldn't be unhappy if he weren't there when I got back because I am taking it really slow."

Nicole talked about his other traits, and the similarities she sees in herself. In describing him, she again contradicts herself slightly, showing the normal ambivalence that develops in many parent-child relationships. "I think he is a neat person, and he is someone I would like to get to know because he is a lot like me and I admire him for some qualities, but I don't trust him yet. He's an artist and has a lot of procrastination habits that I have. He has the fun part that Mom doesn't have, and Mom is learning to be more fun and he is learning to be more serious. He seems to be responsible. He doesn't send any money, but he does pay rent to a friend who he is renting from. Our contacts have been so small. I would miss him if he left. I hope he stays, but I would not be surprised if he didn't."

Allen runs hot and cold about wanting to be interviewed by me, agreeing at one point and then changing his mind at another. I have talked to Nicole's mother, and she believes that when he is not visiting Nicole he is reluctant to talk because he feels guilty. Currently he has sporadic contact and does not own a telephone.

Nicole's story presents many themes that are common among children in these situations, some of which we saw in Mark and Ellen's children:

First is the difficulty a child has in trusting the absent parent when contact is infrequent. Second, and closely related to this, is the issue of communication between the child and that parent: who will write first, the need for the child to be the recipient of communication rather than the initiator, the form that communication will take, whether by letter or by phone, and so on. Two people who feel less comfortable with writing than Nicole and Allen may not consider writing an option. The third theme, which Nicole so clearly articulates, is the carryover between difficulty in trusting one parent and trusting people in other relationships. Fourth, and also like Mark and Ellen's children, is the trauma of reestablishing contact after it has ceased. It was extremely hard for Nicole when Allen showed up unannounced. Her reaction "like I was on drugs" reflects her feeling of being in shock. Fifth, we hear how a child adapts to the relationship with the parent by lowering expectations of that parent. Nicole would expect to be disappointed as a defense against actual disappointment when Allen did not come to her plays. In that way she was not let down. Sixth, we see the role the other parent takes in compensating for the absence of one parent. Nicole's mother is very supportive of Nicole and encourages contact with Allen while also hoping Nicole retains a realistic appraisal of him. Finally, Nicole has a positive view of her mother, thereby giving her a better sense of herself. In some ways it is a protective view, perhaps fostered in an attempt to find protection for herself. This helps her to compensate for the part of herself related to her father that she is uncomfortable with.

When a Father Has been Unfaithful

Whereas the first five children just described had a father or mother who dropped out but was attempting to control the contact seemingly at their whim, the next five illustrate situations in which the child is holding the parent at arm's length. The children are the active ones in modulating the volume for the relationship.

Mimi's Story: The Perspective from Young Adulthood

Mimi refuses to see her father, while he pulls out all the stops trying to reestablish a relationship with her. She feels totally justified in rejecting him.

Mimi is a college senior interested in a career in counseling; her parents (her father is a physician and her mother is a nurse) divorced when she was seven and her older brother was nine. Visitation with her father began on an every-other-weekend basis. When she turned ten, she stopped all visits, while her brother continued visiting. "I was picking up on things that made me feel uncomfortable. My father would have women staying over, which my brother did not see. Also my brother needed more attention. My father would have big parties and would show us off, and my brother liked that. It just didn't feel right, so I didn't want to see him."

As Mimi began withdrawing, she learned from her mother the painful details of why the marriage had ended. "He had been unfaithful to her, and he had also sexually molested his patients." I asked if he had ever been charged with abuse. Mimi did not know but said he was still practicing medicine in the same area of New York where he had always practiced.

When Mimi refused to visit her father, he went to court to have the visitation enforced. She was court-ordered to spend time with him but still refused, a situation we saw from Leif's perspective in chapter 3 when his sons refused court-ordered visitation. "He abused my mother and was mean to me and my brother and had hit me and punished me fairly harshly. I was shocked that after I had told the judge those things about him, the judge still made me visit." Despite Mimi's recalcitrance, he continued to push for visitation. "When I was twelve he married my mom's best friend, and that created a dynamic that added to my desire to avoid him. I had never liked her, so that has not helped things since then. He tried to get us together a few years ago. He asked me out to dinner and brought her along without telling me. That didn't help things, either."

Many custodial parents become caught between the child and the noncustodial parent. I asked Mimi if her mother interfered with or encouraged her to see her father. "My mom pushed me to see him, and when I said I didn't want to, she said it was my decision. She was supportive and did not try and build a wedge between me and my father."

Having lost on a number of fronts in his attempts to see her, Mimi's father tried to bribe her to visit. "He would ask me to stop by after school and then would say his car didn't work and could I stay the night. Or he'd buy me things, which I wouldn't accept. In high school I didn't see him at all unless I bumped into him. He would call every so often and would try to get me to visit, and I'd refuse. My brother began not wanting to see him, either. We used to not answer the phone because we were afraid he would call and harass us to visit."

Contact has not increased since Mimi left for college, though her father's attempts to see her continue. "I got into a big fight with him once when he tried to convince me that I had to have a relationship with him. I said I would love him because he brought me into life but that I would never trust him. I now have to laugh about it because who wants to set up boundaries with your parent?"

As often happens, the way one observes one's parents interacting affects one's own intimate relationships. Mimi is no exception. The ambivalent relationship with her father and the way she saw him treat her mother has had a definite effect. "I dated very little in high school and my first year in college. Then I met a guy I have been dating for over three years. Having been around my father has enabled me to see a lot of things that other people can't see as fast. I have a sixth sense about guys. If they mistreat me or if I see them get mad a lot, I stay away. The guy I date now is a very calm person. I feel lucky but I am still skeptical. I worry what if, in ten years, something happens. My mom didn't know when she married my dad what was going to happen. My mom told me things to look out for—watch how they act with children, for example, and see how they handle money. You can tell about someone from those kinds of things."

One thing Mimi said she learned was that her father gave love conditionally. He mailed her a check for a thousand dollars at high school graduation. She kept it for the whole summer without cashing it and then, just before she went to college, decided to use the money because she was desperate. As she spent it, she worried about the ramifications of accepting the money. True to form, he increased his calls.

As with other children I interviewed, Mimi's future relationships have been affected by her dealings with her father. She wants to avoid involvements in which there are conditions on how love is given and received. She's wary of trusting men and has become protective of her mother. The charges against her father of patient abuse were related to me with a sense of shame and remained unexplored throughout the interview. But, from the way they were disclosed, I could tell they obviously have an impact on her ability to ever trust her father again.

Leon's Story: The Perspective from Middle Age

Not all the "children" interviewed here are just starting out in life. Leon offers a perspective that goes back another generation. Now forty-six, he saw his father twice in twenty years, and, as in Mimi's case, it has been by his own choice. When I met Leon at a mutual friend's son's wedding, I mentioned I was working on this book, and he immediately spilled out his story without any prompting, showing how near to the surface these feelings remain, even for older adults. A car salesman, he is very easy to talk to, gregarious, and full of amusing anecdotes. But once the surface of the salesman is scratched, the feelings come out, tinged with anger and hurt.

Leon is the oldest of two boys; his parents divorced when he was thirteen. For the next three years he lived with his mother and saw his father on weekends. In the late 1950s, divorce was not very common and he felt an enormous discomfort with his evolving family situation. Then his father remarried and tried to incorporate Leon into his new family. "I didn't want any part of it. I stayed away from him after that and essentially did not see or communicate with my father for the next ten years. Then one day he dropped in on my new wife and me. Boy, was that traumatic after ten years," he said, rolling his eyes.

Why did you go for so long without seeing him? I asked. "He had been unfaithful to my mother. I was hurt and felt abandoned. His remarrying forced me to acknowledge his affairs. I didn't want any part of his new family. I didn't see him again for ten years after that visit even though I knew where he was. Then my nephew was Bar Mitzvahed and I saw him again. He has since remarried a second time, and I don't want anything to do with him or his new wife."

Like Mimi and other children who believe one parent has wronged the other, Leon has never forgiven his father. He suffers for it, he told me. Now married for the second time, he has chosen not to have children because of the pain he witnessed in his own family. The mirroring effect referred to earlier is one way of thinking about the self-hatred displayed here. Other parents avoid seeing their children because contact reminds them of their failures. To escape facing this side of his life, Leon chose not to have children. Yet his brother who raised two sons clearly feels differently.

Was Leon who was the oldest and probable protector of his mother more affected than his brother? As we have seen throughout, not only do children from the same family react differently, but the position of the child in the family and perhaps the gender can have an impact. Older children tend to grow up a little faster and play a more parental role in divorce than the younger children if all children are in the home. It is the oldest child who often becomes the pal of the single parent. As a result, that child may learn more about childrearing and adult pain than the younger children. If what they learn is negative, those older children may decide to avoid any future childrearing responsibilities. In Leon's case, he became the "man" of the family when his father left. But he could not escape how he felt about fathering.

When Both Spouses in a Marriage Have Lost Contact with Their Fathers

Every so often twists of fate (or is it conscious planning?) result in two people with unique backgrounds marrying each other. In this case, a young woman, Pam, who has not seen her father for twenty-two years, married a young man, Tom, who went for ten years with little contact with his father. (I also interviewed Tom's younger sister, Candy, whose reactions to her father's absence follow.) The more than two hour interview with Pam and Tom took place in their East Coast apartment. Both in their mid- to late twenties and involved in business, the newlyweds appeared spellbound by each other's stories. Even though they had been married only six months, they knew a great deal about each other, a sign of the enormous amount of communication they had exchanged about their families. They stated they were attracted to each other, in part, because of their similar background in coming from divorced families. They knew that the other person understood and was sensitive to the need to work to keep a family together.

Pam's Story

Pam described her mother and father, Chris, as complete opposites. Chris was very outgoing, attractive, and mercurial. He had been raised by two unstable parents and felt very insecure as a result, Pam believes. Her mother, on the other hand, was a shy "plain Jane" whose personality was not as evident. Opposites did attract, initially, as each provided for the other what was missing. But the marriage did not last. "My father cheated on my mother a lot, would come and go. Every time he would leave I would sleep with my mom in her bed. I could tell, I was three at the time, that she was miserable. My grandmother would encourage her to leave him, but my mom was pretty much a weak person and wouldn't do it. She'd have stayed with him forever. One night he came home late out of the blue and I sat up and said to him, 'You don't sleep here anymore,' and he looked at my mother and asked, 'Is that true?' and she looked at me and said, 'Yep. It's true.' That gave my mom the courage to say the marriage was over."

Pam's mother wanted Pam to have a father and quickly remarried a man [Stan] she knew from the church. Pam was thrilled. She had known Stan and viewed him as a caring person who treated her lovingly.

Chris had visitation rights and would see Pam in her mother and step-father's house. Pam dreaded the visits. "I was petrified of him," Pam said. "He had yelled at my mother and scared her, though he never hit her. I had not been alone with him. One time when the divorce was going through, my mom and I were walking along the beach and he came down with his car and tried to run us over. I think he was just trying to frighten us." This fear set the stage for what was to become their last meeting, when Pam was four.

"I'll never forget it. He pulled up in a white Cadillac convertible with his girlfriend. He got out of the car to pick me up for a two-week visit. He lived in this big house, which I think he had bought through dirty money. He told me about all these beautiful things he had in the house to attract me. Stan was holding me, and I didn't want to go. Chris was pulling me, and Stan stopped holding me because that would be preventing Chris from having visitation, and neither Stan or my mother would do that. So I was hanging on to Stan's neck and screaming that I didn't want to go, and Chris couldn't pull me off. Then Chris said, 'She doesn't want me.' And he just left and I have not seen him since.

"We have spoken once, and that was when Stan wanted to adopt me. We found out from Chris's second ex-wife where he lived and called him to get his permission. He was married to his third wife at the time. My mom got on the phone and said Stan wanted to adopt me, and Chris said, 'I'm her father!' My mom said, 'How can you consider yourself her father, you haven't seen her in twelve years?' He said he wanted to talk to me. So I got on the phone, and he asked me why I considered Stan my father. I said, 'Because he raised me. Biology means nothing to me. I don't know who you are. If I ran into you I wouldn't know you.' [This is a theme Tom echoes.] He said, 'Okay, but I want you to know, you have a brother.' Of course, he had illegitimate kids all over the place. So I said, 'So what?' Then he asked my mother if there was anything I needed because he was a millionaire. She said 'Yes, a car.' He promised to send one up to me if I met him. I agreed to, but, of course, we never heard from him again."

Even in the early 1980s, when divorce was booming, Pam's mother felt it carried a stigma. She wanted her previous marriage kept a secret when the family moved to a different state so that people would think Pam was Stan's daughter. Pam was not even shown pictures of Chris until she was sixteen. She had completely forgotten what he looked like.

When Pam met Tom, she and he realized that she had never been given the opportunity to talk about her father. She associated a great deal of pain with the years of separation. In addition, Pam had to face the enormous guilt she felt from the defining moment in her life when, at three, she stood up to her father and kicked him out of the house. Brief counseling proved to be effective for her in coming to terms with her past before she moved ahead with marriage to Tom.

During our interview I asked Pam whether she had wanted to see Chris when she was younger. Given the strong attachment she had formed with Stan, and the way she felt about Chris, she never asked to see him. She commented that if she had asked to see Chris, she would have been disloyal to her mother, a theme that recurred during the interviews with Tom and Candy. I wondered if she had ever, in the heat of a battle with her stepfather, said she wanted to visit Chris. "No," was her reply. "To me he has been blanked out of my mind. I have a new dad now, and Chris is gone— good riddance. And, as far as I know, he has never tried to see me. He didn't want the responsibility. He was a selfish person and didn't care what happened to me or to my mother. Also, he was angry at my mother and probably thought he didn't want to have anything to do with either of us. He may not even have wanted kids."

How has your experience with your father affected your relationships with men? "I don't think it has at all. It is more with the circumstance," Pam said. "If Tom and I argue, and he leaves, I panic. Is he coming back? Or even with arguments with my mother, I worry if she'll come back. My mom always reassures me she will. It comes from what happened with Chris, and I don't know if I'll ever totally get over that. A different part of me knows that with Tom, if we have an argument, he *will* come back. So it is getting easier. But a part of me has distrust on some issues [a similar theme was raised by Nicole and Mimi]. If Tom and I are having an argument, I'll even follow him into another room to finish it so that no one leaves the house angry."

As discussion turns to Pam and Tom's current relationship, Tom begins to add his perspective and describes his way of interacting when they have a fight. The conversation drifts to his upbringing.

Tom's Story

Tom was ten and Candy was seven when their mother and father split up. The separation was nowhere near as traumatic as Pam's family's, nor was the termination of contact between father and child as abrupt. As in many families, the noncustodial parent and child just drifted apart, according to Tom.

"When my parents got divorced, they had joint custody, and I saw quite a bit of him for the next few years. It was always on weekends, and what bothered my mother was that he always had my sister and me for the fun times, while she had us during the week when the work had to be done. Then he got remarried to a nice woman with kids and all of a sudden, boom, he was gone. They moved to Chicago and we stayed in phone contact, but that deteriorated until we spoke only a few times a year, holidays, birthdays. Finally it just stopped.

"By this point, my mom had remarried, and her husband had really taken over the role of the father. He was paying for everything and I began to think of him as a father. And he was doing a great job. I learned later my biological father was not paying child support we were owed. It is interesting that my biological father and stepfather couldn't be more different. My stepfather was very successful in business and preached responsibility, and my father was not successful and was acting irresponsibly."

For a number of years, Tom's father was essentially out of the picture and living a thousand miles away. "Then my father came home with his tail between his legs, having failed at his second marriage and at his job. At that point we didn't care where he was at. We didn't know how to even get in touch with him, though I guess I could have through my grandparents, with whom I had stayed very close."

Visiting his paternal grandparents while not seeing his father did not seem to pose a problem for Tom until one traumatic day. "My grandparents never talked about him. He wasn't there. He didn't call. And when he finally moved back to town, he just showed up at the house one time. I had seen him twice in eight years. Everyone was very uncomfortable around him. Candy and I saw him and didn't speak the whole time we were there. She cried. We had gotten on with our lives and he was in the way. He was back on our turf and we didn't like it. We felt, 'Look, you cruised for eight years, didn't take care of us, our stepfather did, and now do you think you're going to step in and become Dad again?'"

Not only was he back in the picture after many years, but Tom was left with the impression that nothing significant about him had changed. "When I turned eighteen, my stepfather wanted to adopt me, and we got in touch with my father, who said he would let me be adopted if they forgave the child support he owed them. My mother told him to get screwed. I got on the phone and shouted at him and changed his mind. He signed the papers and we got adopted. But that ticked me off. I don't believe because you gave birth to a child, that makes you a parent. His dropping-by out of the blue fit with his earlier pattern of ducking responsibility."

Despite that incident, within the next two years, Tom and he resumed regular contact, but it was not without a price. "There were very mixed emotions about seeing him again. Then he remarried a very stable woman whom I like. Since then, we have slowly started seeing each other more and more. But I became aware that my attempting to reestablish a relationship with him was upsetting to my mother and stepfather. I still considered my stepfather my father. But my father was there for the first ten years, so it can be really confusing. With Pam's and my wedding, a lot of issues came to a head that revolved around loyalty and what everyone felt was their position in the wedding and in the family."

As often happens with major family events, feelings that can lie dormant for years resurface. The event became a metaphor for family history and a measure of love. Money returned as an issue when Tom and Pam said they were willing to pay for his father and stepmother as guests but not for any of their friends. Seating at the wedding became a problem: Where does a son place his mother and stepfather in relation to his father, from whom he was estranged for many years, and his stepmother? By putting issues out on the table and by removing himself from the middle of any ongoing animosity between his mother and father, Tom, with Pam's help, was able to balance the competing needs of parents and stepparents. Today, Tom continues to want to build a relationship with his father. Yet he never forgets that it was his mother and stepfather who have done so much for him and that their feelings are affected by his actions.

Candy's Story

My interview with Candy confirmed much of what I had heard from Tom. Her life experiences, perhaps because she was younger, a daughter, and a separate person from her older brother, caused her to react in a different way than Tom did. Whereas Tom tended toward stoicism, assuming responsibility of his mother and younger sister during the initial years after the breakup, Candy, only five when her father left, reacted with great anger.

Now twenty-six and the manager of a retail establishment, she has assumed a position of great responsibility. But until her twenties, she felt as if she drifted. "I never remember when my parents were together. When he left, I recall visiting him. We used to go to the zoo and do other things like that. I was happy visiting my father but I was very unhappy inside. I remember when my mom got remarried and how hurt I was. I was very messed up when I was in elementary school. I don't think I fully understood divorce. I always thought that my daddy would come back to me and he would get remarried to my mom, and we would again be one big happy family. But it didn't work that way! My father had left. He basically abandoned us. He called less and less and moved away. None of my friends were divorced and certainly none of them had a father who had left, so it was very difficult, emotionally and financially. I also felt hurt by the way the kids at the school made me feel because we couldn't afford nice clothes."

Candy laments now what she put her new stepfather through when he first entered the family. Her comments offer valuable insight into the impact remarriage has on family members. "I don't know how he put up with it. I was violent to myself. I got into drugs. I didn't know how to control myself and I would have temper tantrums, I was so angry. I had such anger in me and I don't know why. I wanted to hit something to make myself feel better. My mother and brother were the main support, and along comes my stepfather and I worry he's going to take my mom away. Maybe inside, as I got closer to my stepfather, I thought he would leave, too. So I was angry at him, also. I went to therapists, but it didn't help until I finally decided to let the anger go. I was tired of being angry and I realized my father was not coming back.

"I realized that my stepfather was my father. He was the one who raised me. I can't imagine going into a family like he did and taking over. He was remarkable, especially given how bad I was and how unaccepting I was. He never gave up on us."

Candy also vividly remembers seeing her father again at her grandparents' house for the first time in years. "There was Daddy and I was supposed to open my arms to him. I cried hysterically the whole time I was there. And I never trusted my grandparents again in the same way because he was there and they hadn't told us in advance."

Candy felt her grandparents had given her the message that her feelings were not considered important, while her father's needs were. The residue left by her father's actions still haunts her, affecting her feelings about herself and the decisions she makes about her life. "I don't like my father. I never want to be associated with him. My biggest fear in life is that I am going to turn out like him. I see him as such a loser. I work so hard because my father has made nothing of his life and I'm scared that will happen to me. My mother was incredible in how hard she worked to take care of us, but it is that fear of being lazy like my father that drives me. He took the easy way out. You can't throw your children away, which is what he did. I want to be strong and successful like my mother and stepfather.

"When my father came back, I hadn't seen him for over ten years. He's tried to start a relationship with me. I didn't want to be angry at him anymore, so I tried to be friendly. I'm embarrassed to say, and I don't feel good about it, I accepted gifts from him because I felt he owed me. I used him for a long time because I needed the things he would offer me. But I never felt good about it and I finally stopped accepting the gifts. He started telling me he loved me but I couldn't tell him the same thing. I also realized I was sticking a knife into my stepfather, and that made me feel worse."

Since Tom and Pam's wedding, Candy has distanced herself from her father. She felt he was stirring things up between Tom and her and that he even was inserting himself into Candy's relationship with her live-in boyfriend. (Interestingly, her boyfriend's parents are divorced, and he is also out of contact with his father: both Candy and Tom became involved with people whose backgrounds are similar to their own.) As a result, Candy has drifted apart from her father and is not returning his calls anymore. Candy admits she is not interested in seeing him in part because she fears falling back into the pattern of using him, a behavior that reminds her of her fear that she will be like him and unable to take care of herself. In fact, *each* unpleasant contact she has with him renews that fear. As a result of this fear, Candy's self-perception is that, as a defense, she is very focused in her life and hardworking, and, at times, unable to let her hair down and be "wild."

Each success in her business career, and there are many, reinforces for

Candy that she is not like her father. If she were like him, she tells herself, she would sabotage her career. Each time she feels even the slightest bit lazy, it provides an impetus to work harder. She compensates in a healthy way by identifying with her successful mother.

Does Candy want to start a family? Not yet, she said. "I feel like I have too many needs right now to be able to give to someone else. Maybe when I'm older."

With these three adults other points emerge from those already raised. With Pam, we have a child who takes a protective role over a parent as Pam did with her mother by throwing out her father. Was this single act an aberration or the result of a message learned about the power of a child over a weak mother? Unlike in a Greek tragedy, Pam is able to move on with her life, helped by her mother's quick remarriage to a new father. Therefore, she played a beneficial role, not a destructive one. She took the reins and it worked well. Because she is insightful, her difficult situation left her with an accurate perception as to her power in relationships. The perception is coupled with the fear that each angry departure spells the end of contact with that person "forever." While Pam was protecting her mother, Tom, to a much lesser extent, was protecting his sister and mother.

From Candy we hear the common fantasy that children of divorce have that their parents will magically reunite. We also hear the rage that a child feels at the stepparent whose presence epitomizes the death of this fairy tale. Candy takes out her anger on herself, unable to effectively diminish the power that her stepfather has assumed. With a loving and consistent stepfather, the resolution of this conflict is a happy one.

We see enormous rage at Tom and Candy's father. Having finally coped with his abandonment, they now are forced to face his return. This raises the question of when a parent stops being a parent. Does the child always have to stay open to a parent's return? Like an uninvited guest who will not leave, his presence—and the way he reappeared—is highly upsetting. What is the proper response to the returning parent for Tom and Candy? Being decent people, they feel conflicted about seeing him. They react differently, Tom as the patient, mediating son, and Candy as the petulant child demanding her due. Tom attempts to work things out, while Candy rejects him.

The sense of loyalty is difficult to resolve for Tom and Candy, as it is for so many children in this chapter. Time spent with their father can cause pain to the mother and stepfather that have given them so much. Where is the respite for children in these impossible binds?

Finally, we see the fear of growing up like Dad that Tom and Candy experience. They adapt by working hard as a defense against this fear. It is a healthy adaptation because their mother and stepfather have been admirable role models who also work hard. The lesson to be learned is that the success or failure of any parent becomes a lens through which children view themselves. This lens, when there is no contact, may become magnified because there is little other information to counter it. When parents who fail at work are in constant contact with their children, the children can construct a more variegated image of the parent and incorporate the successes and failures into their understanding of the parent. When the parent is absent, it is more likely that a monolithic (and negative) impression is formed.

Conclusion

What can we draw from the stories of these ten children? One impression is that all are in pain to varying degrees. Those who are abandoned and have little control over continued contact with their parents tend to react with hurt, while those who have shut out their parents tend to react with anger. The conditions under which children stop seeing their parents may have an impact on which direction the pain gets channeled—inwardly in the case of those abandoned, and outwardly in the case of those who reject their parents. Regardless of education and class, from the children of physicians to the children of prostitutes, no child escapes untouched. Some social science may suggest that fathers are superfluous to families[20] or that families can cope without a mother's presence.[21] But when the children are interviewed in depth, their message is that while they certainly are coping, they are not always happy about such absences. The children never forget and, in some cases, wear their pain near the surface, willing to share it at the slightest hint.

Two questions nag me from talking to these children:

First, how *should* a child respond to a returning parent? With Sally, Tommy, Polly, and Lee, with Nicole, Leon, Tom, and Candy we see a range of possibilities. And it is a troublesome one. The children feel like Ping-Pong balls whose emotions are at the beck and call of the parent. If the child has adapted to life without Mom or Dad, has found a way to cope with the feelings related to absence, how can he be expected to open his heart again and trust someone he has learned to distrust and live without? Yet what is a parent who wants to reenter a child's life to do in these situations? If the parent stays forever absent, will that cause more pain?

The second nagging question: What does a child do with the torn sense of loyalty when the parent returns? How can a child incorporate the returning parent into his or her life and not offend the custodial parent who has given the child so much more? Tom's example may provide an answer: Talk about it. This is easier for adult children than younger ones but nonetheless provides a clue as to how to begin to approach this conflict.

The message from these interviews is that the pain continues for children when there is no contact. A child may not want to or be able to talk about the absence when it first occurs, as in Pam's case. Eventually, as new relationships emerge, it will become a key area of growth that has been blocked and needs resolution. The child continues to grow but, as in the case of Sid, a piece of the puzzle may be missing. There is a yearning for that absent parent.

We need to find ways to expose children to both parents after divorce without forcing them to shuttle back and forth. We need to find ways to keep both parents in the picture and on optimal terms with the children. Unfortunately, some children after divorce are alienated not just from one parent, but from both.[22] The wheels that a separation puts in motion call all relationships into question. The forward motion can put the relationship with the noncustodial parent at risk and can have a deleterious effect on the child's relationship with the custodial parent, too. Once impermanence is introduced, it can be hard to draw a line. The children interviewed here need permanence in their relationships with their parents so that they will be better able to cope with the vagaries of life.

Having "enough" time with a child after divorce, in and of itself, will not be sufficient. What is needed is for the role of both parents to be meaningful, for the time together to matter and for the influence of both parents to be felt and appreciated by the child. In that way, the child remains connected to both parents.

If that fails and a cutoff occurs, we need to be aware that the children who want to reconnect are often flying solo. As they move to reestablish a tie with the absent parent, they risk losing the parent who has been their major support. We need to find ways to accompany them on that flight so that they do not have to go it alone as they enter new territory.

Chapter 7

Absent Parents, Law, and Social Policy

REBECCA L. HEGAR

What rights do parents have in the situations just described? Issues surrounding the rights of parents with respect to their children, always complex and charged topics in our society, are further complicated when parents separate or divorce, or when one parent is absent. The notion of "parental rights" has evolved over time and has developed differently in various cultures. In countries that share the English (common law) legal tradition, we take it for granted that when children are born, they will live where the parents decide, usually with the parents. We assume that parents must and will authorize medical care and sign other consent documents on behalf of their children, and we know that American parents have considerable latitude in how they educate their children, whether at public, religious, or nonsectarian private schools, or at home.

Not only in medical care and education do parents exercise their rights. As children grow, parents decide how to supervise, discipline, and rear their children, as long as their care does not fall below the minimally acceptable level that can lead to the involvement of child protective services and the juvenile courts. Parents must sign or co-sign most contracts involving even adolescent children, and they can grant or withhold consent for their children's decisions to marry or join the armed forces, as well as to have surgery. Parents legally control their children's income, though most working teens would be horrified to know that!

When married parents divorce, the various rights of parents and the relatively few claims of children must be either divided between the parents or retained by both in joint custody. (The situation for parents who have not been married to each other is somewhat different and will not be covered here.) When one parent absents himself or herself from the lives of the children, it may seem logical to assume that he or she no longer has the right to act as a parent. However, that is not the case. In most situations, absence carries no loss of parental rights, though loss of rights may be possible after an extended absence, if so decided by a court.

This chapter explores how parental rights and obligations are affected when parents who have been absent are involved in controversies over divorce and child custody, visitation, child support, and termination of parental rights due to stepparent adoption. A final section of the chapter assesses the basic fairness of the ways in which our society treats absent parents, residential parents, and their children.

Divorce, Child Custody, and Parental Absence

As noted earlier, the primary focus of this book is on situations where married or divorced parents lose touch with their children. When a married parent, or one with joint custody after divorce, stops seeing the other parent and children, nothing concerning the absent parent's rights changes automatically. Both parents, though living separately, retain the right to act on the child's behalf, for example to have access to medical records, or to withdraw a child from school. To prevent an absent parent from unexpectedly intervening in the life of a child, particularly if that parent might pose some danger, the other parent can file in court for a temporary sole custody order.

"Desertion" of spouse and children is a traditional ground for divorce in most jurisdictions. Although "no-fault" divorce, usually on the basis that the couple has lived separately for a specified period of time, has become increasingly common in the United States, some states retain laws permitting divorce on the basis of traditional grounds, such as adultery, cruelty, or desertion. Very recently, public debate has resumed about the desirability of retaining fault based grounds for divorce in some circumstances. Where possible, filing for divorce on the basis of desertion may allow for a quicker decision than waiting the time required for a no-fault divorce.[1] Both the absent partner and the one left caring for the children of the marriage should be aware that continued absence of one parent will, sooner or later, allow for a divorce, whether on grounds of desertion or under a no-fault provision based upon the length of separation.

Most parents whose ex-spouse is completely absent will want to obtain sole custody of the children, in order to prevent disruption of their lives, should the other parent reappear. When the other parent remains absent and does not contest the divorce and custody petition, this is a likely outcome. However, a number of states now have laws favoring joint custody, and the parent who is raising the children may wish to establish in court that it is not in the children's interest for custody to be shared with the absent parent, or with a parent with a history of absences from the children's lives.[2]

Access, Visitation, and Parents Who Have Been Absent

The right to have access to the children of the marriage is one that almost all parents retain after divorce. The parent who has been absent for some time may have to go to court to obtain an order providing for visitation, but, barring evidence that he or she is a danger to the child, it will ordinarily be granted.

Child abuse allegations. Child abuse, neglect, and especially sexual abuse are particularly difficult and charged issues that sometimes are raised when a custodial parent wants to bar visitation with the noncustodial parent. Other chapters of this book have presented cases where absent parents felt unfairly accused of having harmed children, and the truth may be difficult to discern in such situations. One legal publication notes that six levels of certainty concerning abuse allegations might be used to determine appropriate child custody and visitation. They are that the abuse allegation is either definitely true, probably true, possibly true, possibly false, probably false, or definitely false.[3] This set of categories is obviously problematic. (What is probably true is also possibly false, as is the reverse.)

It is true that it is often difficult for courts and others to be completely certain that abuse occurred, especially when the child involved is very young or is otherwise unable to relate events clearly, or when the child reveals abuse and then later, out of fear or misguided loyalty, denies that it happened. In fact, recantation of an earlier disclosure is a step in the process children frequently go through in coming to terms with actual sexual abuse, and it therefore should not be considered as evidence that abuse did not occur.[4]

In the public concern and publicity over all types of child abuse allegations, it is easy to lose sight of the fact that they actually arise in a tiny proportion of even contested custody and visitation disputes, less than 2 percent, according to one national study.[5] Furthermore, in cases in that study in which sexual abuse allegations were made, they were confirmed by investigators in about half the cases, and abuse could not be ruled out in another 17 percent. In the remaining third of the cases, in which investigators believed no abuse occurred, most of the allegations had been made in good faith, that is by parents who genuinely believed what they alleged.[6]

Despite such research findings, there is a public perception that many efforts to restrict visitation are based on false allegations of abuse, usually, though not exclusively, against fathers.[7] Another commonly held view is the opposite, that women and children who allege abuse in the context of custody or visitation disputes are unlikely to be believed and afforded protection by the courts.[8] What is clearly true in this clash of perspectives is that abuse allegations are now made more often than in earlier decades, and that courts frequently must struggle to sort out their truth.

Access for relatives of absent parents. Not only do some absent parents feel unfairly cut off from visitation with their children, so do some of their relatives. Access for extended family members, especially for grandparents (see also chapter 9), is another issue that has grabbed the attention of the public and of lawmakers in recent years, leading as far as a series of congressional hearings in 1982.[9] In general, access to children is granted by the parents to whichever relatives they wish, but especially in cases of divorce or death of a parent, courts and legislatures have begun to intervene when the custodial or surviving parent denies visitation to grandparents.[10]

During the 1970s and early 1980s, the highest state courts in New Jersey (*Mimkon v. Ford* [1975]) and New York (*Layton v. Foster* [1984]) ruled in favor of grandparent visitation in cases in which custodial parents and adoptive stepparents had objected, and by 1985, forty-nine states had revised their laws to allow grandparents to petition courts for access to their grandchildren when the parents are divorced.[11] Now all U.S. states and the District of Columbia have statutes addressing access for grandparents.[12] While the "grandparents' rights" movement has been highly successful, the legal position of other relatives of absent parents is much less clear. Even grandparents may have little recourse if their son or daughter, while absent from the child's life, is not either divorced from the other parent or deceased.

In addition to visitation for the absent parent and possibly other family members, other rights concerning the child also continue despite parental absence. For example, if the custodial parent dies, custody ordinarily reverts to the absent parent. Custodial parents who wish to avoid this outcome require legal counsel about their options.

Child Support and Enforcement

Issues surrounding financial child support for children of divorce and for others being reared by one parent are among the most pressing and difficult of our time. As the number of children living in single-parent families rises, so does the importance of support provided by nonresidential parents. At the same time, numerous areas of controversy surround the issues of child support and enforcement of child support orders. How should courts determine what parents must pay? How can resulting court orders best be enforced? Should there be a link between paying child support and being permitted to visit one's child? These and related questions are explored in this section. Because child support and its enforcement are highly relevant to most families from which a parent is absent, and because they form the single area of relevant social policy in which there has been substantial federal legislation, they are described in some detail in this section. (See also chapter 1.)

Like other family law matters in the United States, disputes over child support are governed principally by state law and handled in state courts. Although a child support order can be made in any situation in which a child is not living with both parents, until fairly recently it was much less common in situations involving unmarried parents. Before a child support order can be made for a child born outside a marriage, regardless of whether the mother or father is raising the child and requires support from the nonresidential parent, paternity must be legally established.

In the usual case, it is a custodial mother, either formerly married or never married, who seeks support. Since many single parents are poor enough to receive government assistance, in the past twenty years the federal government has become deeply involved in helping the states obtain and enforce child support orders, which, if paid, would help keep children out of poverty and off of the public assistance rolls.

Mechanisms to enforce child support orders are a feature of the federal legislation passed during the 1970s and 1980s. For example, a 1975 law[13] first allowed garnishment (involuntary withholding) of federal wages and payments (such as federal income tax refund checks) when child support payments are past due. Most relevant to the topic of this book, the 1975 law also committed federal assistance to finding absent parents so that child support orders could be obtained and enforced. The state and federal parent locator services cooperate with each other in sharing information from a variety of sources, including state drivers' license and automobile registration records, tax offices, corrections departments, and the federal Social Security Administration, IRS, selective service system, and Veterans Administration.[14] All parent locator services are obtained through the local child support enforcement office serving the parent to whom child support is owed.

Once a child support order is in place and the absent parent has been located, a variety of strategies are available to insure payment of child support, many of them features of the Child Support Enforcement Amendments of 1984. They include involuntary withholding of payments from the parent's paycheck, intercepting state income tax refunds, and obtaining liens against property (which would require payment of child support arrears out of any profit from sale of a house or business, for example). Some enforcement strategies may be available only for AFDC families or only when payments are in arrears, and specific eligibility should be discussed with a local child support enforcement office.

Child support and visitation. A final issue connected with child support is central to the topic of the absent parent. Should child support and visitation be linked in any way? For example, should the parent who fails to pay support have the right to visit? Or if visits are not permitted, should support be required? These questions are debated, not just in the United States and Canada, but also in other western countries with rising divorce rates, such as the United Kingdom and the Netherlands.[15]

In the United States, various states have different histories of connecting child support and visitation, or, as is the most recent trend, making the two matters independent of each other.[16] In New York, for example, it was the practice fifty to a hundred years ago for separated parents to contract with each other that the father would support the children if permitted to visit them. According to one legal scholar, this may originally have been done because New York state laws required child support only when the children were indigent.[17] Although New York's child support laws now apply to all children, a separation contract that links child support and visitation is still enforceable in that state. In contrast, some states, such as California and Pennsylvania, do not permit the right of visitation and the obligation to support to be linked, while others sometimes allow them to be connected.[18]

Some research studies report that visitation and payment of child support by nonresidential parents go hand in hand, though the underlying link behind the association is harder to identify.[19] In one study of cases from five visitation enforcement programs in different regions of the country, sophisticated data analysis identified conflict over child support and payment patterns as among the key variables contributing to parents' resolution of visitation disputes. The programs were not successful in helping parents reach agreement when "there had been a lot of conflict about child support, poor payment, and history of irregular visitation to begin with."[20]

Termination of Parental Rights and Stepparent Adoption

In certain circumstances, the rights of a parent concerning a child can be permanently removed by the court, either with or without the consent of the parent. Voluntary "termination of parental rights" often happens when the absent parent has been replaced in the child's life by a stepparent, and all parties agree that it is best if the stepparent adopts the child (as in the case of Tom and Candy in the previous chapter). The very serious and comparatively rare step of involuntary termination of parental rights is sometimes taken when the court finds that the parent's actions (or inactions) have been seriously harmful to the child, or that the parent is unfit as a parent, and that it is in the child's interest to have the legal relationship ended.

Adoption, for example by a stepparent, is not possible without termination of the rights of at least one parent (a child can have only two legal parents), and parents who have voluntarily absented themselves from their children's lives should be aware of this possibility. State laws and court precedents vary, and termination of the rights of an absent parent may not require evidence of harm to the child. For example, the U.S. Supreme Court allowed adoption by a stepparent over the objection of a biological (unmarried) father because he had only a "meager" relationship with the child (*Quilloin v. Walcott* [1978]). In that case, he had never had custody or sought it, nor had he contributed significant support,[21] unlike many of the parents described in earlier chapters.

The very limited research concerning stepparent adoptions reveals interesting patterns relating to the absence of a biological parent. In one study, five of the fifty-five noncustodial parents whose children were subsequently adopted by stepparents had visited their children regularly.[22] However, sixty-four percent had provided at least some financial support, and the cancellation of the support order was one factor in the decision of some of the noncustodial parents to agree to the adoption. Although in most cases the adoptions were carried out with the consent of the noncustodial parent, parental rights were terminated involuntarily in twenty-three situations.[23]

Assessing Society's Response to Parental Absence

Summary. As presented earlier in this chapter, the parent who is no longer in contact with a spouse and children loses no status or rights automatically. However, the residential parent may file for separation and divorce and obtain custody of the children in most situations in which the absent parent does not contest. Any prior court order for child support, or any new order made in the parent's absence, can usually be enforced if the absent parent's whereabouts and place of employment can be discovered. The grandparents who are related to the children through their absent son or daughter may be able to gain the right to visit, even if the custodial parent refuses. Further, the absent parent who returns after a period of time ordinarily can obtain a court order allowing visitation, unless there is evidence that visits could harm the children. If the custodial parent should die, the absent parent may well end up with custody. However, prolonged lack of contact between a parent and child can provide grounds for termination of parental rights in some states, a scenario that is likely to be played out primarily in situations where a stepparent wishes to adopt the child.

Trends and directions. As we survey the changes that have taken place over the past thirty years in social policy and law affecting absent parents, certain trends stand out. First, although family law matters are governed by state statutes and handled by state courts, there is a tendency toward somewhat greater interstate uniformity in the areas of child custody, visitation, and support, due in part to the influence of federal legislation and model statutes, such as the Uniform Reciprocal Enforcement of Support Act. Second, matters that once were entirely at the discretion of local judges are increasingly regulated by guidelines, formulas, and preferences that limit judicial discretion. This is particularly true of child support, but also can be noted in statutory presumptions favoring joint custody. Finally, gender is disappearing as an official criterion in many legal matters, including custody and child support,[24] although it certainly remains an influential variable in actual decisions made by parents themselves as well as by courts.

Conclusions

To return to the issues raised at the beginning of this chapter, how fair are the ways in which our society treats absent parents, residential parents, and their children? One helpful way to assess policy is to ask how it affects each party, as well as others not so directly involved.[25]

Although decisions concerning child custody, along with related issues of visitation and child support, are supposed to be made in the interest of children and with attention to their needs, it has frequently been observed that this is not the case.[26] When a parent is out of contact, no automatic social scrutiny or intervention on behalf of the children occurs. A court will examine the issues of custody, visitation, and support only if one parent files a petition. That such issues are resolved primarily on the basis of adult interests is illustrated, for example, by the absence of legal representation for children in most divorce situations and by the fact that, as long as divorcing parents are in agreement, courts rarely question custody and related plans for children. Nor can children in most situations either refuse visits ordered by the court or force a parent to carry out visits as ordered. The parent with visitation is free to visit but is not compelled to do so. And only if a child becomes dependent on welfare does the state take the initiative in pursuing child support from the absent parent.

In most cases involving one parent who is out of contact, the residential parent does pursue divorce, custody, and child support, and may also seek to limit visitation by the nonresidential parent. Being or having been out of contact with the child very frequently works to that parent's disadvantage in court. Further, as a number of the family stories presented in this book illustrate, out-of-contact parents often perceive that they have been treated unfairly by the legal system. They may believe that the courts' orders concerning custody, visitation, and child support favor the other parents for reasons unrelated to ability to care for the children (for example, gender bias, political influence), or they may feel they were successfully vilified in court by their former spouses. Many find the child support they are required to pay burdensome, and some resent their lack of control over how it is spent. Ask the absent parents, and hear that the deck is stacked against them.

It should come as no surprise that residential parents also fault the system, not only for inadequate child support orders and weak enforcement, but also for allowing formerly absent parents to resume visitation, to block adoptions by stepparents, and to take other actions they perceive as interference or even harassment. Some think that the courts do little to protect them and their children from abusive former partners. Residential parents may favor linking child support and visitation only when it gives them greater control ("Payments are in arrears, so I shouldn't have to allow visits"), just as out-of-contact parents favor it when it serves their interests ("I'm not permitted to visit, so I shouldn't have to pay").

The larger society is also affected by policies in the areas we have been examining. Everyone's taxes pay for the cost of litigating cases in court, as well as for public assistance to children not supported by absent parents. As more and more children are reared by one parent, our cultural definitions of family change, demanding change in our social institutions and public services. Schools and other community organizations struggle to deal with children from single-parent families, a burden made heavier when children lack emotional and other supports from both parents.

Although it may appear that social policy in response to parental absence satisfies no one (least of all the unhappy parents interviewed here), there have been some major advances in the past twenty to thirty years that increase fairness in the way decisions are reached and enforced. The process of divorce is swifter, decreasing the time families must await resolution of questions related to custody, visitation, and support. There is less distinction made between children born inside and outside marriage concerning their parents' duties toward them. Gender of the parent is now less likely to govern the outcome of a custody contest or child support petition.

Child support awards are more clearly related to parental income, though a remaining shortcoming is reflected in the huge variation in child support obtained by applying the formulas used in different states. Finally, it is much harder than it was twenty years ago to avoid all child support obligations.

On balance, social policy as it affects absent parents, residential parents, and their children is moving in the direction of more predictable outcomes based on rational considerations. This is the case despite the fact that many individuals affected by parental absence continue to feel wronged in the legal process. That they feel wronged is perhaps an artifact of the win/lose nature of court contests, or it may be that, in reaching decisions based on weighing the various interests involved, courts are rarely able to satisfy everyone.

Chapter 8

When Contact Is Reestablished

Where to Go from Here

While the focus has been on parents not in contact with their children, some do reunite after lengthy periods of separation. In a three-year follow-up interview with thirty parents who participated in the original survey (approximately one-sixth the sample), 30 percent stated contact had increased. Half of the mothers and fathers said nothing had changed in their relationship with the child with whom they were not in contact, and the remaining 20 percent said what minimum contact there may have been had decreased further. Some of the parents interviewed in depth in earlier chapters, such as Kerry in chapter 4, called to tell me that her situation with all her children had improved since our interview. For the parents who were back in contact, almost all reported great satisfaction with the renewed relationship. The parents who were not seeing their children were still mourning the loss of contact but had begun to come to terms with their situations. A few reported that the "ball was in their child's court," giving the impression they were not going to vigorously pursue the children any longer. They believed they had tried everything they could and, in some cases, were following the advice of friends and therapists who encouraged them to move on with their lives.

Is it possible to predict who would have reestablished contact from the parents who participated in the survey? While no clear predictors were found, there was a greater likelihood for parents to increase contact with their child if they had other children whom they were visiting. Parents who said they were out of contact with all of their children when originally surveyed were less likely to cite change.

While parents who do reestablish contact are happier with their situations, it is not easy. For some, the children had moved back in with them after difficulties with the custodial parents. For others, when the child left the custodial parent's home for college or a marital relationship, the child and parent were no longer feeling constricted by the child's living with the custodial parent and a renewal occurred. If we consider this from a social exchange perspective as discussed in chapter 1, we can see that the emotional costs of contact have been diminished when the custodial parent is no longer part of the equation. One father reported, "Now that my daughter is in college and out of her house, things are going fantastically well. I visit her and we communicate by E-mail." (It is interesting to consider in the future whether custodial parents will be able to monitor their children's communication with another parent, now that computerized mail is possible. If a noncustodial parent believes his access to his child is being restricted, he or she can always go on-line to the child.)

I have selected five cases—two mothers, two fathers, and one child—to highlight some of the issues that arise with reconciliation. While each of the parents reports struggles, he or she is more content now than when originally contacted. Following the case examples, I offer a series of proposals for change that will hopefully enhance the lives of parents and children who are on the brink of a cutoff.

MIA

The first example is provided by Mia, who after three years of no contact with her children, slowly reentered each of their lives as they reached their late teens and expressed a need for her. Such a pattern of rebuilding a relationship at this age or in the early twenties is not unusual.

Mia was raised by both her parents. The second of five children, she had a horrific childhood, suffering physical abuse at the hands of her brother over the course of a number of years. Her parents, who were not abusive themselves, were never aware of the violence Mia endured. Upon graduation from high school, she married Frank, a man she had met while working as a salesclerk in a local store. He was four years older than she was and had "been around" much more than Mia. Love was not the reason for the marriage, according to Mia—escape from home was.

The marriage was happy initially. A son was born a year later, and two daughters followed within the next few years. Frank worked in a factory and Mia stayed home, playing the traditional domestic role. As the years wore on, Mia became suspicious of Frank's comings and goings. "He often wasn't where he was supposed to be. He wasn't helping out much around the house, and he'd be gone at odd hours. Finally, I came home one day and found him in our bed with another woman. He wanted me to sit there and have a very civilized discussion with him about the whole thing. I wouldn't do that, so I left."

The children, who were then seventeen, fifteen, and thirteen, were given the option of going with Mia to an apartment or staying in their own home with their father. Mia told them the truth: She would have to find work, they probably would not see her much, and they would not have much money. She was so convincing about the state of their economic situation that the children decided to stay with their father. Other factors may have convinced them, also. "My ex would give the kids anything they wanted. He set no rules, didn't care if my son had a girlfriend over or anything. Who wants to be with their mother when they can do all of that?"

Mia made the conscious decision not to seek custody. "It would cost me too much money up front to go to a lawyer and fight for them. Besides, they were teenagers and did not want to be with their mother. Frank also threatened me by saying he wouldn't pay any support, and winter was coming on. I worried that I would not be able to adequately house the children if I kept them. There never was any real custody or visitation agreement. The kids just wanted to go to school and have fun. I was ordered to pay child support, but he was also supposed to pay me maintenance. He didn't pay me, so I didn't pay him. He had everything. I had nothing.

"There was a hearing at one point because of some unpaid bills, and it got into the visitation question. Frank brought up that I never saw the kids, and he twisted everything. The judge was supportive of me but thought that the kids couldn't be forced to see me when they are teens."

Apparently, according to Mia, the children fell into a pattern of not seeing her for the next three years. Mia chalks this up to their father discouraging contact and distracting them with fun and games whenever they discussed wanting to see her. "They just didn't realize how much time had flown by," Mia told me. "There were no arguments, they didn't curse me for leaving. They just wanted their freedom!"

A letter Mia sent me two years before I interviewed her describes this period of her life and shows how misconceptions can be engendered about who left whom. She wrote, "My son is the one I am most concerned about now [because of his alcoholism]. He asked why I left. I didn't want to place blame on his father, though it was his fault. What can I say? I saved myself and tried to face my children. I'm not sorry for what I've done. I was honest with them. It was very difficult for me to let go of them."

During the three year period of no contact, Mia kept up her own battle to visit. She wrote them constantly, sent them notes and small gifts on holidays and birthdays, and let them know she was always willing to talk with them. She also attended school events and watched them from afar, without interfering in their lives.

Her children were having problems, though. Her son (as mentioned in her letter to me) became an alcoholic. Her oldest daughter, Jan, dropped out of high school when Frank would not let her attend an alternative school that may have been better suited to her learning needs.

Mia began working for a newspaper clipping service and noticed her youngest daughter had scored a winning goal during a high school soccer game. She called the child's school and left a message of congratulations and promptly received a phone call from the daughter. They talked for five hours and began rebuilding their relationship. Jan called her a few months later and said she had a surprise for her. She brought over her fiancé and announced she was pregnant. Together, they celebrated the impending birth of the child and the birth of a new mother-daughter relationship. Finally, Mia reconnected with her son when she asked him to help plan his sister's baby shower. Mother and son have been close ever since and talk almost every day. The alcoholism is being worked on.

Mia thinks part of the impetus for her youngest daughter's willingness to call her was the daughter's increasing dissatisfaction with her own home life. Frank had remarried, and the daughter could not stand her new stepmother. Frank would sometimes go carousing for hours and leave the daughter alone. Despite this, the daughter still refuses to move in with Mia, preferring the comforts that her father can afford.

Is there bad blood between Mia and her children after being out of touch for so long? "No. We don't talk about the past. We just pick up on our relationship where it is right now. If we dwelled on the past, we would have to get into a lot of other stuff that I don't think would be helpful to talk about!"

How do the children see this? How do they justify not seeing their mother for a few years?

Jan: A Daughter's Perspective. I interviewed Jan, who is now the mother of two small children. She was eager to speak with me and gave the following rendition of that period of their lives.

"We lost contact with my mom over two and half years. She made us really angry because we [the children] felt she was going to put my father through the wringer, take him for all his money. She was pretty mean during this time. In fact, she has always been pretty mean. When I graduated from high school, she was upset I called to invite her to a graduation party instead of sending her a written invitation. She said she wasn't going to go. Another time I got into a car accident, and she was mad that I called my father first and not her.

"We also stopped talking to her because she would just blow things out of proportion. Or she'd call the house and get real mad on the phone, and we wouldn't want to deal with that, and after a while she stopped calling."

Jan thinks that even though her brother speaks with Mia, he is still angry at her for trying to take all of their father's money. "I have to tell my brother to call because he wouldn't talk to her otherwise."

Both mother and daughter seem to agree to not discuss the past. "I am still angry a bit but don't talk to her about it much. It is pretty much behind us. My father thinks it is okay for us to see her and tries to protect her sometimes by not letting us bad-mouth her. Our relationship has been getting better. Sometimes she flakes out and yells, and I tell her to stop it and that works."

For this family, things are better but it has been a struggle. From the eldest daughter's perspective, the need to rebuild a relationship supersedes any negative feelings she and her brother may have about Mia's behavior. The youngest daughter, who called Mia from school, is the child who reportedly has the best relationship with Mia. They reconnected because Mia continued to push for more contact. Part of their coming to grips with their relationship now is learning what to talk about and what to avoid. The children are also learning how to cope with a mother who they perceive to be difficult. Here we also see the different pictures each generation paints. Mia blames Frank; the children blame Mia's behavior. Personalities obviously clashed. The picture is similar to what we have seen in patterns in earlier chapters. Mia sees it one way and the children another.

CURTIS

Whereas Mia was pushed out of her relationship with her children, Curtis initiated the separation with his eldest daughter while maintaining custody of the youngest (a reminder that these parents often have differential relationships with their children). A forty-six-year-old factory worker, Curtis, unlike all the other parents I have interviewed, appeared totally unfazed by the two-year separation.

His own upbringing was unusual and may offer a clue as to his seemingly indifferent view of parent-child relationships. He was raised by his grandparents after his twenty-one-year-old father left town with another woman. His mother filed for divorce but because of her young age did not win custody of the children. Curtis and his brother went to live with his paternal grandparents. As Curtis told me, "This made my father my brother; my one real brother was sort of like a nephew. My grandparents adopted me because neither my father or my mother was too good a parent."

He met his future wife at the time of his discharge from the service and her graduation from high school. They married three years later and both began working in local factories. The marriage was shaky at first. "She was a spoiled brat. Things improved after a while, and then things got worse when the kids [two daughters] were born."

When Curtis was laid off from his job, the marriage unwound further. For the next few years he began spending a lot of time at home, and, he believes, she became jealous of his relationship with the children. The marriage deteriorated to the point that they had a violent confrontation. "I threatened to leave with my oldest daughter and go to California. My ex screamed at me and I nailed her. It was the only time I hit her. The cops came and everything. After that she straightened out pretty good."

A few months later she refused to have sex with him and began a series of affairs. In retaliation, Curtis said, he also began to fool around. When he was called back to work on the early morning shift, he was able to maintain a high level of involvement with his children that his wife's schedule did not permit. A year later, in 1992, they separated.

"My oldest daughter was in college at the time, and I eventually gained custody of my youngest, who was seventeen. She first lived with her mother because that was close to her school. Then her mother threw her out of the house. I don't know exactly why she was thrown out, but I heard it was because there was a stolen camera and my ex got angry and told her to get the hell out. My ex fought to get her back, but I got custody because I was more responsible. My ex was unstable. Everything was party time, and she wants things when she wants them."

While raising his youngest daughter, a blowup between him and his college-age daughter led to a two-year period during which they never saw each other and barely communicated. Curtis lays the reasons for the cut off on the demise of his marriage. "A girl had moved in with me, and I would talk openly to her about my feelings toward my ex, which weren't positive. She had taken off with another guy. My daughter heard those things and got real angry. Then she was telling me to be more assertive, and she was manipulating her mother. She was having a lot of emotional problems and I got a letter from her college about her problems, and told her to get to a psychologist. Everything was building up. One time she was screaming at me and I told her to get the hell out. I did not see her after that for a few years."

Curtis seemed relieved not to see her because of the turmoil she was causing. He sent her cards on her birthday and Christmas and would get an occasional call, but no time was spent together. Unlike most parents, he did not seem to second-guess himself or feel any pain, loss, or guilt over the distance. "I figured she'll settle down. Then she called me out of the blue to tell me she was getting married, and would I visit her new home? She met someone she liked, and that may have cooled her down a bit. So we started seeing each other again." Typical of his demeanor and the lack of regret he felt at not seeing his daughter, he told me, "It wasn't hard for me to see her again after two years."

In this situation, a divorce added fuel to an already unstable family. Curtis and his daughter would probably not have dropped out of touch with each other if not for the divorce. But a combination of factors—the anger generated from the breakup, the daughter's feeling torn between her divorcing parents, the presence of a new woman in her father's life, and Curtis's bad-mouthing of her mother—pushed the relationship over the edge. The combination of maturation and a family event (the daughter's new home and marriage) sparked the reconciliation. Here the daughter initiated it. It is clear from the kind of person Curtis is that he would not have made the first move. His early upbringing most likely left him well defended from his own feelings. Expressing a desire to see his own daughter may have reignited feelings about his separation from his mother. Feeling out of control in that situation, he was not willing to admit feeling out of control with his daughter (or with the incident in which he hit his wife).

As in the previous case, the relationship started up again without much discussion. It is going smoothly now, according to Curtis.

TYRONE

Tyrone, an African-American father, never married Renee, the mother of his son, Lewis. He might have been viewed at one time as the typical young man who dropped out after insemination. These young men are often described in the social science literature and the media as part of the reason for the rise in the number of young unmarried mothers. They are viewed as the youths who are only out for a good time and who, when faced with parenting responsibilities, disappear into the neighborhood. Nothing would be further from the truth in Tyrone's case. Tyrone was never encouraged to have contact with his child, even though he wanted it. He had to fight for that right in court.

Raised by his mother and stepfather, Tyrone has not seen his own biological father since he was seven and still feels he suffers from his father's departure. Tyrone had known Renee when they were young and growing up on the same block in Baltimore. After high school, Tyrone moved out of state for a year before returning. He and Renee quickly become reacquainted. One year later, Lewis was born. "I was raised to be responsible [while, by implication, his father was not]. As I grew up, the responsibility stayed with me, and it was never a challenge. When my son was born, I was enthusiastic to be a father.

"We had never shared a home," Tyrone told me, "yet we had a child. But Renee didn't want anything to do with me from the start. I could tell when I first visited them in the hospital. She wanted to be in control. She wasn't happy with the idea of sharing anything, least of all Lewis. I felt at that time that I never had the chance to establish a decent relationship with my son. I knew I wouldn't get a chance to see him graduating from school, or to be with him for his first birthday party or on Father's Day. She told me she did not want me around."

It is not uncommon for a mother in this situation to discourage visitation by the father. She may feel that there is no future to their relationship, that the father will be a bad influence, and that her life will be easier if she and her parents raise the child without interference. This happened with Lewis. He was raised by Renee and her parents with little input from Tyrone and his mother, who were allowed only an occasional visit. In addition to the possessiveness at the root of Renee's blocking visitation, according to Tyrone ("She treated him like jewelry or a car, something to show off"), Renee may also have had realistic concerns about the people Tyrone was consorting with and where he was living. Tyrone admitted, "Renee never felt that we were capable of taking full responsibility for him and being adequate parents and grandparents." It is hard to know why she had these concerns.

The pattern of infrequent contact continued for years, with Tyrone often going many months without seeing Lewis. Finally, and after considerable reflection about his own loss of contact with his biological father, Tyrone became fed up. "I couldn't tolerate not having the opportunity to establish a relationship with my son." Tyrone was also in a new relationship with a woman who was supportive of his seeing Lewis. He sued for visitation.

"When I went to court, Renee tried to convince the judge that she had no problems with him seeing me but she did not want the child around certain people and in certain neighborhoods. My position is that as long as he is in my custody, nothing will happen. It doesn't matter who I'm with, I will protect him." After a lengthy battle, and an unsubstantiated allegation of child abuse against Tyrone by Renee, he won regular visitation.

Reuniting with Lewis was not easy at first. "He was six and he didn't really know me. He would cry when his mother would leave him here. But with time, it has gotten easier. I have had to work hard as a father. I know he needs to be with other children and I'll take him to the park to play with them. He was shy at first, but now we are getting along better. Even when I don't feel like taking him, I know I have to motivate myself to do it. It is part of being a father. I love my son very much: he is able to see that I was a loving father to him."

In this situation, as in patterns identified in earlier chapters, the custodial parent was blocking contact. Only through the father's legal action was visitation established. The child was passive in the decision making about contact, unlike Mia's and Curtis's situations, where the children's personalities played a significant role. Unlike other cases, there is no substantial indication of incompetence on the mother's part. She seems to have been acting in what she perceived to be Lewis's best interests, though she was described as being possessive. She had concerns about the environment Lewis was going to be placed in when visiting Tyrone. Tyrone's own coming of age, his insight into his relationship with his father, and the support of another woman propelled him to want greater involvement. Tyrone readily described Lewis's initial problems with reestablishing contact, which he correctly labels as normal for a child that age. His awareness and accurate understanding of Lewis's emotions should pave the way for an easy transition.

BEATRICE

This last case is complicated by the number of children involved, the seeming intransigence of the custodial father, the shifting loyalties of the family members, and the perceived ineptitude of the legal representation. Beatrice ultimately gave up her custody rights so that she could see her children again and yet still faces adversities.

Beatrice did not see four of her seven children for almost two years. The oldest, Nicolle, was born while Beatrice was single and in high school. The four she lost contact with were the product of her first marriage. Two more children were the product of a second marriage. Now raising a grandson from Nicolle's marriage, and her two youngest, Beatrice's house is quite full. Two years before I conducted our lengthy interview, she sought me out after reading one of my articles. At the time, she was not seeing the four children. She lamented the state of her court case and identified the quintessential issue facing women who seek custody in court. "I did not know how emotional to be in presenting my case. I always thought the courts were there to protect both sides, but they are not. If we react or don't react [in court], we don't love our kids." In other words, if a mother wants custody and is emotional in presentation, the judge may decide she is too hysterical and unfit. But if a mother is unemotional, the judge may think she is not warm and loving enough. Now, two years later, she has reestablished contact and is struggling to rebuild what she has lost. It has not been easy.

Born in the late 1950s, Beatrice was one of three children raised by both parents. Her father, coincidentally, lost contact with two children of his from a previous marriage, causing Beatrice to wonder if history repeats itself. She never met her half siblings. "I know he tried to contact them at one point, but his first wife wanted nothing to do with him. Whenever I tried to ask him about them, he didn't want to talk about it."

Beatrice's adolescent years were disrupted when she dropped out of school to give birth following an unplanned pregnancy. She and her parents raised her daughter until Beatrice could move out on her own. She met her future husband, Duke, while both were working at a nearby motel. They married two years later when she was twenty-one. He had just started law school.

"The marriage was unhappy from the start. I didn't know anybody in the law school community. I got pregnant right away and Duke had a bad temper and felt he was too young to be tied down. He adopted Nicolle, which was nice, but it may have added to his feeling trapped." The marriage never improved, even though three other children were born over the next seven years.

Finally, Duke's flagrant infidelity brought the relationship to a close. "He cheated on me—and with his secretary. I ignored some of his affairs, but when he was carrying on in our house, that was it. I had been an angel until that point, but when I learned about his behavior I took off on a different course. He only became violent with me when I asked him to leave. At first he refused but then, finally, he agreed."

The battle for the children did not start immediately with Duke's departure. The couple went to mediation. Duke had never been interested in the five children until the breakup and was content to have Beatrice raise them the first three years after the divorce. During this time both remarried.

Life for Beatrice, her new husband, her five children, and her two new children from the second marriage was not easy. Her eldest son, then fourteen, began acting out and playing hooky. Her second son was expelled when he brought a gun to school. He was eleven at the time.

It got worse. "We were in family therapy, and my first son became verbally abusive to my husband and me. I tried to work it out, but I felt like a bad mother. He called me a bitch, a slut, a whore, and my husband a no-good bum. Duke told my son he would try for custody, and that he wouldn't get in so much trouble if he changed homes.

"Then things happened so fast. The four children I had with Duke came home from visitation one night and told me that Duke was going to get custody. My attorney received papers demanding a custody review, but I was told there wouldn't be a hearing. Then I was told there would be a hearing. I changed attorneys, and the new one did not show up for court. I lost custody of all four because the kids and I didn't show up. It was illegal but they did it."

The story becomes more complicated here. Beatrice was granted temporary visitation by Duke while a court date was pending to determine visitation. Then her eldest son became violent with Duke and tried to choke him to death. A hastily called court date concluded with the pronouncement that Beatrice should not have visitation because she was trying to encourage violence between her son and Duke. Beatrice blames her new attorney for allowing this to happen. "We had switched judges, and my attorney was lax in taking care of this. My ex finally said I could see the kids if I agreed to not go for custody. I could see them on his terms. I got the order barring visitation stricken, but I couldn't get the kids returned. I was allowed to go to the kids' activities if I could find out about them, but it was difficult to get their schedules. I went to one game and kissed my son hello, and his stepmother stepped in and whisked him away. I begged her, 'Just let me say hello to my son.'"

Beatrice then went for months without seeing them because the children refused visitation. Her attorney advised her to not call because they would consider that harassment. She moved to a new home and could not get the children her new number. Court evaluations were ordered as battles over visitation raged. The court-appointed psychologist favored mother–child visits, according to Beatrice, yet she still could not get her due.

After a year of legal wrangling and psychiatric evaluations, Duke won sole custody. The reasons were that Beatrice was not emotionally competent and did not have the financial resources that the children's father did. "But we were not in the same psychological situation. He had custody and I did not. Of course he would cope better! At that point, my attorney was not doing anything and couldn't even set up visitation. I decided to write a letter to my ex and say I would not go for custody. So I went back on his terms. He held all the cards. With that established, I began to see my children again. Since then I have seen them in counseling and I have visitation; sometimes I even have them for the whole summer. My visitation with the kids should not depend on my relationship with my ex, but it does."

When there is a reconciliation after so much acrimony, it can be a slow process with fits and starts. Resentment can take a long time to clear up. "My eldest son is back living with me now. I wish things could be different for the other children. I still get a lot of 'why can't we live with you instead of Dad?' They never did request to live with him instead of me, though they did refuse to see me for a while—probably because of Duke's influence. I'm seeing them again, but things aren't great. I got kicked in the crotch three months ago by my ten-year-old daughter.

"I wish my children and I had more to say to each other, but we don't and I get resentful. My new husband won't go to sessions. He's nice when Duke is here, but we lost two babies through miscarriages during the fighting with Duke and he has seen me go through a lot of pain, so it's hard for him."

Renewed contact often opens up new conflicts for ex-spouses. Triangulation between Beatrice, her ex-husband, and the children was one manifestation. "Things are going well between us some of the time, but I don't like my ten-year-old saying she'll go tell Dad if things are not going well. We aren't automatically over what we were going through. Maybe I am a slow healer. But the pain of not seeing the children was worse and still lingers. I wish their feelings were more acknowledged by the counselor and Duke."

In looking back on the experience of not seeing her children, Beatrice says, "I never had the chance to present my side of the case in court. It doesn't matter anymore but it does make me feel incomplete, like the situation wasn't finished. No one could understand what was going on. A lot of research is being done on grief, and I cannot figure out why, if you have a baby born dead, every one is understanding, yet there is no understanding of the loss of children that you have been taking care of after a custody fight. I was treated like a loony tune because I was grief-stricken. And I held up better than a lot of people I have seen."

Nicolle: A Daughter's Perspective. I received permission from Beatrice to call her twenty-year-old daughter, Nicolle, the child Beatrice conceived while still in high school. I thought her view would be helpful in corroborating Beatrice's story.

I asked Nicolle why her mother had lost contact with the other children.

"I believe it happened because Duke was being vindictive. He said he wanted custody because he was concerned about their schooling. But when we were younger he never cared about our education. He was too wrapped up in his own life and in TV."

Nicolle has tried to establish a separate relationship with her half siblings, one that would not be affected by the problems her mother was having with Duke. Duke initially agreed to her visiting, and then stipulated that the visits had to be short and he and his new wife had to be present. Hearing that, Nicolle backed down and went for eighteen months without seeing them.

The children were not passive in their attempts to see Nicolle. "One time one of the boys ran away but couldn't find us. When Duke found him, he beat him up." I asked why the children did not know where she and her mother lived. "Because we had moved during that period of time to get away from my dad. My mom and her husband couldn't afford to keep the house, and she had to move because Dad was spying on them. If we moved out of the county in which he had contacts, my mom thought the custody case would be heard by a more favorable judge!"

Nicolle was not optimistic about the other children's well-being. "The kids are scared because Dad is abusive and intimidating. He and his new wife went to their school and said their biological mother was killed and that one of the boys was delusional when he mentioned her. He really screwed with the kids' minds.

"I'm a threat to him, so he is leery about talking to me because it will come out about the emotional abuse. We kind of mutually hated each other, so he didn't seek custody of me. He talked to the school guidance counselor about how nutty I was, so I dropped out of school. He gained custody illegally. Mom sunk thousands of dollars into the custody battles, and her health wasn't any good. In the end she just signed away almost all her rights to see them again."

These are painful situations born of years of fighting and vindictiveness. As can be seen, especially from the perspective of a child in the family, the fallout from a cutoff and attempts at reconciliation can be enormous. If the parent with custody wants to block contact (one of the most common patterns) and continues to make life hellish for the other parent, he can.

While these four cases are presented primarily from the parents' perspectives, in keeping with the spirit of the book, I would like to conclude with a brief view offered solely by a child.

JULIE

Julie, a ten-year-old, illustrates the part that significant family events, unrelated to a relationship, can play in bridging the gap between family members.

Julie stopped seeing her father after her parents broke up. She began having difficulties in school and at home. Her mother sought help from a local mental health clinic, and Julie willingly entered a therapy group for children of divorce. With the help of the therapist, she began writing letters to her father, a common activity in these types of groups. Her letters usually described how she was spending her day and ended with a plea for him to call her. He was unresponsive. The therapist working with her hypothesizes that, as time wore on, it became increasingly difficult for him to admit he had messed up their relationship. Reconnecting with Julie and making such an admission was too painful for him and would have required him to examine other mistakes he may have made in the father-daughter relationship and in the marriage. Ignoring her was easier.

When Julie's paternal grandmother died, she went to the funeral and saw her father for the first time in two years. That became the impetus for the reconciliation. Now in therapy together, they are working on their burgeoning relationship. She had reached out to him and was rejected. Had it not been for some other family event, something as unfortunate as a grandmother's death, it is impossible to know how long he would have gone before responding to her cries for attention.

Each of these is an example of a cutoff and then reconnection between parent and child. For some, it is working out, while for others, such as Beatrice, the relationship remains tenuous. As mentioned, we possess no models or images for how parents and children can reunite after months or years of separation. Images of children cooking and playing with their parents, or being read to or playing catch abound. But where are the pictures of children and parents who have been separated by divorce and then reconnect? We need to construct them out of reality so that family members can know what to expect.

Where to Go from Here

It is obvious that disjunctures between parents and children after divorce happen for a variety of reasons. These include issues related to the absent parent—wanting to avoid paying child support, having substance abuse or emotional problems, and shirking parental responsibility. But they also include the more complicated ones that are the focus of this book—being blocked from contact, dealing with allegations of abuse, having relationship difficulties with children, and being seen as incompetent by the custodial parent.

These cutoffs present a serious problem for our society and have long-term implications for the growth and development of children and families. Some parents and their children suffer enormously when there is no contact. Even when contact resumes, the pain continues, as is shown in this chapter. Once a break occurs, resewing the family ties in a way that is comfortable for all is a daunting task.

Six proposals, broader in scope than the individually directed suggestions provided in the next chapter, can be put forth to help with these issues, but first, two statements need to be made.

1. Divorce will not stop in the foreseeable future. Some community leaders as well as authors of recent books attack the notion of divorce, citing it as the core of American social problems. It is too easy to get a divorce when "no-fault" reasons can be given for separating, it is argued. Given the chicken-egg nature of this point (Are divorce and single parenthood causing social problems or are social problems causing single parenthood?), this is hard to debate. Making it harder to get a divorce is not the answer, except for the person who wants to hold on to the marriage. The process is far from pain-free. Certainly emphasizing the importance of family and keeping the family together can reap significant benefits. Making it easier for couples to work out marital problems will save some relationships. But attempts at family preservation should not come at the expense of those who need to divorce because they are desperately unhappy or in danger or have divorced. Focusing on the strengths of family togetherness and not the weaknesses of the single-parent family is one approach to dealing with the terribly complex set of behaviors that accompany family life. If the emphasis on keeping families together results in single-parent families being ignored or stigmatized (although in some neighborhoods, such families are the norm, rather than the exception),[1] we have failed to provide a healthier atmosphere for families.

2. Not all cut-offs between parent and child can be prevented. Wise social interventions attempt to meet the needs of the greatest number of people while recognizing that not all people can be reached by those interventions. We will always have children and parents who lose contact after divorce. Not all relationships can be worked out or should be expected to within a required time period. Humans are complicated beings and have to cope with multiple stressors after a breakup. Such is our nature. This is not

to say that attempts should not be made to improve relationships either through social policy reform or personal attempts (a point I will return to). Rather, it is to caution that some problems will be unsolvable or difficult to resolve.

Proposal Number 1

An aggressive approach I favor would be to require some marital counseling before granting a divorce. This might help those marriages that could be saved. In an attempt to stop problems even before they develop, some states are going further and are considering charging more for a marriage license if the couple does not go for pre-marital counseling. If that fails, at the time of the breakup, we should reinforce for parents the importance of both having contact. This can be accomplished by requiring everyone who gets separated to attend a lecture or discussion group about the aftermath of separation and divorce (many states already have in place some type of formal intervention). At least two different educational-type programs, focusing on the short term, have proven successful.[2] Such group programs could speak specifically to the ongoing needs of children to have contact with both parents.

Yet what the interviews in this book show is that these particular problematic relationships evolve over time. While a range of individual and programmatic interventions are the basis for addressing them, they must be undertaken with an awareness of how people change within months of a breakup.

With this in mind, mediation alone for cases of divorce is not sufficient. *Timely* mediation is what is needed. By this I mean that many families would benefit from returning at six-month intervals after a settlement so that the wisdom of that arrangement can be assessed and kinks in it can be ironed out.[3] Maccoby and Mnookin write of the value of mediation followed by evaluation in California. Divorce is an emotional process, and people often are less receptive to education about divorce in its earliest stages. When the dust settles and new issues arise, interventions may also prove effective. A program designed to automatically assist families after six months may have helped some of those families I interviewed. Perhaps festering wounds could have been lanced and cleaned, or miscommunication could have been straightened out. Even eighteen months after separation, the time when some states grant a divorce, could be an opportunity again for intervention.

Problems also develop years later, when children reach new developmental stages, as needs change, or parents remarry. No government-sponsored programmatic solution that tracks down people after a divorce is finalized is realistic. Only community-sponsored approaches (run by churches, schools, et cetera) addressing potential pitfalls and attended on a voluntary basis would be possible.

Proposal Number 2

We must fully appreciate the great diversity of experiences in this troubled sample of parents.[4] I interviewed families who are struggling with such diverse issues as child support payments, alcoholism, drug abuse, domestic violence, infidelity, physical health problems (both acute and chronic), mental health issues, physical and sexual abuse, neglect, prostitution, physical distance, emotional distance, theft, court systems that were unresponsive, child protection agencies and police departments that were unhelpful, runaway behavior, remarriage and divided loyalties, feelings akin to posttraumatic stress, and refusal to follow court orders. The parents came from a variety of racial and ethnic backgrounds, had a great deal or little education, and ranged from being poor to financially well-off. Children I spoke with were angry, hurt, disillusioned, wary, and untrusting of the adults in their lives. I also interviewed families with enormous strengths who, even though they had encountered the above, were able to overcome the impediments that such issues posed for them. Yet almost every single person with whom I spoke felt great pain from being out of touch with a child or a parent.

While these families have all arrived at the same point of no contact, their paths there are remarkably different. We need to reconceptualize how we think about and how we act toward these parents and their children. Our reactions to and treatment of the parents will affect how the children feel about themselves. As we all struggle to understand who we are, we need to have an accurate portrayal of who our parents or guardians are. Assuming a bias a priori against an out-of-contact parent can only be harmful.

When we think about the diversity of parents and loss of contact, the following specific points should be considered:

• At least four different themes can be found underpinning the reasons why parents do not have contact. Mothers' and fathers' reasons differ to some degree, and children often present a variation on the parents' stories.
• Parents sometimes lose contact with one child but not with the next. This point is worth reiterating because it counters the notion that parents who are out of touch are monolithically bad people. Variability and, again, diversity of experiences are more the themes.

• Reconnecting so that children and parents feel comfortable with each other is difficult to accomplish.

Proposal Number 3

Because of the diversity of families, an array of interventions is needed as we try to alleviate some of the problems associated with parents and children losing contact. One approach is to reach out to fathers. All over the country fathering programs are being set up geared toward specific subpopulations of fathers, ranging from African-American fathers to Head Start fathers, poor fathers, middle-income fathers, and divorced fathers. They focus both on those living away from as well as those living with their children. These programs offer everything from individual and group support to family counseling, parenting classes, mentoring by other fathers, and legal advice. With fatherlessness being called one of the major problems facing America, and with there being, according to one estimate, 180 neighborhoods where father-absence characterizes at least 90 percent of the families, grassroots and national efforts need to be supported.[5] The work of the National Institute for Responsible Fatherhood and Family Development is one such effort reporting success in building notions of responsible fatherhood in African-American males.[6] These approaches should not include pushing mothers out of their role in the family.

Another broad approach is to form stronger relationships with mothers. While teen and welfare mothers have historically been the targets of parenting classes and many social programs designed to enhance parenting skills and the quality of life for those with low incomes, little seems to exist for mothers who are not in those particular populations. The exceptions are grassroots efforts offered by such organizations as Parents without Partners and Mothers without Custody. Perhaps because mothers are "supposed" to know how to parent and usually have custody, such efforts as cited to involve fathers are assumed to not be needed for mothers. Yet I wonder how many of the women I have interviewed would have been helped by institutionalized programs for women, by support centers for mothers in their twenties to fifties that are there when the mothers need them, rather than when they happen to be generated on an ad hoc basis. Are mothers who are on the cusp of losing custody being left in the dust in the rush to bring the father back into the family? Consideration of their situation is obviously needed.

Finally, the situation of the children needs to approached through a variety of school, community, and religious-based experiences that range from the educative to therapeutic. We cannot approach these families just through the adults. Discussions in schools, for example, about the great diversity in families, about the impact of divorce on feelings and the development of relationships, may help to ease the difficult transitions that children face. While open discussion of these issues is occurring in some communities, others fear that such discussions will tear at the fabric of the family. I believe denial of the reality of divorce will only contribute to the growth of a generation unable to cope with the potential uncertainties of long-term relationships.

Proposal Number 4

Court personnel, including judges and mental health evaluators, need to recognize the emotional processes that parents like these in this book are going through with a divorce. While much has been written about divorce in general, little is known about the parents who have lost touch and want to reestablish contact. For example, if a parent is having a strong emotional reaction to not seeing his or her child for a while and displays that reaction in court or during the custody evaluation process, it might work against the parent increasing contact. By the same token, if the parent does not seem particularly upset about the custody arrangement, especially if it is a mother, that in turn may work against the parent because the impression may be left that the parent is unfeeling.

The court personnel also need to be aware of how parents who are out of contact may be in a state of unrecognized mourning, as were many of the parents I interviewed. This state goes unacknowledged because society tends to stigmatize these parents and not give them permission to express loss. No ritual exists that identifies this type of loss as normative. With death, neighbors and friends pay their condolences, send flowers or food. A series of common steps are taken. Not when a parent stops seeing a child. An understanding that this mourning process may be occurring can make court evaluations and interventions more effective. These parents are a unique population.

Proposal Number 5

Tone down the rhetoric about "deadbeat" fathers and mothers. I hope it is clear that in many cases it is more complicated than an election-year sound bite. Replace "deadbeat" with something more descriptive, such as "parents who are not paying the support they owe." We need child support payments from those who can pay but refuse. This is a serious problem. But let us not tar every absent father and mother with the same brush and treat them as if their issues are similar. Some parents are in arrears financially, but still provide attention. Others send money but never visit. Absent may mean different things in different contexts.[7] If money is all we are interested in collecting from these parents, if we are not interested in their giving love, support, and attention to their children, then money is all that we are likely to get in the best of circumstances.

At the same time, some fathers' rights organizations (and some mothers' rights organizations) need to clarify their mission and tone down their rhetoric.[8] Communication between the sexes, rather than retribution, should be the goal. Meetings that turn into free-for-alls and attacks on women (or men) can be destructive to everyone involved. They lead to an armed-camp mentality, rather than to a focus on reconciliation.

Final Proposal

When the proposition is put forth that children should not see the visiting parent if there is conflict between the parents, the answer is not to cut out the visiting parent—it is to work on the parents' relationship to the extent possible so the child can have the benefit of a mother and a father. In many of these cases, mediation had not occurred. In others, therapeutic interventions had failed. But should the result of such failures be to stop visitation? Parents need to operate under the assumption that other methods should be tried to gain resolution if initial attempts fail. Over time, emotions may cool and clearer heads may prevail (as happened with some of the parents here). When divorcing parents make a commitment to work on their continuing parenting relationship for the benefit of the child, a strong message is sent to the child about the nature of responsibility and the possibilities in life for growth and change.

It is the responsibility of parents to do everything in their power to ease the pain for their children. Children's needs must remain primary because it is they who are apt to suffer the most from the loss of contact. One would hope that, through greater understanding about how parent-child relations after divorce can falter, we can shore them up!

Chapter 9

Prevention and Resolution

Advice for Parents and Children

The previous eight chapters represent the results of a study and a commentary on legal and social policy issues. There is much that can be learned from the parents interviewed for this book and from literature on divorce and mental health counseling. In this chapter, I draw on these sources and offer concrete suggestions to parents in a self-help format for prevention of a loss of contact and for resolution when a loss does occur.

Legion are the stories in this book from fathers, mothers, and children who are suffering enormous pain due to a lack of contact. For some parents, the cessation of contact becomes a defining event in their life. It is as if a part of them stopped developing. The months go by but their lives cannot get on track. A valuable source of definition is gone from their lives and the future possibility of a child as a resource in old age is severely jeopardized. For children, the same can be true. Attempts to grow up and sustain intimate relations are hindered. Every setback in a relationship is viewed as being the result of parental absenteeism. The parent as resource, influence, and caretaker is missing. For some children, the wounds may never heal.

Financially, with a divorce comes a diminution in resources, even if the visiting parent is paying support. If that parent is absent, money and other in-kind assistance (gifts, clothing, et cetera) may have stopped completely. When child support is not paid, the family can face great hardships. We have heard of children going to school feeling poorly clothed, others being withdrawn from private schooling, and families selling cherished homes. Legal battles soak up money as warring parents pour their resources into others' pockets rather than into the family savings accounts. Time off from work for court appearances, psychological testing, and mediation are costly on both financial and emotional levels.

The struggle over contact often comes on the heels of a marital separation and divorce, which exacts a significant toll in and of itself. The breakup signals a time of great ambivalence for both partners. One or both partners may have been threatening such a move for months or years, thereby weakening the resolve each brought to the relationship and the benefits derived from it. The final decision to separate usually accompanies a time of great hurt, loss, and anger. With the separation, partners often go through an identity crisis, which may be minor or significant depending on the level of emotional development each has achieved individually.[1] For divorcing parents, even as decisions about parent-child contact are evolving, emotional stability is tenuous.

Life Spheres

Knowing this, how can we stop parents and children from losing touch with each other? Before I give suggestions for intervention, it is important to consider the social, structural, emotional, and legal spheres of these parents' lives. Like concentric circles, each sphere influences the others and affects the parents' abilities to maintain contact with their children. Whatever suggestions are made must be considered in the context of these spheres. These influences often work to pull families apart rather then keep them together. A cutoff between a parent and child does not take place in a vacuum.

The Social Sphere: Its Effect on Contact

The social sphere of divorce refers to the public side of life as influenced by friends and community standards. Reactions and messages a parent or child receives from family members, friends, and the community about divorce or about another family member will have an impact on contact. The following are ways these messages might appear:

- Friends and family are telling a child he is better off without his mother because she is interested in having a career *and* motherhood.
- A teacher conveys to a custodial mother that both parents are not needed for a conference.
- Fathers are a rare sight in a community and are made to feel uncomfortable when they do appear.
- Narrow gender roles are assigned to both mothers and fathers, and those who move out of those roles are seen as unfeminine or unmasculine.

Whereas these are negative inducements for contact, the wider community can have a positive influence, too. If a religious leader or the president of the United States uses his or her position of authority and emphasizes the importance of fathers and mothers staying involved, the message can affect the actions of parents and children after divorce. Clergy can teach congregants about the importance of their commitment to their children. Prenuptial counseling can reinforce this message. The parents of newborns who are receiving religious rites can be told that their obligation to their child is lifelong. Grassroots efforts can assist here, also.[2] In these ways, in the social sphere, the community in its broadest sense can work for or against a parent staying in contact.

The Structural Sphere: Its Effect on Contact

The structural aspects of divorce refer to the physical dimensions that separate parents and children. Family developments always impose some impediments to contact on divorced parents and their children. Typically after a breakup, physical distance grows between family members as one parent moves first to a new home, then to another home, and to a different job or a new relationship. Each move can be a few miles away or across the United States. The greater the distance (and the more difficult the transportation between the two areas), the higher the likelihood that contact will diminish. If a mother visited her children every other weekend and once during the week when she lived five minutes away, a new home two hours away will have a significant impact on the midweek visits. Age will also interfere with contact. Some separation, with the advent of the teen years, occurs even in never-divorced families. The older the children, the more likely that school and peer activities will provide attractive alternatives. These are expectable changes that all families can anticipate. They naturally set the stage for diminished parent-child contact.

The Emotional Sphere: Its Effect on Contact

It is this sphere, centered on feelings, that arguably has the strongest influence on the relationship between parent and child. Parents cannot escape their own upbringing, their beliefs, and their reactions when it comes to handling divorce and its aftermath. Feelings guide actions. They also, along with experience, help to establish a sense of identity. The way a parent assimilates a wealth of experiences from the past and responds to current interactions with the other parent and the child will strongly affect the continuing relationship between both parents and the child. For example, if the custodial parent believes that divorce is fundamentally wrong and was opposed to it from the beginning, he or she may harbor sufficient anger at the other parent to cloud judgement about visitation. Every phone call by the noncustodial parent to the child may be treated with disdain or rejected. That parent's feelings are guiding the contact.

If the visiting parent feels that he or she is incompetent as a parent because of past failures or social conditioning, he or she may withdraw (as happened with some of the parents in earlier chapters), believing the child will be better off. If the visiting parent feels hurt because of the lack of contact, he or she may respond angrily and escalate the conflict or withdraw further. If the parent is paralyzed emotionally and has not adequately mourned the loss of the relationship (or is experiencing a post-traumatic stress-like reaction, as a high percentage of those in the survey were), that will affect communication. The point is that feelings are basic to whether the parent-child relationship will flourish.

The Legal Sphere: Its Effect on Contact

Consider the laws in a particular state. Are they designed to make contact between parent and child easy after a divorce or are they tearing at the fabric of the relationship? Is shared custody a presumption? How are child support and visitation handled? Are the rights of parents considered? Is the financial status of a parent taken into account? Are lawyers encouraging or discouraging litigation? Do the court personnel seem interested in helping parents work out differences, or are they more interested in quickly discharging the case because they are overworked? Is there a long wait to settle disputes? Are the rights of either party being ignored? Is mediation required? Can one parent insist on therapy for a child if the other parent does not agree therapy is needed?[3]

The law has an impact on these relationships. (See chapter 7.) We know some parents break the law because they are unhappy with the court's response to their requests for custody. Parents who kidnap their children and go into hiding often say that their own needs have been ignored by the courts and that their attempts for assistance have gone unheeded.[4] The way the law is written and practiced will have a profound impact on whether parents are encouraged about or discouraged from staying in contact.

An awareness of these four spheres helps set the context for understanding the pressures on parents and children after the breakup. They form the bases for intervention.

Prevention: Stopping the Loss of Contact

Whereas there are parents who do not want anything to do with their children, here we focus on situations potentially correctable from the parents' perspective. Two prevention-related questions guide the discussion: What if the noncustodial parent wants to maintain contact? and, what can a custodial parent do to help keep the noncustodial parent involved with the child?

What follows are common scenarios that hinder ongoing contact between parent and child. Included are specific issues to consider in preventing the cutoffs from developing.

When the Custodial Parent Wants to Restrict or Stop Contact

To prevent loss of contact, efforts are needed by all parties. The situation must be considered from the perspective of the custodial as well as the noncustodial parent before recommendations for change can be made.

Custodial parents have a wealth of reasons, which range from the noble to the selfish, for wanting contact between the other parent and child to cease. Most often the reasons are based in reality, other times on perceptions that are misguided, and occasionally on conscious distortions. They include concern for the child's safety or emotional well-being, respect for the child's wishes, a desire for retribution, and fear of competing with the other parent for the child's affections.

What are the initial signs that contact will be impeded? The noncustodial parent experiences the beginnings of the restriction by finding it increasingly difficult to visit or speak with the child. The child may not be home when it is the responsibility of the custodial parent to have the child ready for visitation. Telephone calls to the home may be blocked. Gifts and letters are returned unopened. The child may appear increasingly angry or sullen during visitation, giving the visiting parent the impression the child is being unduly influenced by the custodial parent. The child may be accusing the visiting parent of things that sound as if they are being parroted from the custodial parent. The custodial parent may be threatening to cut off contact or warning that child support payment and contact will be linked.

Recommendations if You Are the Custodial Parent. If you are considering cutting off contact between your child and the other parent, honestly explore the reasons with a trusted friend or family member not involved with the situation, a leader in your church, or a professional. Make sure you are not acting out of a desire for revenge, anger, or fear of a burgeoning relationship between your child and the other parent. Consider the impact of the four spheres described earlier in this chapter. Failure on the other parent's part to pay child support is *not* a reason to prevent visitation. Anger at the other parent for ending the marriage, disagreements with the other parent's lifestyle (as long as it is not illegal), or unhappiness with a new relationship your ex-spouse has initiated are not sufficient causes to interrupt your child's opportunity to see his or her parent.

More specifically, as Johnston and Campbell write, it is useful for parents to consider "how they are using the custody dispute to forestall painful feelings of loss, to repair an injured self-esteem, or to restore a sense of power."[5] Parents can help themselves if they "mourn the loss, reconstitute a better self-image, and regain control over their lives in more appropriate ways."[6] Reality-based decisions can be made when divorce-engendered conflicts are separated from earlier unresolved ones.

When you are making a decision based on information you received from your child, make sure it is accurate and is not being parroted from information the child heard from someone else. Document as many facts as you can before acting on impressions. Check out perceptions. If a law has been broken by the other parent, as in cases of child abuse or neglect, the parent should be reported to the appropriate authorities so that action can be taken. Your child should be referred to professionals for evaluation and potential treatment.

Before cutting off contact, a reasonable step is to begin an ongoing conversation with the other parent about visitation, parenting expectations, and your child's development. Lack of communication will only exacerbate the worsening relationship. Try to prevent issues from building up. Seek outside mediation for intervention if you need help with communication. If you circle the wagons around yourself and your child too soon, and before a full understanding of what has transpired is gained, there may be enormous suffering.

Recommendations if You Are the Noncustodial Parent. Many parents I interviewed said their attempts to visit were being blocked and that the children were poisoned against them (one of the patterns discussed in chapters 3 and 5.) If you believe this is happening and that it is unfair (some parents admit to having problems and purposely distance themselves), consider the following steps:

First, check it out with the other parent. This is the easiest and least acrimonious first step. Many divorced people assume the worst about their ex-partner. In that climate, all interactions take on a negative tone. If you enter the discussion with an open mind and are not defensive (that is particularly difficult if there has been an acrimonious history), things may go more smoothly. Try to describe in a nonadversarial fashion what you are observing. You might say, "The last few times I have been scheduled to see Johnny, he hasn't been there. Is there some issue we need to talk about with our visitations?" A number of books are available in your local bookstore or library that describe specific approaches to nonadversarial discussions. One therapist offers the following advice for how to mediate such difficult situations.

- Keep to the here and now; do not bring up past problems when you are having a discussion with your ex-spouse and need to solve a current problem.
- Keep to one issue; people often get in trouble in discussions if they bring in outside issues.
- Speak in the first person; it is safer to say "I feel this way" rather than "you feel this way."
- Do not attack or counterattack; describe the ex-spouse's behavior you disagree with rather than impugning his or her character. If he makes a point that has merit, don't strike back.
- Deal with issues quickly; do not let things build up.
- Do not try to win every argument; there does not always have to be a loser.[7]

If the problem is miscommunication or some misunderstanding, this approach opens up the potential for it to be resolved easily without either side of the argument escalating.

Second, if there is a concerted effort to block your contact, consider involving another party to help you. Friends and relatives may be able to mediate on your behalf. Involving children as go-betweens is not a good idea, for reasons argued earlier in this book.

Third, if the previous steps have failed, seek out a professional to help you. Clergy or professional counselors can help to mediate family problems, particularly if they have known your family in the past. You can also suggest going to an unbiased third party for family counseling, perhaps to a person the other parent chooses from a list of professionals you supply. An objective third party can offer advice to both of you that may provide a new perspective.

Fourth, seek legal help if your rights are being denied. Mediators, professionals who foster nonadversarial problem-solving and are schooled in both law and human relations should be the first choice. Knowledgeable of divorce, custody laws, and mental health, mediators can save you money and a great deal of heartache if they work with both you and your ex-spouse. If you need the name of one with a professional affiliation, call the

Association of Family and Conciliation Courts at (608) 833-4009 and ask for a referral in your area.

One note of caution: do not expect your child to rush to your side. If you suspect the child is being prevented from seeing you by the other parent but would otherwise want to visit, be careful how you proceed. The child may be telling you one thing and the other parent something else. The child may be lying to avoid being caught in the middle. The child may want to withdraw from parental conflict by not seeing you. As discussed in chapter 6, the age of the child will govern some of his reactions.

When the Child Wants to Stop Seeing the Noncustodial Parent

Children sometimes are the ones who are resistant to continuing visitation. This is especially true in the following cases: when the noncustodial parent is blamed for the divorce and the child feels angry or abandoned; when parents are fighting and it is easier for the child to withdraw than to continue to be in the center of the conflict; when the child feels loyalty conflicts and a show of affection for the visiting parent may hurt the feelings of the custodial parent; when the noncustodial parent and child disagree about parenting issues; when distance is a barrier; when peer relations become more important than seeing the other parent; when the child feels discomfort being alone with the visiting parent, due perhaps to that parent's drinking or drug-taking behavior, a shift in religious affiliation, or any other lifestyle change; or when the child is threatened by the visiting parent's new relationship with an adult or a stepchild.[8]

Recommendations if You Are the Custodial Parent. The emphasis here is on prevention of a major rift between your child and the other parent. Your job is to find out why your child wants to stop seeing the other parent and determine if that reaction should be supported. Here it gets tricky. As a parent, you may want to support the *feelings* your child has while giving the message that the result of those feelings, not seeing the other parent, is unjustified.

For example, a child may want to stop seeing a parent because the parent is too strict, has become involved with a new partner, or is not spending "quality time" with the child during visitation. The child may say, "It's no fun going to see Mom because there isn't anything to do there." Or, "Dad's always on the phone or with his stepchildren when I visit, so I don't want to go anymore." In these examples, the feelings that the children have, of being bored or replaced, are justified. But if they act on them and cease visiting, the result may be a significant diminution in parent-child contact, which can have unintended negative consequences.

If the child is *not* being harmed, you want to assume a posture that will increase communication between your child and the other parent. Ideally, you would encourage your child to share his feelings with the other parent. In this way you are staying out of the middle of their relationship. You are also modeling for your child that he should be able to solve his own problems with the other parent. You could say, "It must not feel very good to be ignored. Rather than not going back again, let's brainstorm about how to discuss this with your father."

If that has been tried and failed, you will next need to talk to the other parent on behalf of the child. If you approach the other parent in an accusing manner ("Why aren't you spending more time with her?"), you will probably not be as helpful as if you say, "Your daughter misses not having as much time with you." You may need to practice starting a conversation in a way that communicates the importance the other parent holds for your child.

The framing question for you is "What can I do to facilitate this relationship in both the short and the long run while still being supportive of my child and the other parent?" A consideration of what the other parent is feeling is necessary. Are you and the parent having a disagreement about parenting practices? If so, you both will need to talk about and possibly modify those practices to reach a middle ground. Is the other parent feeling replaced by a new relationship you are involved in? If so, be sensitive to that.

If your child is being abused or neglected (whether the child wants to stop visitation or not), a different course has to be taken that will *at least* temporarily restrict access. Notifying child protective services is imperative.

One cautionary note: Be wary when the perceived rejection your child experiences at the hands of the other parent is a replay of rejection *you* may be feeling from the other parent. If you find yourself having too strong a reaction to their relationship, it may be a sign that there are issues that have not been resolved between you and the other parent. It also may be a sign that you are consciously or unconsciously encouraging your child not to visit. You may do this by emphasizing the importance of after school activities that interfere with visitation. You may be subtly disparaging the other parent in front of the child or complaining about how hard it is to maintain the visitation schedule. If so, you are fueling the flames.

Sometimes your child may have serious concerns about visiting that are not easily resolved. The other parent may be verbally abusive. That parent may accuse the child of taking sides or make the child feel uncomfortable by grilling him about your activities. Family counseling at this time may help prevent these issues from escalating and should be considered.

Recommendations if You Are the Noncustodial Parent. If your child does not want to see you because of your own problematic behavior, get professional help. If you have a substance abuse problem or have been abusive (emotionally, physically, or sexually), do not expect to be able to change your behavior on your own. Do not anticipate continuing visitation without at least getting help and having a third party supervise. Your child's fears of you are justified and should be respected. If your child has an intense attachment to you even though you have been abusive, that does not exonerate you. Rather it is a sign that this stage in your child's development is marked by normal feelings of ambivalence. You were once a trusted parent who betrayed that trust. Your child will have difficulty sorting out those feelings and may send you mixed messages. He is confused. Do not force continued visitation on your child. Again, without professional help and honesty on your part, you risk inflicting more harm and losing all contact with your child, including telephone and written communication.

Assuming that you have been a caring and responsible parent and your child wants to stop visits, try to find out why. You need to learn if there has been some miscommunication between the two of you. Children often want to cut off contact for "adolescent" reasons: Your rules are too strict; they can't watch their favorite TV show at your house; they aren't near their friends, et cetera. While these are not viable reasons for cutting off contact, they may be signs that your child is growing up and is seeking activities that do not involve you as much. These desires would have emerged if you were still living with your child. Be careful to not take them as a rejection of you as a parent.

You may be losing out to more attractive alternatives as well as to the march of time. The child who liked to snuggle with you when he was seven will not feel comfortable doing that at eleven, and would rather be at the movies with friends. If contact is starting to slip away, it may need to be renegotiated so that the time you spend together does not interfere as much with other things.

Your child may have entered a new stage in which she is angry at you for imagined or real slights. Your promotion or shift in work schedule will mean less time with her. Your dating someone new and taking that person's children to the zoo constitute direct competition to her. A natural reaction would be for her to retaliate by withholding her time from you.

Talk to your child about the changes you are observing in the desire to be with you. Get suggestions from the custodial parent. Examine your own behavior to see if you are giving off messages that you are not interested in seeing your child. Conversely, you may be sending the message that your child is occupying too central a role in your life. It may be that you lack balance between involvement in your own activities and absorption in your child. Such a message can be frightening to a child, who may withdraw out of protection. Finally, be sensitive to your child, listen, and respect what he is saying.

One therapist provides the following hints:

- Keep a calendar that clearly indicates when visitations are to occur so that there is no confusion about the schedule.
- Make the visitations meaningful without overloading activities; find a nice pace for activities that you and your child can enjoy.
- If you have a younger child, make visitations shorter and more frequent.
- Do not overreact to a child's refusal to see you at some point.
- When picking up your child for visitation, stay in the child's house for a few minutes so that the child can begin to switch gears.
- Never miss a visit unless you have called in advance; trust can easily dissolve if you skip visits without prior notification.
- Do not take the child against her or his will, but instead seek help if refusal to visit continues.[9]

Managing Issues That May Interfere with Contact

It may sound simplistic, but the best first steps to take with the next series of problems are similar to those already mentioned. Just as the three most important considerations in buying a house are location, location, location, the most important steps in preventing problems from occurring after divorce are communication, communication, communication. Remember that any interaction with the other parent is influenced by the four spheres of the social, structural, emotional, and legal.

When the Visiting Parent Is Drifting Away

Many parents and children want the visiting mother or father to stay in touch for all the right reasons: He or she is a loved figure, a respected and valued addition to the family, a help with child care and economic contributions, and a positive influence on the child. His or her presence is emblematic of all that can be worked through in relationships. If the visiting parent stays in touch, the message is sent to the children that even though the marriage has ended, with work and communication, conscientious and consistent caring can continue.

But as we have seen in so many cases, the visiting parent starts to drift away, either because of emotional problems, anger at the breakup, problems with visitation, miscommunication, or the desire/need to avoid financial obligation.

Recommendations if You Are the Custodial Parent. Certainly legal obligations concerning child support have to be met. But the message has to be given that it is the *person*, not just the pocketbook or chauffeur, that is needed. Nothing will more likely drive a father (and increasingly a mother) away than the impression that his only value to the family is as bread-winner.

How do you convey to the noncustodial parent that he or she is needed? Include the parent in decisions about the children by keeping her or him informed. Ask the parent's advice. If you think the parent is starting to drift away, talk about it. Try to remove any impediments to involvement. Examine your own behavior and think how it might be interpreted by the other parent. Separate your feelings about the breakup from your belief in the importance of keeping the parent involved. Remember that the culture around divorce often makes it hard for that parent to stay in touch.

If the parent is behaving inappropriately, talk to the parent about becoming more responsible. Tell him (or her) that his child needs him to act responsibly and that you want his input.

Keep communication flowing between your child and the parent. Help your child send cards on holidays. Help your child interpret the other parent's behavior in a way that builds self-esteem in the child and is reality-based. It is part of your responsibility to your child to do everything to keep a visiting parent who is behaving appropriately involved.

Recommendations if You Are the Noncustodial Parent. If you feel yourself drifting away from your child, take an honest look at what you are doing. Some parents I interviewed cut off contact because they were too embarrassed with their own behavior. Essentially, as I wrote in chapter 2, they did not know how to love or how to express love. They believed that a parent has to be perfect to stay in contact. When they ran into personal problems, they believed they were sparing their children by removing themselves.

Some parents who drift away hold themselves up to some Olympian standard and take an "If only I had..." approach: If only they had hung in there longer, done more when the kids were younger, set different priorities, or been stronger emotionally, they would not experience any problems being with their children now.[10] It is hard to second-guess yourself. If you have made mistakes, acknowledge them and move ahead to the future. Do not let the past handcuff you.

Recognize your value to your child, even if it is sometimes hard to see. Your presence stops a lot of myth building about you from developing. Reality, no matter how harsh, is usually easier for a child to deal with than the myths that build up around your absence.

Children of divorce often have misconceptions about what happened between their parents. Talk to them so that they know that their behavior did not cause the divorce. Do not attack the other parent. That will only cause the children to choose sides and feel loyalty conflicts. Finally, do not shy away from being a parent.[11] That is your responsibility.

When Family Members Encourage the Custodial Parent to Cease Contact

Sometimes parents and friends do not have the same picture of the other parent as the custodial parent (social sphere). They become a force in discouraging the custodial parent from allowing the noncustodial parent visitation. In some of these situations, the custodial parent may have pertinent information and impressions from the child that friends and relatives do not have. Sometimes relatives are not aware of positive changes in the noncustodial parent so that he or she no longer needs to be avoided.

It may not be a friend or relative encouraging cessation of contact. As we heard from at least one parent in an earlier chapter, a new wife with no children of her own may want to raise her stepchildren without the interference of the biological mother. In these cases she may encourage the father to reduce the mother's contact.

Recommendations. If you are the custodial parent, listen to your support system and decide if they have accurate, up-to-date information. You ultimately have to decide where the boundaries should be drawn between yourself and your support system. Weigh your child's needs. If you do not want the noncustodial parent to drift away, and in most cases you should not, you may have to go to bat for that parent with your relatives, particularly with your own parents. Your child's grandparents can have a powerful influence on your child. You will need to explain to them about the importance of this parent-child contact. Without that information, they may unwittingly drive a wedge into that relationship. Your new spouse may have motives that he or she is unaware of. If you are receiving a strong message from that spouse, examine its underpinnings carefully before deciding how to proceed.

When a New Spouse Discourages the Noncustodial Parent from Having Contact with the Child

If the noncustodial parent has remarried, a subtle or overt message may be coming from the new spouse about the desirability of visiting children from the previous marriage. Visitation is an expensive proposition when travel and gift giving are involved, as they often are. The new spouse, either purposefully or unconsciously, may drive a wedge between the noncustodial parent and children in hopes that a lack of involvement will reduce the desire to pay child support and the costs of visitation. The new spouse may also discourage visitation if the new spouse has brought children into the marriage and loyalty conflicts emerge. The new spouse would prefer to have the noncustodial parent home rather than off seeing the children from the previous union.

Recommendations

As with the prior suggestions, listen to your support systems and then decide whether reducing contact makes sense. There is rarely a time when it does. Keep your child's interests primary. Many noncustodial parents I have talked with take great solace in knowing that, no matter what happened, they consistently attempted to keep the lines of communication open with their children. If you are the first one to close them off, you may never get them reopened.

When Distance Makes an Already Tenuous Relationship between the Noncustodial Parent and Child Even Weaker

Over time after divorce, family members tend to move away from each other. A job promotion or relocation, remarriage, new housing opportunities, or better schools may result in physical distancing. Sometimes moves coincide by chance with a declining parent-child relationship. A job opportunity comes out of the blue for the ideal position. But other times, people move away because they are not getting along, and they feel like failures in their relationship with their child. Living near the child and not having a satisfactory relationship becomes too painful.

Recommendations. Using distance as an excuse for reducing contact may be teaching your child that effort should not be made in working through difficult relationships. You are saying, in essence, "I can't handle things, so I am leaving." The child who may have been refusing contact will read that as rejection or as justification for rejecting you. It might confirm what the child already felt—that you do not care. Do not let distance become an easy excuse for reducing contact. If a move has to be made, invest in creative ways of communicating long-distance. Some ideas: mailing funny cards to each other (homemade or store-bought), sending video or audiotapes back and forth, having a set time to speak on the phone every week; and saving money carefully so that plane, train, or car travel is affordable. Remember, if the relationship is painful, running from it will most likely make it worse.

A number of parents in the survey said that distance contributed to the downfall of the relationship. It does not have to. Certainly distance makes it easier for the relationship to fade and provides a ready excuse. But it also can be seen as an opportunity to forge a different kind of relationship. Face-to-face communication is replaced by spoken or written communication (by letter or computer). Daily contact is replaced by one- or two-week vacations together. Be aware that distance will intensify the communication that does occur because every minute seems more precious. But it does not have to terminate it.

When Distancing Is Used to Weaken a Relationship

Sometimes a move to a new location is used intentionally by a custodial or noncustodial parent to shift a parent-child balance. If the custodial parent believes the visiting parent and child have formed too strong a bond, the custodial parent may move or take a job somewhere else explicitly to diminish contact. On the other side, a visiting parent who has a strong bond with the child may relocate intentionally to force an issue around continued contact. As long as the visiting parent is in the area, the child does not have to make choices. But with the move, the child may be asked to again choose where he wants to live, a choice the visiting parent hopes will reverse an earlier custody decision in favor of the custodian. This may happen more frequently as a child reaches the age at which he can choose where he wants to live.

Recommendations. When distance is a weapon, the stakes in the relationship are running too high. Everyone will suffer. It is time, as with many of the other issues mentioned, to de-escalate. Think of the child's well-being. Moving a child to a new home or having the child travel a great distance for visitation *as a ploy* to gain an advantage in a relationship is unlikely to produce a happier and healthier child.

As someone who has studied the extremes of divorce, I realize that passions can run high and that it is believed some children need protection from the other parent. A move can be a legal way of providing that protection. The key here for a parent is to sort through anger at the other parent and the child's best interests before making a decision about relocation.

When the Custodial Parent's Feelings Inappropriately Block Contact

Most of the preceding issues have to do with outside events and pressures as interpreted by the custodial or noncustodial parent. On a basic level it is the *feelings* of each parent that have the greatest impact (the emotional sphere). Feelings shape perceptions. Feelings, as already mentioned, derive from a history of "long past" and "recent past" events. The way a parent saw his or her parents interact, the way the parent was treated as a child, and experiences in relationships as an adult, coupled with the parent's own history of successes and failures in life, combine to affect the feelings that parent holds about the self and others. If one parent feels hurt, angry, lonely, and wronged by the other parent, it will be difficult to view the actions of that parent with anything but distrust. In these situations, the role of parent gets confused with the role of ex-spouse. Every action in relation to the child has the potential of reverberating into the personal domain of the parent who feels wronged. This gets played out in various ways. For example, a mother wants to increase the time she spends with the child after a breakup. The father perceives that behavior as being motivated by a desire to hurt him, rather than out of the mother's wish to be with the child. He blocks her request in order to protect himself.

A cycle is set up in which each parent does not trust the motives of the other. The cycle destroys the ability of both to work together. A second example involves a custodial mother who has been hurt a sufficient number of times by the father that she comes to expect the worst. Sincere efforts over months or years to change are discounted. The father gives up, citing all the positives he has accomplished recently and complaining he cannot get a break. The mother, accustomed to broken promises, has her feelings about him confirmed when he backs out. As emotions take over, the custodial parent leaves a narrow range within which the visiting parent can operate and be accepted. One parent may have started the cycle, though in most relationships this is hard to tell, while the other parent continues it.

To complicate matters, children get caught up unwittingly in these cycles. Their normal expressions of displeasure or exasperation with a custodial parent may be viewed as something deeper. They may reject a mother with the same tone or words that the mother heard from the children's father. This causes an immediate escalation of problems because it appears the children and father are ganging up on the mother.

Of course, there are times that this is exactly what is happening. The parent on the receiving end is being ganged up on, rejected, or subjected to language heard before in a purposeful attack. I have seen this with both a custodial and a noncustodial parent on the receiving end. If it is the custodial parent, he or she may retaliate by restricting visitation or disciplining more harshly. If it is the noncustodial parent, he or she may withdraw or return to court. Either way, when emotions are affecting rational discourse, there are problems.

Recommendations. If your feelings are interfering, do not kid yourself—they are not easy to change. If you find yourself continually angry at your ex-spouse, it will be hard to enjoy life and to be an effective parent.

To change, there are three common approaches to take, and you can take all three. One calls for insight, one for cognitive change, and one for behavioral change. Briefly, to achieve insight into your feelings you need to examine past patterns and think honestly about *why* you feel a certain way. Once you ascertain why you have, for example, feelings of anger toward your ex-spouse (probably not difficult to do), you need to consider the connections between those feelings and your parenting behaviors. It will also be helpful to consider why your child or ex-spouse is acting a certain way. If you have insight into your ex's feelings, they may become easier to handle (though not necessarily easier to accept). Insight can, but not always, lead to change.

To change cognitively, you need to train yourself to *think* differently about past and current events. Whereas insight is connected with feelings, cognitive changes are connected to thoughts. Try to step back and look at your situation objectively. You may want to train yourself to remove negative thoughts about past interactions with your ex-spouse, or to think positively about your child's visitation with your ex. One mother placed a rubber band around her wrist and snapped it whenever she was tempted to ask her daughter about what her father had said about her during father-daughter visitation. She had a red wrist, but it worked. This approach is geared toward reducing the emotions associated with a situation and to retrain your thinking.

Along these same lines, think about ways to "reframe" your own behavior and that of your ex-spouse. Reframes are designed to provide a different view of behavior. People get locked into viewing the other parent in a certain way. One father saw all of his ex-wife's behavior as an attempt to get back at him. It was suggested that perhaps the behavior was an honest attempt on her part to get closer to the children. By reframing the mother's behavior, the father was able to (sometimes) see her actions more favorably.

Changing behaviorally is the easiest for some people. This means changing *what you do.* If you find that you are *always* getting into a shouting match with your ex-spouse on the phone, you may want to change the part of the conversation at which you think the shouting starts. One parent told me he can talk with his ex about visitation and summer vacations, but that holidays, because of the family traditions and emotions involved, always cause problems. If you are in this situation, anticipate your own reaction and then make sure you do not scream at the other parent if he starts to shout first. You may want to write out a script of what you want to change in the conversation. If you find you are grilling your child too much about the other parent, you may want to make a private star chart for yourself where you give yourself a star for each day that goes by without your asking about the other parent.

Many parents can predict in advance when a problem might arise. In those cases, it is easier to gain control of yourself before the problem occurs and then try and change some aspect of the upcoming situation. Once you find you are behaving in a way that makes you feel better about yourself, it will be easy to continue. Behavioral changes often lead to changes in feeling and thinking.

When a Custodial or Noncustodial Parent's Legal Rights are Jeopardized

There will be times, as cited in chapter 7, when a parent's rights are flagrantly violated and other times when they are subtly encroached upon. A custodial parent may be blocking contact all or some of the time or not delivering mail sent to the child. A visiting parent may be slow in returning a child after visitation or constantly litigating as a form of harassment.

Recommendations. The first step is to make sure that you have an accurate perception of the events that are unfolding. *Consider* communicating your concerns to your ex-spouse. Ideally, improved communication can rectify problems that are arising. Realistically, though, if you believe your rights are being abrogated, consult a lawyer. Be careful. Depending upon the situation, communicating initially with your ex-spouse before you consult a lawyer may be detrimental to your position if your ex-spouse stalls and uses that time to strengthen his or her legal position. This happens when one parent operates in a good faith and the other does not. I interviewed one woman for another book who kidnapped her daughter and hid for eleven years after being tricked into believing her ex-husband wanted a reconciliation. She signed away rights to property in the process, going against her lawyer's advice. She backed herself into a corner and broke the law to retaliate and gain possession of her child. Had she followed her lawyer's advice, she may not have gone on the run.

Mediation is a less adversarial route than hiring a lawyer. Mediation can work, even with the most difficult cases. One study of high conflict divorces reports that over 80 percent had been helped by intense mediation to negotiate an agreement. Two years later, almost two-thirds had stuck with the agreement or negotiated a new one.[12]

While this book has been written in a way that highlights the differences as well as the similarities between mothers and fathers, a word is still needed about the social conditioning that men and women bring to their postmarital and parenting experiences. Conditioning affects how each parent will interpret and respond to tense situations as they arise. John Gottman, a researcher on marital interaction, states that women are given the training as children to negotiate emotional issues, while men are not. Men have the ability to stonewall, essentially to be nonresponsive to a woman's comments. Stonewallers claim they are acting that way to be neutral, while in reality they are perceived as being nonresponsive, smug, and disapproving. Women are more apt to follow a cycle of demanding something and then withdrawing if they do not get it. Unless a man and a woman can understand both during and after a marriage that they each have different ways of handling emotions that grow out of their relationship, they are doomed to greater difficulties. For dealing with difficult situations in a marriage, Gottman recommends four key steps that, I believe, can also be applied to working with postmarital relationships that have the capacity for change. First, calm down and think relaxing thoughts. Attempts should be made to reverse old ways of thinking about your ex-spouse. Second, he recommends speaking nondefensively. Third, make sure you validate the feelings of your ex-spouse. Fourth, if you can resolve conflict through these steps, continue to try them again and again, what Gottman calls overlearning.[13]

It is possible to prevent a parent from drifting away or from being blocked from continued access. But it takes a concerted effort, and all parties must be willing to communicate.

Resolution: Bringing Parent and Child Together

This section discusses approaches to take *if a parent has been out of contact with a child for a lengthy period of time and some or all of the parties are interested in contact being reestablished.* Here I speak to the custodial parent, the noncustodial parent, the child, and the grandparent. The social, structural, emotional, and legal spheres affected in these situations will also be discussed. In fact, all may have combined to keep parent and child apart and to impede reconciliation.

The reasons reconciliations occur are as numerous as those that cause breakups. (Case studies illustrating the reconciliation process appear in the previous chapter.) Most commonly, though, reconciliations happen for four reasons: maturation of the child, a family event that makes reconciliation desirable or becomes an excuse for it, a custodial or visiting parent's emotional change, and a shift in living situations.

Maturation of the child. Children's needs and attachments can vary by age. For example, research shows that preadolescent daughters are the easiest for single fathers to raise, in part, it is hypothesized, because they are interested at that age in being "daddy's girl."[14] A daughter living with her father may have become attached to him to the exclusion of the mother for this reason. But when the daughter nears puberty, she may want to move out and be with her mother, who can be a gender role model for her. This would be a normal shift in identification. Past difficulties (and lack of contact) between daughter and mother would be forgotten as they rebuild ties. In other cases, a child grows up, leaves home, and is not directly influenced by the custodial parent anymore before he reconciles with the absent parent. These types of reconciliations, due to normal development, happen all the time.

Family event. A marriage, birth, or death may compel family members to reunite or may be the excuse for them to see each other again. (We heard about this with Julie in chapter 8.) Lacking a significant event, battling family members often have little reason to get together. But under the protective umbrella of family tradition, some family members who have been separated are able to let bygones be bygones. It is usually an event having to do with the child (or the death of a grandparent), rather than either of the parents, that sets the stage for reconciliation. Such an event often signals the child's becoming an adult (graduation, marriage, birth). This rite of passage frees him or her to visit both parents without experiencing extensive loyalty conflicts.

Emotional change. Parents and children are not fixed entities. We change in both our behavior and our perceptions. What may have been an insult or a hurt one year can be forgiven the next as a different perspective on life or on the other person is acquired. A son may want to see his father when baseball season rolls around and call him out of the blue after months of no communication. A mother who may have absented herself may decide to pick up the phone on the spur of the moment and check in on the children. Perhaps she talked to a friend who had done a similar thing. Maybe she watched a poignant movie about parenting. Such seemingly unplanned events are often the result of a readiness for change and can have positive effects.

Therapy can also have played a part here. People who are open to change may have been assisted by talking with an objective and trained listener. With that help may have come the ability to reconnect with a family member in a new way that facilitated a relationship.

Yet it is not always so clear cut. Some therapists, parents have told me, encourage the parent to *stop* trying to seeing the child after a while. If the parent has tried and failed continuously over the years to see the child, or if the child is constantly rejecting the parent, this approach can make sense—for a while. It may, in fact, help the parent to draw a clear boundary between himself and the child, which may reverse a trend toward emotional self-flagellation. A few parents I interviewed took this stance. By responding to rejection by ceasing to beg for reconciliation, some parents regain self-respect, which works to their advantage in the relationship. They cease to be a doormat, which helps the child to see them in a new light. As a result, new interactions can sometimes begin, leading toward reconciliation. A parent, in any case, should never close off completely to the possibility of change in himself or the child. Each new developmental stage in a child's life offers an opportunity for growth and for reconnection.

Change in living situations. The remarriage of the custodial parent, a move to a new city, or a departure of a child for college (also a maturational issue), sometimes results in the child or absent parent initiating contact. For example, a stepfather moving into the home can be stressful for the child and raise anew unresolved feelings about the biological father. Being asked to call a stepfather "Daddy" may make a child long for her biological father and be an impetus to bridge the gap. A custodial parent being transferred out of town may cause a child to reconsider the other parent as a viable way of staying with familiar friends and school settings.

There are other reasons a parent and child might reconcile, ranging from the onset of a major illness of one parent to the resolution of a parent or child's substance abuse problems, a legal decision involving child support and visitation, and so on. Often there are multiple factors. How can a parent or child bring about a reconciliation and make it comfortable for everyone?

Effecting a Reconciliation

Any family member may decide to work toward a rapprochement. A custodial parent may try to bridge the gap between his child and the absent parent when he sees how upset his child is from not seeing his mother (for example, the child is asking about her, cries when her name comes up, stares at her picture, et cetera). The custodial parent, even when there is no reaction from the child, may have changed his feelings about the absent parent and want to encourage contact. Perhaps he has received new information about that parent (for instance, she is now employed, is not living with a person who is a bad influence, has been abstinent, et cetera). The custodial parent's change of heart can open the door for the return of the absent parent if that custodial parent has been discouraging contact.

The absent parent may have a change of heart, also. He may feel differently about the child, the custodial parent, or himself and move to reconnect. If the absent parent has struggled with substance abuse or emotional problems, recovery from them may coincide with a willingness for greater intimacy. These can be particularly sticky for all involved. In one situation, a father who had a significant drug abuse problem for years stayed away from his children because he was ashamed and did not have room for a relationship with both his children and his drugs. He was described by the mother as "a great manipulator and charming." When he finally entered rehab, he wanted contact with his children again, a natural outgrowth of entering treatment. The mother was, in turn, understandably ambivalent. While she wanted him back in the children's lives, she was wary of him because of his past.

A new significant other in the absent parent's life can also cause a change of feeling, just as the departure of someone from the custodial parent's life may. Other pressures may also be an influence. A child support enforcement agency may begin to garnish a father's wages. As a result, he may respond by insisting on resuming visits. Parents who have been out of touch, when forced to pay, may reinsert themselves into their child's lives, feeling it is their due.

The child may decide that he wants the absent parent at a graduation, awards ceremony, or wedding. Such a rite of passage becomes a time of reconsideration and renewal. The event is the impetus and/or excuse for a reconsideration of the absent parent. In other situations, the child may feel cloistered by or over-involved with the custodial parent and attempt to reunite with the absent parent to provide some distance. Here the child is hoping to use the absent parent as a buffer in balancing the relationship with the custodial parent. Finally, the child may need something from that parent—money, a signature on adoption papers, contacts for work—and bridge the gap.

If you are in the situation where you want to open the door for recontact, consider the following steps (depending upon the nature of your situation and the people involved). Remember, beginning a relationship again after a long period can be traumatic.

1. Write expressing your interest in renewing a relationship and the rea-

son for the change in your feeling about visits (if you have been the one who has blocked or stopped contact).[15] Specify in the letter that you will call in a few days, after the recipient has had time to consider your request.

Some sample letters are provided here:

(From a nonvisiting parent to a custodial parent)

Dear _____,

I know I have not called or seen "Susie" for too long a period of time. I am unhappy about that. I would like to make a fresh start now. I would like to put aside our differences for the good of Susie. I (depending on the situation) (a) am in a better place now; (b) apologize for my past behaviors; (c) feel differently about things now and hope you do, too, et cetera. After you have a chance to think about this for a few days, I will call so that we can talk and hopefully consider a meeting.

Sincerely,

(From a nonvisiting parent to a teenager)

Dear _____,

I know I have not called or seen you for too long a period of time. I am unhappy about that. I would like to make a fresh start now. I (depending on the situation) (a) am in a better place now; (b) apologize for my past behaviors; (c) feel differently about things now, et cetera. After you have a chance to think about this for a few days, I will call you so that we can talk and hopefully consider a meeting.

Love/Sincerely,

(From a custodial parent to an absent parent)

Dear _____,

I know you have not called or seen "Susie" for too long a period of time. I am unhappy about that and think it is time we tried to make a fresh start now for Susie's good. I (depending on the situation) (a) see you are in a healthier place now; (b) have come to realize how much Susie needs you, even though I have not always agreed with your actions; (c) have thought more about my part in all of this; (d) apologize for my past behaviors, et cetera. After you have a chance to think about this for a few days, I will call so that we can talk and hopefully consider a meeting.

Sincerely,

(From a child to a nonvisiting parent)

Dear _____,

I know we have not seen each other for too long a period of time. I am unhappy about that and think it is time we tried to make a fresh start. I (depending on the situation) (a) hope you will consider seeing me again; (b) hear you are in a healthier place now; (c) have not always agreed with your actions and have been hurt by them but want to try again; (d) have thought more about my part in all of this; (e) apologize for my past behaviors, et cetera.

After you have a chance to think about this for a few days, I will call so that we can talk and hopefully consider a meeting.

Love/Sincerely,

Consider these as a guide and design your own letter using your language and your situation. Be honest and nonjudgmental with your writing.

2. Do not expect that your wishes for a meeting will be immediately acceded to. Change takes time and you may be approaching the other parent or the child when he or she least expects it.

3. After you telephone, if the other parties are willing, plan a meeting at a neutral place where everyone will feel safe and where each party has the ability to leave. The "safety" is very important, particularly when there has been violence or the threat of it. Some family members may feel they have had little control over the events that have led to the cutoff. Thus, they need to feel that they have some control during this initial meeting.

4. Try and tune in to the other people in advance. Consider what they may be feeling and thinking prior to the meeting.

5. Inform other relevant family members of the potential for a reconciliation. Your relatives, as part of your support system, have an investment in what happens and need to be kept up to date.

6. If yours is a high-profile reconciliation, avoid the talk shows. I have seen families reunited under the glare of TV lights; don't do it that way regardless of how enticing a free trip to New York or Chicago may be. It rarely works out well for everyone.

7. Clarify with a lawyer any legal issues that may still be pending from the relationship. Consider how to respond to or raise questions about child support and past potential transgressions (lack of visitation, blocked visitation, restraining orders, warrants, et cetera).

8. Consistently identify for yourself the strengths that you can bring to the relationship with your family members. Focus on the positives and not the negatives as you move forward.

Actions to Consider During Reconciliation

Once the decision is made and the reconciliation process is going forward as planned, consider the following:

1. At the first meeting, regardless of your role in the cutoff, do not be defensive or accusatory. Give each person a chance to speak and to hear what others have been experiencing during the absence. People will be checking each other out and looking for signs of change. Not everyone will be willing to go forward with more contact, and those who are willing may be ambivalent. Do not hold high expectations for the first meeting. Change comes slowly. Many parents and children I interviewed recounted having a single contact, planned or otherwise, and then returning to a pattern of little or no contact. The single meeting is not a panacea for the past. The more extreme one person's position, the less likely things are to be resolved;

2. Do not feel that you have to replay or resolve past problems. Some people need to get everything out on the table before they can move on; others cope better with ignoring the past and starting fresh. The need to talk about such issues varies by family.

3. Move slowly and do not try to achieve a close relationship quickly. Do not expect to hear, "I love you." Physical contact such as hugging or kissing may be uncomfortable for some people at the beginning. Others will not want to share important feelings until a new level of trust has been established.

4. Anticipate that the other person will have changed during the time you have not seen him or her. Those changes will be physical and emotional and may be for the better or for the worse. Children grow more rapidly than adults, so seeing a child after a lengthy absence can be particularly traumatic, particularly if a child has gone through adolescence during that time.

5. Learn from any past mistakes that you or other family members have made. If people return to past destructive or unproductive patterns of communication, it is hard to move forward.

6. Unless necessary, do not include people who are not directly involved or who you are not sure can be helpful. (Grandparents, new spouses, and stepchildren are examples.) This can be a period of great miscommunication, and each additional person can add to the confusion. A child, though, may feel most comfortable bringing along a friend at an initial visit. One eighteen-year-old who had been abducted and hidden from her mother for twelve years brought two friends with her to the airport when she saw her mother for the reunification. The friends, as her support system, were important to her, especially as her father's abducting behavior had caused her

to mistrust him. Her friends were the only touchstone to reality she had as she struggled to reconnect with her mother after so many years.

7. Be supportive of everyone involved throughout the process. Whether you are the custodial or noncustodial parent, do not bad-mouth the other parent because that will place the child in the middle. If you are the child, be aware that you will affect your relationship with the custodial parent by spending increased amounts of time with the absent parent, as was mentioned by Tom and Candy in chapter 6.

8. Clearly separate legal and nonlegal issues; if child support is due, for example, keep that issue separate from visitation.

9. Don't overwhelm the other person with feelings; share slowly.

10. Remember that your personal past history can repeat itself in your present. The types of experiences you had growing up can have an impact on how you approach a reconciliation. An adult whose parents divorced, leaving him with tenuous contact with one parent, will have a framework in his mind about how his own reconciliation with his child might work. That might be a far cry from the reality of the current situation, though.

A Note for Children

If you have been in the position of not seeing your mother or father for a while, you are not alone. Many of the children I have interviewed in this book have had experiences that are most likely similar to yours. They have discussed them in previous chapters and, in some cases, offer advice to other children. For example, one child I interviewed advises, "Give your parents a chance and let them try to build a relationship instead of shutting them out." Alan in chapter 2 offers, "Don't take the guilt just because they're your parents." Patty, in chapter 4, states, "If possible, try to love both parents the same and try to not put yourself in the middle. Don't think it is your fault you are in the middle. Try to talk about things and don't keep them inside."

Good advice. The children send consistent messages in their stories, messages that any child (and parent) reading this should keep in mind. Borrowing from David Letterman, I offer here the top ten things to do if you are not seeing one of your parents and reconciliation seems possible:

1. Do not blame yourself for the divorce.

2. Do not feel guilty about what has happened. You are the child, those around you are the adults and are the most responsible for the events.

3. Stay out of the middle of your parents' fights.

4. Find someone you trust to talk to.

5. Keep the door open to a reconciliation. People do change. If you have

been traumatized by the absent parent, be careful before you begin contact again and be wary about letting down your guard too quickly. (As was mentioned in the previous suggestion, find someone to talk to about it.)

6. You may have been told that your mother or father is a bad person; that does not mean you are a bad person. Try to fight the tendency to internalize the negative images you may have of the absent parent.

7. If you are offered money or gifts, consider the pros and cons of accepting them. You have a right to them but they may come with certain expectations.

8. Do not try to rush into a new relationship with the absent parent; it will take time. Visitation may seem awkward at first and lack the spontaneity that can make it more enjoyable. Go at a speed with which you are comfortable.

9. Expect that your reestablishing contact with one parent may raise issues of loyalty for you (you may feel disloyal to your custodial parent) and may cause competition between your parents.

10. Accept your feelings; you have the right to feel angry, happy, sad, or ambivalent about your situation. You also have a right to change how you feel. Say how you feel and keep communication open as long as it is not too painful for you.

It may be helpful to make a list of the pros and cons that you will experience with each parent if you start to see one of them again. Sometimes writing things out in an objective way can help to clear away some of the fog.

A Note for Grandparents

I have focused on parents and children in this chapter, but it is important to add a note for grandparents who, when a child is not seeing a parent, are usually in one of four positions:

- You are siding with the custodial parent and often help out with child care and finances.
- You are siding with the visiting parent (your child) and have infrequent or no contact with your grandchildren.
- You have regular contact with your grandchildren, even though your child does not. (See Tom and Candy, chapter 6.)
- You raise your grandchildren in your home and one or none of those grandchildren's parents is present. (About five percent of all children in the United States are living in such situations.)[16]

Grandparents without Contact

If you are a grandparent who has a grandchild not visiting you or your child, you are in a painful, but common situation. Many of the parents I interviewed in the book lamented not only their own loss of contact with their children, but also the loss their parents experienced. (See Rachel, chapter 1). A movement is growing slowly in the United States concerning grandparents' rights after a divorce, and, as mentioned in chapter 7, you may have a legal right to access to your grandchild.

Many grandparents are upset over the loss of contact with their grandchildren that sometimes accompanies a divorce. Grandparents report that they do not see their grandchildren because the youngsters have been poisoned against them by the custodial parent or because the grandparents are closely associated with the absent parent. Sometimes grandparents are forced to take sides and support their own child in custody disputes, even though it results in a cutoff from their grandchildren if the court case is lost. This can take an extreme turn. In one case, the grandparents were "enabling" their son in not seeing his children. The father of the children refused to see them until their mother changed in some amorphous way. But the mother was never clear what was wrong and why the father would not visit his children. She did not know what to do. The children were hurting. The grandparents blindly supported their son, the father. They completely accepted his behavior without question. No one was the winner.

In another situation, a grandmother established contact with her granddaughter seventeen years after the granddaughter's out-of-wedlock birth. The grandmother's son had a brief relationship with the granddaughter's mother, had parted on friendly terms, but had never seen his daughter. The grandmother wondered what had happened to her granddaughter, sought her out, and eventually, following a long series of written communications, established a loving relationship with her. Because of the older woman's actions, the granddaughter and the father started to build a relationship.

If you are not having contact, try the following:

1. Look for support from other grandparents and explore your legal options.

2. Keep communication open with all the parties.

3. If you fear being disloyal to your child by initiating communication with your grandchildren, discuss this with your child. Your child may be happy that you are establishing contact. Make sure your support of your child in not seeing the children is not encouraging behavior that should be questioned.

4. Do not attack the custodial parent if you are trying for visitation. That will serve only to further solidify his or her defenses.

5. If you are seeing your grandchildren sporadically, do not make your time together into an inquisition. They will be feeling torn between their parents and will not appreciate your prying or accusations. Guilt-inducing comments—such as, "You know your father misses you a great deal; you are making life miserable for him"—are not recommended. Instead try, "I am sure there is a lot of pain for everyone when people do not see each other. Hopefully, when you all feel ready, you can work something out."

Grandparents with Contact

Some grandparents keep in touch with grandchildren, even though their child does not. These grandparents often refuse to get involved in the custody disputes and do not take sides. They then continue their relationship with their grandchildren, often to the chagrin and anger of their own child.[17] Some grandchildren can be very happy for a while visiting their grandparents but not their parent. At some point, the piper may have to be paid, though, as it was for Tom and Candy (see chapter 6), who ultimately felt used by their grandparents and never trusted them again.

If you are a grandparent who has contact, while your child does not, contemplate these suggestions:

1. Talk openly with your child about your actions and your reasons for them.

2. Do not try to always steer conversations with your grandchildren toward their mother or father unless the children bring up questions or concerns. Be careful to not make the grandchild feel guilty for rejecting your child. If abandoned by your son or daughter, the grandchildren should hear from you that they are loveable and are not to blame for the lack of contact.

3. Do not bad-mouth the custodial parent or your own child; that will not help your grandchildren's self-esteem. You can disagree with behaviors without performing a character assassination.

4. Be careful about siding with the custodial parent against your child, as sometimes happens. Your child may have acted inappropriately, and your former daughter or son-in-law may need support. You can be supportive, but do it in a manner that does not close the door to future rapprochements, unless the behavior of your child has been so inappropriate that future contact is out of the question.

5. Remember to keep the boundaries as clear as possible. Explain to everyone involved (your child, your ex-son-in-law or daughter-in-law and

his or her parents, and your grandchildren) what your role will and will not be. For example, are you to be a go-between? Are you expected to bring information back and forth between warring parties? Are you expected to listen to one or the other parent being attacked? Or will you say that you are interested in hearing the speaker's feelings but are not interested in hearing negatives about someone?

6. Do not shy away from seeking professional assistance. Therapy can help at any of the stages that I have discussed. Whether individual, group, or family therapy is advised is a decision that needs to be made based on your situation. Each can help in different ways depending upon the circumstances. In addition, the timing of therapy can be key. Parents may feel differently about children they are battling over in court once the case is resolved. For example, during a court contest, the parent may have a need to see the child in a favorable light.[18] A few months later, a different impression may develop, one that may be more reality-based or may develop as a result of the court case. Therapy at this point may be advised, whereas immediately following a contest, it may not have seemed indicated.

Grandparents with Custody

If you are a grandparent with custody, you probably have had to pick up the pieces from your son or daughter's relationship. From your vantage point you may have the wisdom to have predicted what was going to happen. Now you are raising the grandchild alone or with the help of your child full or part-time. You will need to read some of the earlier parts of the chapter written for the custodial parent to get a sense of the importance of your role. As one of the key adults in your child's life, your influence is great.

If you are working to prevent a cutoff or to resolve one that has occurred, consider the following:

1. Your approval will probably be important to the parents involved.

2. While you may need to provide protection for your grandchild in some cases, most of the time you should assume a position that will encourage contact between that child and the parent(s).

3. You may be in the position of putting yourself out of a parenting job. If contact resumes between the child and the absent parent or parents, it may result in your losing custody or daily living contact with that child. That can be very difficult for grandparents who have become attached to the child. Prepare yourself for that eventuality by examining your own role and motivation in any ongoing visitation disputes.

4. Be supportive of your grandchild's feelings during the process of trying to reestablish a relationship with the parent(s).

5. Do not bad-mouth the absent parent. Doing so is also an attack on the child. Describe the behavior that may be troublesome to you without attacking the person. Your feedback to the child about the other parent has to be accurate. At the same time, it can be neutral. In one grandparent support group I led, we spent a great deal of time discussing what a grandparent should tell a young child about why Mommy did not visit. (The mother was a drug addict.) The grandparent decided to tell her grandchild that her mother had problems but that the mother loved her very much. She reassured the child that her mother's absence had nothing to do with her, a fantasy that children often harbor.

A Note for New Spouses and Significant Others

Stepparents and others who are significantly involved are usually in a tricky position. If you are married to the custodial parent (most of the noncustodial parents I interviewed said their ex had remarried), you may be seen as having replaced the noncustodial parent. Your life has come to revolve around your stepchildren, and you may also have children of your own you are raising. If you are married to the noncustodial parent, you have no doubt come to understand the pain he or she feels in being out of the child's life. Some people may be blaming you for the lack of contact, stating that the child does not like you or that you have changed your spouse in a way that makes that spouse not able to relate to his or her child anymore. If you have brought children into the marriage, you may also hear that your spouse is now more interested in your children than in his or hers.

Tough position for you to be in. If you are a person of integrity and are not undermining any of the parties in these situations, you will consider these points:

1. You have your own feelings and ideas about what has transpired in the family into which you have married. You have a right to express those to your spouse in a way that is supportive of him or her while also supporting your own position. But while you share your feelings, the more you can see things in the multifaceted way in which they have unfolded, the less sticky things will get. Remember, when it comes to your spouse's children, he or she is ultimately responsible.

2. Whether you are with the custodial or noncustodial parent, the children will have significant feelings about the other parent. They will be checking you out to see where you stand. Making negative statements about the other parent in front of the children is, to some extent, an attack on the children. Be an active listener. Support the children's expression of feelings without necessarily supporting what they are saying. You might

say something like "I can understand your being angry at your father/ mother. You feel as though he doesn't treat you well. That must be hard." Such a statement is different from saying, "Your father has been a bad person."

3. Be careful about being caught between warring family members. The possibilities are many. You could be caught between your spouse and his ex-spouse, with both blaming you for their difficulties rather than accepting their responsibility. You could be caught between your stepchild and your spouse, or between your stepchild and the other parent. If this is happening, you can tell them you feel uncomfortable being placed in the middle and work with the other family members to reduce this occurrence. Active listening here can be especially helpful.

4. Finally, maintain a sense of humor. Negative stories about stepparents are rampant. You do not have to act in a way that reinforces them.

Conclusions

Whether you are the visiting parent, the custodial parent, child, grandparent, or new spouse/significant other, your behavior will have an impact on the evolving relationships. Parents and children do not have to reach the point of no return, even when harm has been done.[19] Pressures will arise in the social, structural, emotional, and legal spheres that may conspire to pull you apart. The goal is to be aware of those pressures, keep working at staying in touch, and strive for change.

Notes

Preface

1. Schneiderman (1990).
2. The questionnaire is available from the author

CHAPTER ONE *Divorce and How Parents Lose Contact*

1. U.S. Bureau of the Census (1995a).
2. Ibid.
3. U.S. Bureau of the Census (1994). The actual number of children and parents living away from each other is higher because the figure of forty-seven million children in two-parent homes includes those living in remarried families. Of children in single-parent families, 37 percent are living with a divorced parent, 30 percent with a never married parent, and 23 percent with a separated parent (U.S. Bureau of the Census, 1996a).
4. Zill & Nord (1994). The effect of the 1996 welfare bill is unclear.
5. By comparison, the median income was over $43,500 when both parents are in the home, according to a recent Census Bureau report. See Holmes (1994).
6. U.S. Bureau of the Census (1995b). While custodial mothers received more child support on average ($3,011) than fathers ($2,292), they were more apt to be in poverty (U.S. Bureau of the Census, 1996b).
7. Goldberg (1995).
8. Lewin (1995).
9. Del Carmen & Virgo (1993).
10. Ibid.
11. For an interesting and often painful in-depth look at daughters of 269 divorced women and absent fathers, see Wakerman (1984), who uses a volunteer middle-class convenience sample.
12. Furstenberg, Peterson, Nord, & Zill (1983).

13. Seltzer (1991), using a national sample, places the figure of noncustodial fathers who do not visit at close to 30 percent, while Minton & Pasley (1996), using a convenience sample, place it at 9 percent, and Maccoby & Mnookin (1992), using a California sample from the 1980s, give it as 18 percent. The Census Bureau data were gathered from Lydia Scoon-Rogers, July 17, 1996. A change in the rule concerning a custodial parent's right to move out of state (as recently happened in New York) could reduce visitation further.

14. Seltzer (1991).

15. Lydia Scoon-Rogers, July 17, 1996.

16. Mothers without Custody, developed in the 1980s, is intended to provide emotional support and advocacy for noncustodial mothers. It has a national board, revolving presidents, and an occasional newsletter that assists in linking a loose network of locally run support groups. It can be called at 1-800-457-MWOC. Fathers United for Equal Rights, also spawned in the 1980s, is oriented more toward advocacy. No national board exists, but there is a greater proliferation of local support groups throughout the United States, a probable reflection of the greater number of fathers living away from their children.

17. Adjusted for 1991 dollars, median income of both black and white males working full-time declined between 1979 and 1991, while for black and white females it increased. (U.S. Bureau of the Census, 1993a).

18. U.S. Bureau of the Census (1993b).

19. Davis & Emory (1995).

20. U.S. Department of Health and Human Services (1993).

21. Aldarondo (1996).

22. Zill & Nord (1994).

23. Bianchi (1995).

24. There are exceptions, of course, as was noted recently in this news report: "A veteran state trooper sued the Maryland State Police over a policy that he says denies family leave benefits for fathers solely because of their gender. . . . one administrator told him that 'God decided only women can give birth,' and denied his request." (Meyers, 1995.)

25. Menaghan & Parcel (1990).

26. Blankenhorn (1995).

27. Chesler (1986).

28. Lamb (1995).

29. U.S. Bureau of the Census (1992a).

30. U.S. Bureau of the Census (1984).

31. Zill & Nord (1994).

32. Ibid.

33. Chesler (1984).

34. Hogrefe (1992).

35. Weinraub (1994).

36. Saposnek (1991); Maccoby & Mnookin (1992).

37. Hoffman (1995). In one study, the removal of the maternal preference was not found to reduce the rate of mother custody (Bahr, Howe, Mann, & Bahr, 1994).

38. Hoffman (1995).

39. West & Samuels (1995); Annie E. Casey Foundation (1995).
40. Burmeister (1992).
41. Stanley (1992); Dillon (1992).
42. Father poisoned his 5 children, police say (1993).
43. Hanley (1994).
44. Nieves (1992).
45. Greif & Pabst (1988).
46. Braver, Wolchik, Sandler, & Sheets (1993).
47. Ibid.
48. Ibid, pp. 94–95.
49. Personal communication with Tarrie Condon, Child Support Enforcement Agency of California, April 12, 1995. Ms. Condon reported receiving on average fifty calls a week from parents in California seeking assistance with recovering child support. Following an article in *Time Magazine* (April 3, 1995) that mentioned her private, for-profit agency, the number of calls doubled.
50. Ibid.
51. See Greif & Pabst (1988); Greif (1990).
52. Paasch & Teachman (1991).
53. Teachman (1991).
54. Pirog-Good & Brown (1996).
55. Bartfeld & Meyer (1994). For other research using Wisconsin as a basis, see Kost, Meyer, Corbett, & Brown (1996) and Meyer, Bartfeld, Garfinkel, and Brown (1996).

Maryland is one example of a state that is providing training, education, and counseling to the nonpaying parent for the purposes of increasing payments. In Anne Arundel County, after a parent is located following a charge of noncompliance, he or she is evaluated by the program. The cases that are heard by the court often involve men and women who are hard to employ due to lack of education and training, employment history, personal problems often related to substance abuse, and legal problems. These are the stereotypical hard-core nonpayers who drop out of contact with their children. Counselors provide a multimodal approach to get them training and education, work, relief from their court problems, and substance abuse treatment when needed. The program is more cost effective than incarceration and often provides personal as well as programmatic successes. (Three of the parents interviewed for this book, two mothers and one father, have participated in the program.)

Stepped-up enforcement of child support collections could result in the money so gained being offset by the increased spending in collections (Bragg, 1995).

Child support payments are, of course, not just an issue in the United States. Great Britain, for example, has recently overhauled its child support collection process and is more rigidly pursuing those who owe (Stevenson, 1994).

56. Greif & Pabst (1988).
57. Just as mothers are usually the source of information on nonpaying fathers, a convenience sample I collected of over eleven hundred fathers with custody provides some information about noncustodial mothers' patterns. The poorer the father, the more likely he was to receive payment. He was especially apt to receive payment if his ex-wife outearned him. Less than half of the fathers who were court-ordered child support say they always received it, and one third said they never received it,

figures comparable to national figures and to what mothers who are owed child support report (Greif & DeMaris, 1991).

58. See Seltzer & Brandreth (1994) for a discussion of this point. In addition, they also ask what measures are best used to determine the result of the contact—questionnaire responses, test scores, in-depth interviews?

59. Mott (1990).

60. Furstenberg, Peterson, Nord, & Zill (1983).

61. See Seltzer (1991) for more information on this point.

62. Ihinger-Tallman, Pasley, & Buehler (1995).

63. Tepp (1983).

64. Nelson & Valliant (1993).

65. King (1994) found few benefits of father involvement after a breakup outside of the positive effect on academic achievement. She concedes, though, that her research sample did not tap into the quality of the father-child relationship.

66. Amato & Rezac (1994).

67. Furstenberg, Morgan, & Allison (1987).

68. A similar idea about the complexity of the issues being assessed is raised by another group of researchers. They examined frequency of visitation, regularity of visitation, and closeness of father and child among over 100 children and found no clear trends for all the children. Differences were discovered within subsets of the sample. For example, young boys benefitted from contact with their fathers more than younger girls, and neither older boys nor older girls appeared to benefit, with there being a lowering of self-esteem among the older groups when there was contact. In understanding why girls fared worse with visitation, the researchers suggest that such contact might intensify conflict between the custodial mother and daughter. Being involved in legal conflict resulted in a negative outcome for all of the children (Healy, Malley, & Stewart, 1990).

69. Wallerstein & Kelly (1980).

70. Jacobs (1982).

71. Kruk (1991; 1994).

72. Tepp (1983).

73. Wallerstein & Kelly (1980).

74. Dudley (1991a; 1991b).

75. Ballard (1995), p. 67.

76. Greif (1995b).

77. Santrock & Warshak (1979).

78. Downey & Powell (1993).

79. Depner (1993).

80. Greif & Pabst (1988).

81. Arditti & Madden-Derdich (1993).

82. Despite, or perhaps because of this stigma (or due to financial difficulties), mothers without custody may live closer to their children than fathers without custody. Seventy-one percent of noncustodial mothers as compared with sixty-five percent of noncustodial fathers live in the same state as the custodial parent (U.S. Bureau of the Census, 1995b). Living in the same state does not necessarily mean there is more visitation, but it is likely to mean the distance between parent and child is reduced.

CHAPTER TWO *When Fathers and Children No Longer Visit: Feelings of Inadequacy and Rejection*

1. Alvarez (1995), p. B4.
2. Rachmael Tobesman. Personal communication, May 24, 1994.
3. Allen-Hagen, Sickmund, & Snyer (1994).
4. U.S. Bureau of the Census (1992b).
5. Kaufman (1985).
6. Straus, Gelles, & Steinmetz (1980).
7. Some of the fathers in this last group are similar to those who did not want more contact with their children, constituting about 13 percent of the sample. Fathers who do not want more contact differed from the other fathers in the study who want more contact in the following ways: They were less involved with the children during the marriage, were more satisfied with their relationship with the children now, believed the children were happier not seeing them now, and had not kept up with their children. See Greif (1995a).
8. See Ihinger-Tallman, Pasley, & Buehler (1995), who mention this issue and the father's emotional stability as variables in father involvement.
9. Ibid.
10. I wish to mention one more situation related to why a cutoff occurs. At the time of the breakup, a father was enraged at the mother, for reasons that were left unspecified. He wanted absolutely nothing to do with her and was willing to give up all contact with his six month old son in order to avoid seeing her which visitation would have necessitated. Never married to the mother, he soon married a neighbor who, interestingly enough, had a child the same age as his own son. The two families live in the same neighborhood, the children play together, but the child does not know that his friend's stepfather is his own father.

This situation is emblematic of the kinds of extreme reactions that fathers can have after the end of a relationship, and how those reactions will affect the child. To the son, his father abandoned him. The father sees himself as capable of establishing a meaningful relationship with a child (his stepson), but, because of his feelings toward his son's mother, refuses contact. The father's actions are not justifiable; he should have worked through his feelings toward the mother by now for the benefit of the son.

CHAPTER THREE *When Fathers and Children No Longer Visit: The More Acrimonious Cases*

1. Gardner (1987).
2. Greif (1990).

CHAPTER FOUR *When Mothers and Children No Longer Visit: Feelings of Rejection and Betrayal*

1. Furstenberg, Peterson, Nord, & Zill (1983).
2. Reasons could also be related to the fact that women are more apt to be the spouse that ends the marriage, and in so doing, would be severing the relationship with the father at the same time he leaves the home. He loses his family and home and might feel too rejected to attempt to maintain contact. It also could be that chil-

dren, most accustomed to spending time with their mothers, might seek her out more.

3. Jennifer Isham. Personal communication, March 1, 1995.

4. See, for example, Greif (1987); Greif & Emad (1989); Greif & Pabst (1988).

5. Greif & Pabst (1988).

6. Families & Work Institute (1995).

7. U.S. Bureau of the Census (1995c).

8. See Greif (1995b) for a discussion of fathers who did not want contact. All comparisons in Table 1 are significant at the p.05 level.

9. Horowitz, Wilner, & Alvarez (1979).

10. This is meant to be merely suggestive; these were also parents who were divorced. It could be the combination of being divorced and then having no contact with the child that causes the reaction.

CHAPTER FIVE *When Mothers and Children No Longer Visit: When Others Raise Concerns*

1. It is interesting to note that mothers are much more apt to be accused of neglect than fathers. Fathers in the survey were much less apt to have sole custody before they lost contact than mothers, as is mentioned in the previous chapter, so the opportunity for neglect *is* less.

2. See Zuravin and Greif (1989) for a further discussion of AFDC mothers who lost custody after the involvement of child protective services.

3. Thoennes (1988).

4. See Wylie's (1993) balanced discussion.

5. Other mothers who fit this category were also interviewed but are not included here as Ferne's case captures many of their situations' characteristics.

CHAPTER SIX *The Children's Views*

1. Kurdek, Fine, & Sinclair (1995).

2. Wall & Levy (1994).

3. Hertsgaard (1995).

4. Rosseby & Johnston (1995), p. 49.

5. Johnston (1993), pp. 121–124.

6. Johnston, Kline, & Tschann (1991).

7. Folberg (1991a); Maccoby & Mnookin (1992).

8. Johnston, Campbell, & Mayes (1985).

9. Cooney, Smyer, Hagestad, & Klock (1986).

10. Greif & Emad (1989).

11. Associated Press (1995b).

12. Biringen (1994).

13. Ibid.

14. Lund (1995).

15. Johnston (1993).

16. Gardner (1987), pp. xix–xx.

17. Ibid. pp. 67–68.

18. Lund (1995).

19. Greif (1990), pp. 15–21.
20. Blankenhorn (1995).
21. Greif (1995a) .
22. Nicholas Zill, during testimony before U.S. Commission on Child and Family Welfare, March 29, 1995.

CHAPTER SEVEN *Absent Parents, Law, and Social Policy*

1. Krause (1995).
2. Folberg (1991b); Krause (1995).
3. Threatt (1993).
4. Morison & Greene (1992); Rieser (1991); Sorensen & Snow (1991).
5. Thoennes (1988).
6. Thoennes (1988).
7. See, for example, Gardner (1987).
8. See, for example, Pennington (1990).
9. *Grandparents* (1982).
10. Czapanskiy (1994); Myers & Perrin (1993); Thompson, Scalora, Limber, & Castrianno (1991); McCrimmon & Howell (1989).
11. Kotkin (1985).
12. McCrimmon & Howell (1989).
13. Title IV-D to the Social Security Act.
14. Lima & Harris (1988).
15. Corlyon (1990).
16. Czapanskiy (1989).
17. Czapanskiy (1989).
18. Czapanskiy (1989).
19. Pearson & Anhalt (1994); see, for example, Seltzer (1991).
20. Pearson & Anhalt (1994), p. 104.
21. Kotkin (1985).
22. Wolf & Mast (1987).
23. Wolf & Mast (1987).
24. See, for example, Bregande (1989).
25. Turnbull (1981).
26. See, for example, Goldstein, Freud & Solnit (1979); Guggenheim (1994).

CHAPTER EIGHT *When Contact Is Reestablished: Where to Go from Here*

1. Annie E. Casey Foundation (1995).
2. Buehler, Beth, Ryan, Legg, & Trotter (1992); Kramer & Washo (1993).
3. Ahrons & Rogers (1993) suggest paying particular attention to the year after the divorce as the time to intervene to iron out conflict.
4. This point is made in an excellent article by Arditti (1995).
5. Lewin (1995)
6. Ballard (1995).
7. Phares (1996).
8. Bertoia & Drakich (1995).

CHAPTER NINE *Prevention and Resolution: Advice for Parents and Children*

1. Rice & Rice (1986).

2. See Hutchins (1995) for a discussion of some of the grassroots efforts to enhance father involvement that are being tried around the country.

3. Brown (1996) outlines some of the basic considerations concerning the rights of divorced parents and inpatient and outpatient therapy for their children. Consultation with a lawyer in the family's home state is recommended.

4. Greif & Hegar (1993).

5. Johnston & Campbell (1988), p. 200.

6. Ibid., p. 200.

7. Friesen (1985), p. 83.

8. Berg (1993).

9. Neuman (1993).

10. Toder (1986).

11. Adair (1985).

12. Johnston & Campbell (1988), p. 246.

13. Gottman (1994).

14. DeMaris & Greif (1992). It should also be noted that, according to one study, preadolescent children being raised by single mothers exhibited significant adjustment difficulties as they reached preadolescence that the same children had not exhibited when evaluated at an earlier age (Gringlas & Weinraub, 1995). This further attests to the variability of age in measuring adjustment of children in single-parent families.

15. See also Sloman & Pipitone (1991).

16. U.S. Bureau of the Census (1996a).

17. Greif & Kristall (1993).

18. Solomon (1991).

19. In cases where a parent has harmed a child or others, communication by letter or phone may be possible, though monitoring may be advisable.

References

Adair, C. 1985. Noncustodial connections. *Single Parent, 23*(6), 26, 27, 30.

Ahrons, C.R. & Miller, R.B. 1993. The effect of the post divorce relationship on paternal involvement: A longitudinal analysis. *American Journal of Orthopsychiatry, 63,* 441–450.

Aldarondo, E. 1996. Cessation and persistence of wife assault: A longitudinal analysis. *American Journal of Orthopsychiatry, 66,* 141–151.

Allen–Hagen, B., M. Sickmund, H. N. Snyer. 1994, November. Juveniles and violence: Juvenile offending and victimization. Fact Sheet 19. Washington, DC: Office of Juvenile Justice and Delinquency Prevention.

Alvarez, L. 1995. September 8. When dad wants to be more than just a check. *New York Times,* pp. B1, B4.

Amato, P. R., & Rezac, S. J. 1994. Contact with nonresident parents, interparental conflict, and children's behavior. *Journal of Family Issues 15,* 191–207.

Arditti, J. 1995. Noncustodial parents: Emergent issues of diversity and process. *Marriage and Family Review,* 20(3/4), 283–304.

Arditti, J., & Madden-Derdich, D. A. 1993. Noncustodial mothers: Developing strategies of support. *Family Relations, 42,* 305–314.

Associated Press. 1995, August 4. Sorting siblings: Postal co-workers discover they are sister and brother. *Baltimore Sun,* A2.

Bahr, S. J., Howe, J. D., Mann, M. M., & Bahr, M. S. 1994. Trends in child custody awards: Has the removal of maternal preference made a difference. *Family Law Quarterly, 28,* 247–259.

Ballard, C. A. 1995. Prodigal dad: How we bring fathers home to their children. *Policy Review, 71,* 66–70.

Bartfeld, J., & Meyer, D. R. 1994. Are there really deadbeat dads? The relationship between ability to pay, enforcement, and compliance in nonmarital child support cases. *Social Service Review, 68,* 219–235.

Berg, B. R. 1993. Children who resist or refuse visitation. *Single Parent,* 36(3), 13–14.

Bertoia, C. E. & Drakich, J. 1995. The fathers' rights movement: Contradictions in rhetoric and practice. In W. Marsiglio, (Ed.), *Fatherhood: Contemporary theory, research, and social policy* (pp. 230–254). Thousand Oaks: CA: Sage.

Bianchi, S. M. 1995. The changing demographic and socioeconomic characteristics of single parent families. *Marriage and Family Review,* 20(1/2), 71–97.

Biringen, Z. 1994. Attachment theory and research: Application to clinical practice. *American Journal of Orthopsychiatry, 64,* 404–420.

Blankenhorn, D. 1995. *Fatherless America.* New York: Basic Books.

Bragg, R. 1995, April 14. Georgia, pursuing child support, discovers its potential and limits. *New York Times,* pp. AL, D18.

Braver, S. L., Wolchik, S. A., Sandler, I. N., & Sheets, V. L. 1993. A social exchange model of nonresidential parent involvement. In C. E. Depner & J. H. Bray, (Eds.), *Nonresidential parenting: New vistas in family living* (pp. 87–108). Newbury Park, CA: Sage.

Braver, S. L., Wolchik, S. A., Sandler, I. N., Sheets, V. L., Fogas, B., & Bay, R. C. 1993. A longitudinal study of noncustodial parents: Parents without children. *Journal of Family Psychology, 7,* 9–23.

Brown, M. J. 1996. Joint custody and the minor client: Inpatient and outpatient therapy. *Family Therapy News,* 27(1), 9.

Buehler, C., Betz, C., Ryan, C. M., Legg, B. H., & Trotter, B. B. 1992. description and evaluation of the orientation for divorcing parents: Implications for postdivorce prevention programs. *Family Relations, 41,* 154–162.

Burmeister, H. W. 1992. Murder at the courthouse. *Voices of Children,* 2(7/8), 16.

Bregande, M. 1989. No longer the father's primary duty to support: Legal equality or economic disparity among the sexes? *Saint Louis University Law Journal, 34,* 133–147.

Annie E. Casey Foundation. 1995. *Kids count data book.* Baltimore: Author.

Charlow, A. 1994. Awarding custody: The best interests of the child and other fictions. In S. R. Humm, B. A. Ort, M. M. Anbari, W. S. Lader, & W. S. Biel (Eds.), *Child, parent, & state: Law and policy reader* (pp. 3–26). Philadelphia: Temple University Press.

Chesler, P. 1986. *Mothers on trial.* New York: McGraw–Hill.

Cooney, T. M., Smyer, M. A., Hagestad, G. O., & Klock, R. 1986. Parental divorce in young adulthood: Some preliminary findings. *American Journal of Orthopsychiatry, 56,* 470–477.

Corlyon, J. 1990. From rights to responsibilities for parents: The emancipation of children. *Family Law, 20,* 380–393.

Czpanskiy, K. 1989. Child support and visitation: Rethinking the connections. *Rutgers Law Journal, 20,* 619–665.

Czpanskiy, K. 1994. Grandparents, parents and grandchildren: Actualizing interdependency in law. *Connecticut Law Review, 26,* 1315–1375.

Davis, M., & Emory, E. 1995. Sex differences in neonatal stress reactivity. *Child Development, 66,* 14–27.

Del Carmen, R. & Virgo, G. N. 1993. Marital disruption and nonresidential parenting: A multicultural perspective. In C. E. Depner & J. H. Bray (Eds.), *Nonresidential parenting: New vistas in family living* (pp. 13–36). Newbury Park, CA: Sage.

DeMaris, A., & Greif, G .L. 1992. The relationship between family structure and parent-child relationship problems in single father households. *Journal of Divorce and Remarriage, 18*(1/2), 55–78.

Depner, C. E. 1993. Parental role reversal: Mothers as nonresidential parents. In C. E. Depner & J. H. Bray (Eds.), *Nonresidential parenting: New vistas in family living* (pp. 37–57). Newbury Park, CA: Sage.

Dillon, S. 1992, October 17. Shooting followed tougher efforts to collect child support. *New York Times,* pp. 27, 32.

Downey, D. B., & Powell, B. 1993. Do children in single-parent households fare better living with same-sex parents? *Journal of Marriage and the Family, 55,* 55–71.

Dudley, J. R. 1991a. Increasing our understanding of divorced fathers who have infrequent contact with their children. *Family Relations, 40,* 279–285.

Dudley, J. R. 1991b. The consequences of divorce proceedings for divorced fathers. *Journal of Divorce and Remarriage, 16*(3/4), 171–193.

Families & Work Institute. 1995. *Women: The new providers.* Whirlpool Foundation Study. Benton Harbor, MI: Whirlpool Foundation.

Father poisoned his 5 children, police say. 1993, January 5. *New York Times,* p. A10.

Folberg, J. 1991a. Custody overview. In J. Folberg (Ed.), *Joint custody & shared parenting, 2d ed.* (pp. 3–10). New York: Guilford.

Folberg, J., (Ed.) 1991b. Joint custody and shared parenting. New York: Guilford.

Friesen, J. D. 1985. *Structural-strategic marriage and family therapy.* New York: Guilford.

Furstenberg, F. F., & Cherlin, A. J. 1991. *Divided families: What happens to children when parents part.* Cambridge: Harvard University Press.

Furstenberg, F. F., Morgan, S. P., & Allison, P. D. 1987. Parental participation and children's well–being after marital dissolution, *American Sociological Review, 52,* 695–701.

Furstenberg, F. F., Peterson, J. L., Nord, C. W., & Zill, N. 1983. The life course of children of divorce: Marital disruption and parental contact. *American Sociological Review, 48,* 656–668.

Gardner, R. 1987. *The parental alienation syndrome and the differentiation between fabricated and genuine child sex abuse.* Creskill, NJ: Creative Therapeutics.

Goldberg, J. R. 1995. Reconnecting missing fathers to their children. *Family Therapy News, 26*(3), 16, 17, 27, 29.

Goldstein, J., Freud, A., & Solnit, A. J. 1979. *Beyond the best interests of the child* (2d ed.). New York: Free Press.

Gottman, L. 1994. *Why marriages succeed or fail.* New York: Simon & Schuster.

Grandparents: The Other Victims of Divorce and Custody Disputes. Hearings before the Subcommittee on Human Services of the Select Committee on Aging, U.S. House of Representatives, 97th Congress, 2d Session (1982).

Greif, G. L. 1987. Mothers without custody. *Social Work, 32,* 11–17.

Greif, G. L. 1990. *The daddy track and the single father.* New York: Lexington/Free Press.

Greif, G. L. 1995a. Single fathers with custody following separation and divorce. *Marriage and Family Review,* 20(1/2), 213–232.

Greif, G. L. 1995b. When divorced fathers want no contact with their children. *Journal of Divorce and Remarriage,* 23(1/2), 75–84.

Greif, G. L., & DeMaris, A. 1991. When a single custodial father receives child support. *American Journal of Family Therapy, 19,* 167–176.

Greif, G. L., & Emad, F. 1989. A longitudinal examination of mothers without custody: Implications for treatment. *American Journal of Family Therapy, 17,* 155–163.

Greif, G. L., & Hegar, R.L. 1993. *When parents kidnap: The families behind the headlines.* New York: Free Press.

Greif, G. L., & Kristall, J. 1993. A support group for non–custodial parents. *Families in Society, 74,* 240–245.

Greif, G. L., & Pabst, M. S. 1988. *Mothers without custody.* New York: Lexington/Free Press.

Gringlas, M., & Weinraub, M. 1995. The more things change. . . Single parenting revisited. *Journal of Family Issues, 16,* 29–52.

Guggenheim, M. 1994. The best interests of the child: Much ado about nothing. In S. R. Humm, B. A. Ort, M. M. Anbari, W. S. Lader, & W. S. Biel (Eds.), *Child, parent, & state: law and policy reader* (pp. 27–35). Philadelphia: Temple University Press.

Guidera, M. 1994, September 3. Boss, 2 children defend child support 'deadbeat.' *Baltimore Sun,* pp. 1B,16B.

Hanley, R. 1994, June 28. Divorced father accused of killing his 2 children. *New York Times,* p. B5.

Healy, J. M., Malley, J. E., Stewart, A. J. 1990. Children and their fathers after parental separation. *American Journal of Orthopsychiatry, 60,* 531–543.

Hertsgaard, M. 1995. *A day in the life: The music and artistry of the Beatles.* New York: Delacorte.

Hoffman, J. 1995, April 26. Divorced fathers make gains in battles to increase rights. *New York Times,* pp. AL, B5.

Hogrefe, J. 1992. *O'Keeffe: The life of an American legend.* New York: Bantam.

Holmes, S. A. 1994, July, 21. Birthrate for unwed women up 70% since 1983, study says. *New York Times,* p. Al.

Horowitz, M., Wilner, N., & Alvarez, W. 1979. The impact of events scale: A measure of subjective stress. *Psychosomatic Medicine, 41,* 209–218.

Hutchins, J. 1995. "Disconnected dads" draws big crowd for family impact seminar. *Family Therapy News, 26*(4), 27–28.

Ihinger-Tallman, M., Pasley, K., & Buehler, C. 1995. Developing a middle–range theory of father involvement postdivorce. In W. Marsiglio (Ed.), *Fatherhood: Contemporary theory, research, and social policy* (pp. 57–77). Thousand Oaks, CA: Sage.

Jacobs, J. W. 1982. The effect of divorce on fathers: An overview of the literature. *American Journal of Psychiatry, 139,* 1235–1239.

Johnston, J. R. 1993. Children who refuse visitation. In C. E. Depner & J. H. Bray (Eds.), *Nonresidential parenting: New vistas in family living* (pp. 109–135). Newbury Park, CA: Sage.

Johnston, J. R., and Campbell, L. E. G. 1988. *Impasses of divorce.* New York: Free Press.

Johnston, J. R., Campbell, L. E. G., & Mayes, S. S. 1985. Latency children in post-separation and divorce disputes. *Journal of the American Academy of Child Psychiatry, 24,* 563–574.

Johnston, J. R., Kline, M., & Tschann, J. M. 1991. Ongoing post–divorce conflict in families contesting custody: Do joint custody and frequent access help? In J. Folberg (Ed.), *Joint custody & shared parenting,* 2d ed. (pp.177–184). New York: Guilford.

Kaufman, E. 1985. *Substance abuse and family therapy.* Orlando: Grune & Stratton.

King, V. 1994. Nonresident father involvement and child well-being: Can dads make a difference? *Journal of Family Issues, 15,* 78–96.

Kost, K. A., Meyer, D. R., Corbett, T., & Brown, P. R. 1996. Revising child support orders: The Wisconsin experience. *Family Relations, 45,* 19–26.

Kotkin, R. 1985. Grandparents versus the state: A constitutional right to custody. *Hofstra Law Review, 13,* 375–406.

Kramer, B. J., & Washo, K. 1993. Evaluation of a court-mandated prevention program for divorcing parents: The Children First Program. *Family Relations, 42,* 179–186.

Krause, H. 1995. *Family Law in a Nutshell.* (3d ed.) St. Paul, MN: West Publishing.

Kruk, E. 1991. Discontinuity between pre- and post-divorce father-child relationships: New evidence regarding paternal disengagement. *Journal of Divorce and Remarriage,* 16(3/4), 195–227.

Kruk, E. 1994. The disengaged noncustodial father: Implications for social work practice with the divorced family. *Social Work, 39,* 15–25.

Kurdek, L. A., Fine, M. A., & Sinclair, R. J. 1995. School adjustment in sixth graders: Parenting transitions, family climate, and peer norm effects. *Child Development, 66,* 430–445.

Lamb, M. E. 1995. The changing role of father. In J. L. Shapiro, M. J. Diamond, & M. Greenberg (Eds.), *Becoming a father* (pp. 18–35). New York: Springer.

Layton v. Foster, 61 N.Y.2d 747, 460 N.E.2d 1351, 472 N.Y.S.2d 916 (1984).

Lewin, T. 1995, June 18. Creating fathers out of men with children. *New York Times,*pp. A1, A20.

Lima, L. H. & Harris, R. C. 1988. The child support enforcement program in the United States. In A. J. Kahn & S. B. Kamerman (Eds.), *Child support: From debt collection to social policy* (pp. 20–44). Newbury Park, CA: Sage.

Lund, M. 1995. A therapist's view of parental alienation syndrome. *Family and Conciliation Courts Review, 33,* 308–316.

Maccoby, E. E., & Mnookin, R. H. 1992. *Dividing the child: Social and legal dilemmas of custody.* Cambridge: Harvard University.

McCrimmon, C. A., & Howell, R. J. 1989. Grandparents' legal rights to visitation in the fifty states and the District of Columbia. *Bulletin of the American Academy of Psychiatry and the Law, 17*(4), 355–366.

Menaghan, E. G., & Parcel, T. L. 1990. Parental employment and family life: Research in the 1980s. *Journal of Marriage and the Family, 52,* 1079–1098.

Meyer, D. R., Bartfeld, J., Garfinkel, I., & Brown, P. 1996. Child support reform: Lessons from Wisconsin. *Family Relations, 45,* 11–18.

Meyers, M. 1995, April 29. Trooper sues over policy denying men family leave. *Baltimore Sun,* p. B2.

Mimkon v. Ford, 66 N.J. 426, 332 A.2d 199 (1975).

Minton, C., & Pasley, K. 1996. Fathers' parenting role identity and father involvement: A comparison of nondivorced and divorced, nonresident fathers. *Journal of Family Issues, 17,* 26–45.

Morison, S., & Greene, E. 1992. Juror and expert knowledge of child sexual abuse. *Child Abuse & Neglect, 16,* 595–613.

Mott, F. L. 1990. When is a father really gone? Paternal-child contact in father-absent homes. *Demography, 27,* 499–517.

Myers, J. E., & Perrin, N. 1993. Grandparents affected by parental divorce: A population at risk? *Journal of Counseling and Development, 72,* 62–66.

Nelson, C., & Valliant, P. M. 1993. Personality dynamics of adolescent boys where the father was absent. *Perceptual and Motor Skills, 76,* 435–443.

Neuman, M. G. 1993. When your child refuses visitation. *Single Parent, 36*(3), 15–16.

Nieves, E. 1992, November 12. Funeral held for mother from Edison. *New York Times,* p. B7.

Paasch, K. M., & Teachman, J. D. 1991. Gender of children and receipt of assistance from absent fathers. *Journal of Social Issues, 12,* 450–466.

Pearson, J., & Anhalt, J. 1994. Examining the connection between child access and child support. *Family and Conciliation Courts Review, 32,* 93–109.

Pennington, H. J. 1990. Representing women who conceal or who are considering concealing their children: The underground movement. In C. H. Lefcourt (Ed.), *Women and the Law* (pp. 6A1–6A36). New York: Clark Boardman.

Phares, V. 1996. *Fathers and developmental psychopathology.* New York: John Wiley & Sons.

Pirog–Good, M. A., & Brown, P. R. 1996. Accuracy and ambiguity in the application of state child support guidelines. *Family Relations, 45,* 3–10.

Quilloin v. Walcott, 434 U.S. 26 (1978).

Rice, D. G., & Rice, J. K. 1986. Separation and divorce therapy. In N. S. Jacobson & A. S. Gurman (Eds.). *Clinical handbook of marital therapy* (pp. 279–300). New York: Guilford.

Rieser, M. 1991. Recantation in child sexual abuse cases. *Child Welfare, 70,* 611–621.

Rosseby, V., & Johnston, J. R. 1995. Clinical interventions with latency-age children in high conflict and violence. *American Journal of Orthopsychiatry, 65,* 48–59.

Santrock, J. W., & Warshak, R. A. 1979. Father custody and social development in boys and girls. *Journal of Social Issues, 35,* 112–125.

Saposnek, D. T. 1991. A guide to decisions about joint custody: The needs of children of divorce. In J. Folberg (Ed.), *Joint custody & shared parenting,* 2d ed. (pp. 29–40). New York: Guilford.

Schneiderman, L. 1990. Modern fictional protagonists: Motherless children, fatherless waifs. *American Journal of Psychoanalysis, 50,* 215–229.

Seltzer, J. A. 1991. Relationships between fathers and children who live apart: The father's role after separation. *Journal of Marriage and the Family, 53,* 79–101.

Seltzer, J. A., & Brandreth, Y. 1994. What fathers say about involvement with children after separation. *Journal of Family Issues, 15,* 49–77.

Sloman, L., & Pipitone, J. 1991. Letter writing in family therapy. *American Journal of Family Therapy, 19,* 77–82.

Solomon, C. R. 1991. A critical moment for intervention: After the smoke of the battle clears and custody has been won. *Journal of Divorce and Remarriage, 16,* 325–335.

Sorensen, T., & Snow, B. 1991. How children tell: The process of disclosure in child sexual abuse. *Child Welfare, 70,* 3–15.

Stanley, A. 1992, October 16. Angry at child-support demands, gunman kills 4 in county office. *New York Times,* pp. A1, B4.

Stevenson, R. W. 1994, February 7. In tough mood, Britain pursues absent parents. *New York Times,* pp. A1, A6.

Straus, M., Gelles, R., & Steinmetz, S. K. 1980. *Behind closed doors: Violence in the American family.* Garden City, NY: Anchor.

Teachman, J. D. 1991. Contributions to children by divorced fathers. *Social Problems, 38,* 358–371.

Tepp, A. V. 1983. Divorced fathers: Predictors of continued paternal involvement. *American Journal of Psychiatry, 140,* 1465–1469.

Thoennes, N. 1988. Child sexual abuse: Whom should a judge believe? What should a judge believe? *Judges' Journal, 27*(3), 14–18.

Thompson, R. A., Scalora, M. J., Limber, S. P., Castrianno, L. 1991. Grandparent visitation rights: A psycholegal analysis. *Family and Conciliation Courts Review, 29,* 9–25.

Threatt, B. 1993. Abuse allegations during custody litigation. *Texas Legal Resource Center for Child Abuse & Neglect, 3* (1), 1, 4.

Toder, F. 1986. Recognizing and managing guilt. *Single Parent, 24*(3), 32–34.

Turnbull, H. R. 1981. Two legal analysis techniques and public policy analysis. In R. Haskins and J. J. Gallagher (Eds.), *Models for Analysis of Social Policy* (pp. 153–173). Norwood, NJ: Ablex.

U. S. Bureau of the Census. 1984. *Statistical Abstract of the United States: 1985.* Washington, DC: Government Printing Office.

U. S. Bureau of the Census. 1987. Child support and alimony: 1985. *Current Population Reports,* Series P-23-152, August. Washington, DC: Government Printing Office.

U. S. Bureau of the Census. 1992a. Marital status and living arrangements: March 1992. *Current Population Reports,* Series P-20-468, December. Washington, DC: Government Printing Office.

U. S. Bureau of the Census. 1992b. *Statistical Abstract of the United States: 1992.* Washington, DC: Government Printing Office.

U. S. Bureau of the Census. 1993a. The black population in the United States: 1992. *Current Population Reports,* P-20-471, September. Washington, DC: Government Printing Office.

U. S. Bureau of the Census. 1993b. Household and family characteristics: March 1992. *Current Population Reports,* P-20-467, April. Washington, DC: Government Printing Office.

U. S. Bureau of the Census. 1994. Marital status and living arrangements: March 1993. *Current Population Reports,* P-20-478, May. Washington, DC: Government Printing Office.

U. S. Bureau of the Census. 1995a. Household and family characteristics: March 1994. *Current Population Reports,* P-20-483, September. Washington, DC: Government Printing Office.

U. S. Bureau of the Census. 1995b. Child support for custodial mothers and fathers: 1991. *Current Population Reports,* P-60-187, August. Washington, DC: Government Printing Office.

U. S. Bureau of the Census. 1995c. How much we earn—Factors that make a difference. *Statistical Brief,* SB/95-17, June. Washington, DC: Government Printing Office.

U. S. Bureau of the Census. 1996a. Marital status and living arrangements: March 1994. *Current Population Reports,* P-20-484, February. Washington, DC: Government Printing Office.

U. S. Bureau of the Census. 1996b. How we're changing: Demographic state of the nation: 1996. *Current Population Reports,* Series P23-191, February. Washington, DC: Government Printing Office.

U. S. Department of Health and Human Services. 1993. Annual summary of births, marriages, divorces and deaths: United States, 1992. *Monthly Vital Statistics,* 41 (13). Washington, DC: Government Printing Office.

Wakerman, E. 1984. *Father loss: Daughters discuss the man that got away.* New York: Doubleday.

Wall, J. C., & Levy, A. J. 1994. Treatment of noncustodial fathers: Gender issues and clinical dilemmas. *Child and Adolescent Social Work Journal, 11,* 295–313.

Wallerstein, J. S., & Kelly, J. B. 1980. Effects of divorce on the visiting father-child relationship. *American Journal of Psychiatry, 137,* 1534–1539.

Weinraub, B. 1994, December 12. A happy life on the set, and that says it all. *New York Times,* pp. C13, C18.

West, N. P., & Samuels, A. 1995, May 1. Low-income dads seen in vital role. *Baltimore Sun,* pp. BL, B3.

Wolf, P. A., & Mast, E. 1987. Counseling issues in adoptions by stepparents. *Social Work, 32,* 69–74.

Wylie, M. S. 1993. The shadow of a doubt. *Family Therapy Networker, 17* (5), 18–29, 70, 73.

Zill, N., & Nord, C. 1994. *Running in place: How American families are faring in a changing economy and an individualistic society.* Washington, DC: Child Trends.

Zuravin, S., & Greif, G. L. 1989. Low-income mothers without custody: Who are they and where are their children? *Journal of Sociology and Social Welfare, 16,* 163–180.

Index

About the Authors

GEOFFREY L. GREIF is associate dean and professor, School of Social Work, University of Maryland, Baltimore. He is the author or coauthor of four other books on single parents and a coeditor of a textbook. He has also written extensively in professional journals and has contributed chapters to a number of books.

Contributor REBECCA L. HEGAR is associate professor, at the School of Social Work, University of Texas at Arlington. She has coauthored a book and published numerous articles in the areas of child welfare and social policy.